MW00944296

The Unseen Walls
Overland solo across Africa on a Motorbike
1st Edition
©Christian W Brix
Cover by Guy Nicholson

ISBN: 9781731437693
Independently published by C W Brix

THE UNSEEN WALLS

Overland solo across Africa on a motorbike

by Christian Brix

'This is my world, my stomping ground. I must run free, mad-hearted, bellowing with pain and ecstasy, charging with lowered horns, ripping up the barricades that hem me in and stifle me. I must have room to expand, vast, silent spaces to charge in so my voice may be heard to the outermost limits and shake the unseen walls of this cruel universe.'

Henry Miller

Dedicated to Chris Cornell

'The grass is always greener where the dogs are shitting.'

CONTENTS

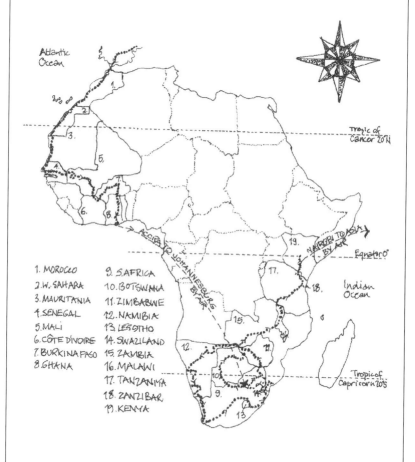

1. MOROCCO
2. W. SAHARA
3. MAURITANIA
4. SENEGAL
5. MALI
6. CÔTE D'IVOIRE
7. BURKINA FASO
8. GHANA
9. S.AFRICA
10. BOTSWANA
11. ZIMBABWE
12. NAMIBIA
13. LESOTHO
14. SWAZILAND
15. ZAMBIA
16. MALAWI
17. TANZANIA
18. ZANZIBAR
19. KENYA

INTRODUCTION

'It is no measure of health to be well adjusted to a profoundly sick society.'
Jiddu Krishnamurti

From base principles, and in the interest of full disclosure – I am a Nihilist. I love my family and friends, but in my lifetime I have not been able to decipher the purpose of human existence. Unlike Nietzsche, however, I would call myself a 'happy nihilist'. I try to be, anyways. I don't know why humans are here on earth, or what we are doing here. I don't think anyone knows for sure, although many have ideas and 'faith'. I don't believe logic to be absolute. As others have noted, it is a crooked set of principles, from which nothing straight can be built. Truth is similarly an illusion, which I have given up trying to find.

The human system of logic can only create paradoxes and false realities. Life is full of contractions, and hence so is this book. I believe more in 'emotional intelligence', and following our animal instinct. Finding meaning in life is something that haunts humanity. However, it can also set us free at times, and that is very much the impulse of this journey – chasing the liberating element. We think we know our world, but in reality we just know our 'little worlds'.

This is both a mental and a physical journey, as the physical movement enables mental movement. Changing your physical viewpoint will directly challenge your mental viewpoint, and when you travel your world becomes bigger. This account is about my journey across parts of Africa, and my thoughts (and struggles) along the way. It is about running from the ills of the Western world, unintentionally and unfortunately headlong into the bigger ills of the Third World. Then trying to navigate back out of them. It's a rejection of modern life, that through many miles on the open road becomes a muted celebration of comfort and some kind of abstract identity. A fumbled reaffirmation of sorts. Life may not make sense, but at least we can be comfortable, and enjoy it as we try to figure it out.

This is not really a celebration of culture and foreign lands. Many 'overlanders' and 'true' travellers will not credit me with 'proper' travel. My response of course is that this is my trip and I did it my way. I couldn't give a shit how they think it should be done. This trip is about my culture, which is about riding a magnificent motorbike great distances, and thinking about it all.

I am not a sociologist or a historian. I am nothing but a confused introverted person stumbling around in this odd extrovert world, searching for something as yet unfound. You could call it meaning, or truth, or peace – perhaps all, or none of these. It's my response to this life. I have heard the calling of this journey for many years, and I am joyously following where it takes me. Maybe I'm just bored and need something to do. I am not really happy, and this trip helped me find happiness, long before departing. It has become my identity, for now.

We live in a hyper life, and I'm calling hyper bullshit on it. I don't think this journey will solve my problems and frustrations, but perhaps it can unlock some of them. It's surely an epic distraction from them, but maybe that distraction is also called 'life'. Just once I want to go somewhere in life I completely made happen, somewhere fate would have never placed me, had I not changed my course so profoundly.

It is about determination and will, about setting a goal and achieving it, running free of the modern envelope and trying to understand this complex world. About having a general direction, but not worrying exactly where the road goes to get there. It's about rejecting this way of life – yet not giving up. Trying to reframe it, and somehow make sense of it, in a way that I can be satisfied within it.

Zanzibar, February 2017

ONE

NON-REVENUE SPACE AVAILABLE
Plan for the worst

'One's destination is never a place, but a new way of seeing things.'
Henry Miller

If our lives start with our formative years, mine was clear. My mother was a flight attendant for the greatest airline of all time – Pan Am. My father was not really present, so did not have much of an impact on me. Watching my mother, I learned about the airline and hospitality industry from a young age. It soon framed how I view the world. From those early days my mother taught me 'how' to travel. She taught me what to look out for and what to avoid, how to have fun, but keep your guard up. As a young man I was mesmerised by the language used, the appreciation of cultures and the sheer distances being covered. I remember talking to someone who was based in San Fransisco, yet lived in Tokyo and commuted to work once a week. It blew my mind. It still does, and 'long haul' carries a deep resonance.

We travelled under the 'NRSA' label – Non-Revenue Space Available – wherever we went. To manage this you quickly had to learn flight routes, schedules, plane loads and seasonality to have much luck at getting anywhere. It was Pre 9-11, before the digital age, in the era of paper timetables. They tried to make them thin and easy to carry, but they were like a little copy of the Yellow Pages. We were always overjoyed to receive the latest copy and be in possession of the next four months of air travel – the world at our finger tips. The tickets were blank and came in booklets of four, little folders of freedom. We simply wrote in where we wanted to go. We had to dress for the occasion as we were 'representing' the company. Aged ten, I would often be found wandering through an airport in smart trousers, dress shoes and a shirt. Bloody uncomfortable, but full of wonder. We spoke in airport designator codes, routes, airplane types and seat capacities. We still do.

We moved to the UK from the US when I was ten, and for nearly ten years I would return to the US three to four times a year, moving from relative to relative during holidays. One trip home could result in ten flights from one side of the country to the other and back again. Always under this framework of employee travel, and I soon loathed it. It was stressful, inconsistent and you never knew if you were going anywhere. You could sit in the airport for days waiting for a flight. Often you flew the other way, as chances were better getting to your ultimate destination from another place. Then there was the silly clothing and travelling as 'UM', or 'unaccompanied minor'. It was a revelation when I turned fourteen and could finally travel unfettered from place to place without a flight attendant chaperoning me. Still, after all this, travel was a stressful and an uninspiring enterprise for me. It was something that had to be done, and not really a choice.

Things changed in my late teen years when I discovered you could travel other places besides the US. I can't say why this basic revelation took so long to occur. Suddenly the whole world opened up and it was not long until I was travelling around the South Pacific learning about the fascinating cultures and countries of the world. I flew almost everywhere possible on the airline network, for next to nothing. My eyes were opened to the world, and somewhere along the line I unhitched myself from the idea of 'nationality' and became uncertain of exactly 'where' I came from. I still am. Nationality is never something I fully understood or felt personally, yet I can clearly see it. People often talk about 'third culture kids'; I can't say I was one of those. More of a 'no culture kid', I guess. It wasn't a negative feeling, more one of freedom. It was liberating.

I had never done well in school. I despised it. For me, travel was an independent school, based on reality. There were no draconian teachers, going on at length about things I would never need to know. I could understand things better when compared and contrasted to other things in front of me, not theoretically in a classroom. Walking the streets of another country is a practical lesson in life, where the lessons are immediately applicable. Standing in front of things, they tend to make sense instantly. A 'cultural feeling' will never be properly expressed in a text book. If our limbic brain – the part that controls emotion and memories – cannot process language then we can only ever really comprehend a place by being in it. I was clearly lucky to experience this at such a young age. It was fascinating to learn a house, for example, can be made a hundred different ways. The main thing is that it provides shelter and stands for a long period of time. How one country does it can be endlessly different from another. The same can be said of everything one country does, and I found it fascinating how simple everyday things can be so wildly different in different countries. It taught me there is no 'right way' to do anything. As long as something works for the task at hand, that is all that really matters. It made me think about everything, and it still does. School never did that for me.

After university I lived in France for a time and bought a camper van to travel around, convinced this was the best way to see the world. Learning about the world had become my identity. For what end I didn't know and like most things I still don't – but the compulsion to do it is still very much there. If you do it long enough, see and experience enough, perhaps you can unlock the meaning of life, or at least your own life. I dreamt one day I would arrive somewhere suddenly and everything would be just right. A place for me. Where I would simply stop, and never leave as there would be no need. It was of course a silly dream: no single place is perfect, just like a human, but it never stops us looking.

Many years later, on a flight back from Italy, I was looking over the airline magazines route map when the idea struck me: *has anyone ever been to every country in Europe?* Just like that, I had to do it. Many people have done it, of course, but I liked the idea. I had already been to about half of the countries in Europe, but still had over twenty to go in the forty-four (disputed) countries of Europe. I recently had been naturalised as a UK citizen and my new EU passport would make this easier. Along the way I became a fan of travel writers. As a boy I was fascinated with Hemingway and Jack London, and loved tall tales of adventure like any child. As a man I started to read more thought-provoking stuff like Henry Miller and Che Guevara, where there was a psychical journey, as well as a mental one.

While aimlessly wandering around a bookshop in London one day I picked up *Jupiter's Travels* by Ted Simon. No one had recommended it; it simply stuck out to me. Several people have described the impact this book had on them, so I won't go into detail, but credit where credit is due. Soon after, I took my CBT and got my first 125cc bike. Zipping around London on a bike was a joy. No more buses, no more traffic, no more inner city gridlock. In the middle of a busy city there was an immense sense of freedom. Like the road was empty and you were simply flying; the road markings didn't seem to apply. A year later I passed my full bike test and bought my first proper motorbike – a Yamaha FZ600. Within a week I was off around Europe, crossing the channel tunnel with £1000 in cash and two weeks of pure freedom. With nothing booked and no firm plans. At thirty years old it was like being a teenager again. I roared off to the Alps and used the bike to visit the last remaining counties of Europe I hadn't been to. Through Luxembourg, Liechtenstein, San Mario and Andorra. It was a heady two weeks of adventure and I was truly hooked. It was a natural fusion for me of the motorbike, learning, adventure and exploratory travel. The motorbike possessed a raw sense of freedom which had a strong pull for me.

I often wonder, is there still adventure in the world? My travels had taken me across most of the developed world at this point, touching six of the seven continents but only lightly on Northern Africa (which doesn't really count). Africa proper seemed the last remaining place on earth with genuine mystery and adventure. Just the word 'Africa' piques the imagination. There was a natural pull to the enigma of Africa for me. It seemed a place I would never naturally go. *The Heart of Darkness* had a profound effect on me. It is one of the most difficult places to access, where life is fundamentally different. It seemed the furthest possible place we could go from our culture and still be on planet Earth. Africa is to the traveller what Nietzsche is to the philosopher – not for the faint-hearted. I wanted to learn it, know it and walk it. I wanted to see places most people would never see. I wanted to learn more about the world, hoping one day I could finally understand it. I had done my early lessons and felt ready for graduation.

I thought of Frank Sinatra's famous lyrics in the song 'New York, New York': *'If you can make it here, you can make it anywhere.'* Except in my twisted mind I had applied it to Africa somehow. If you can make it in Africa, then you can make it anywhere. If you can't, however, you can disappear and die a horrible death, having your skin picked off by birds in the desert.

It's the big leagues, and this is how I got there.

THE PLAN

'The most effective way to do it, is to do it.'
Amelia Earhart

The route

Africa was the destination, but could it be done in a circular fashion and in one trip without air travel? In my ultimate fantasy trip I saw three years: one year to circle Africa, and into the Middle East. One year to cross India and South-East Asia into Australia/New Zealand (boat travel was an acceptable part of it). One final year to follow he Pan-American Highway from the southern tip of South America, up to and across North America before returning to the UK. Clearly a bit of a fantasy. I had no idea if I would even like travelling for this long, or being in some of these places.

I decided to commit to one year and focus on Africa. London to Cape Town seemed an excellent overland route to truly see some of the world and throughly test my skills. There are four classic routes to Cape Town, two central Sahara Desert crossings, and the two coastal routes. The central routes are by far the most adventurous, but are currently are a strict 'no-go' due to instability in the area. Solo, at least. Parts of Algeria, Mali and Mauritania are attempting to break away and form a new independent Islamic republic, which they are calling 'Azawad'. The intense poverty and non-existent social services lead to porous borders. It's a fertile ground for radicalised criminal activity and freedom fighting, with a deep hatred of the Western world. It was widely reported that any Westerner who wandered into the Sahara proper over the last four years had been kidnapped, and either ransomed or killed. I would be more bullish in a group, but solo travel in these parts has different considerations.

I chose to travel on my UK passport, as the Foreign & Commonwealth Office (FCO) has a handy traffic light system of travel advisories, giving you scope to move around a country. The US conversely just rules the whole country out – red or green – and often sits at the same advisory level for extended periods. The UK system is updated more often, and is more responsive. If you are in a green zone, or even a yellow (with good reason) you will be covered by the safety net of the UK government (they will come and rescue you if required/possible). Travelling in a red zone invalidates your insurance and also means you are on your own, without potential rescue. Not the end of the world in a group, but something to obviously be mindful of when alone.

Avoiding red entirely was impossible, but I worked a route that was approximately 90% green, 9% yellow and only 1% red. I was happy with this, and bought a laminated wall map to sketch it out. That map stayed on the wall for over two years as I began to study the changes in advisories for all the countries on the way, learning the hot spots and issues of the region as I went. I tuned into part of the world I knew little about, reading the 'Africa' portion of BBC News online daily, and soaked up all I could. I marked terrorist attacks and kidnappings on the map and, if required, altered the route ever so slightly. Despite a torrent of bad news, I saw the main issues are typically centred around the same trouble spots. The vast majority of Africa is safe day-to-day. It just has the potential to flare up in minutes nearly everywhere, unlike our stability in the West. A simple election can result in riots, borders closing and deaths. I would have to pay attention to the news both before departure, and actively while on the road to steer around potential unrest. The full run to Cape Town from the UK was around ten thousand miles, and over time I felt like I came to know every stretch of that road, as if it was imprinted on my mind.

At this stage I had a foolish notion of 'routes' – like there were options. I had yet to learn that there is not much in the way of roads in this part of the world. Small changes in the road can mean a deviation of hundreds of miles in West Africa. Off-road capability is key, as is travelling around the weather. I was also new to the term 'rainy season'. We have rain in the UK, lots of it, but nothing of the biblical proportions of Africa. A muddy road is very hard work on a bike, hence its best to avoid the rainy season. September and October were the ideal time to make it through the poor road 'network' of West Africa, nature providing my starting date.

Further south I would come into spring, which would be cooler to travel in than summer. I had no illusions about reaching Cape Town as quickly as possible. Apart from Namibia, the vast bulk of the countries were questionable, hostile and likely to be mixed in their 'welcoming' (at least that's how they are portrayed). Nigeria worried me the most, despite its smallish size. Its population is one-fifth of Africa and is well known for aggressive scamming. As an unavoidable country on the way, I figured the best thing to do was push as hard as possible through it. If I was comfortable somewhere I would stay and have a look around. If not, I would push south quickly. I hoped to be in Cape Town by Christmas, which gave me three months. I had heard of people making the journey in six weeks, and the record is currently eleven days, but clearly that's mad. I reasoned three months should be plenty of time.

When reaching the safer region of Southern Africa, I would take my time and be the tourist. The east side is a lot more travelled by tourists, and tourism in general exists there. In West Africa it's non-existent. My English sister and her family were in Kenya, just North of Nairobi. It was a logical stop-off point, and I guesstimated to arrive somewhere around Easter, likely in need of a rest and some familiarity. From there I would see how I felt, but the plan was to head north to Sudan and try to cross into Saudi Arabia and over to Oman. Saudi is a strict country to visit and an escort would be required the entire time. Therefore I aimed to cross it in three big days to keep the cost low. From there I would see the UAE, and into Oman to ride the mountains there. I figured it would all take around a year, perhaps ten months. Sitting at your kitchen table, it's very easy and fun to plan like this. I would soon find out on the road such a journey is never a simple line drawn on a map. Beyond Cape Town seemed so far away, I couldn't seriously consider it at the time.

My work has a fantastic sabbatical policy. If you have worked for them for over ten years you are eligible for a year of unpaid leave. I happily 'did my ten', with a long-term vision to my year off. September 1 2016 was my last day of work, and I would return on September 1 2017. Unless I got a serious taste for the road, and was holding up well in finance and health. They didn't need to know that part of course. I would not be paid, but I had been working hard on the property game, with a couple of flats rented out to fund the trip. I refinanced my mortgages before departure and freed enough capital to afford the trip outright by my estimation. Retrospectively this was an error, as there was way too much money in my hands and this led to some lavishness. Had the money been better allocated, it would have gone a lot further to help keep me stay within my means day by day. Life could obviously be worse.

Many people advised I should raise money for charity, or seek sponsorship by companies. For me the urge was to travel under my own steam, on my own dime and my own time. Just once, just one year. As an adult with means, I wanted to be free of everything. No work, no relationship, no house to run, no place to 'be'. It's a rare thing to be able to achieve. I wanted to run truly *free* in all senses of the word, just to know what it felt like.

The Bike

With a route selected, I could start work on choosing a bike. My mechanic of some time, one mildly famous Nick Lloyd of Andover, helped me consider my options. Like most of the world, I was considering a BMW – perhaps the newer GS800. It wasn't an active choice, more a default one. When you mention 'adventure bike' to anyone everyone mentions the famous BMW GS. I heard they had a lot of problems and required a lot of maintenance, which did not sound appealing. I leaned to the Japanese manufacturers as I had great success and affection for my Yamaha Fazer, so looked to see how Yamaha stacked up in the adventure bike department. I was not about speed and knew I would be dropping the bike a lot and having to pick it up on my own. A single cylinder machine around 600 cc was ideal, the simpler the engine the better. I had limited technical skills, so Nick kindly offered (*well*, I might of talked him into it) to tutor me on the basics. This brought me to the Yamaha XT660Z Tenere, a bike with years of proven pedigree. The name 'Tenere' comes from a region of mountains in the Sahara – where unfortunately due to current politics I would not take the bike. It was a shame, but I'd still give the thing a damn good run.

Still green in the art of off-roading, I booked myself onto a course officially sponsored by Yamaha in Wales. Here I could learn the basics of off-roading and test-ride the Tenere at the same time. Despite being scared shitless several times, I had a blast. I'll never forget the safety briefing: 'If anyone is not comfortable doing a piece of terrain just raise your hand. You can hang back and we will loop around for you'.

Of all the things to tell eight nervous alpha males! Unsurprisingly, not one hand went up all day. It was scary most of the time, but the best way to confront your fears. Soon we were riding up small rivers and doing 50 mph on stuff I would not even ride on normally. We rode on surfaces I didn't think it was possible to. I was highly impressed with the bike; it was huge but it was bulletproof. I threw it into the bank on the side of the trail twice, and it just fired straight back up again. It's the Toyota Hi-lux of bikes – indestructible and simple. A perfect mix for the harsh road ahead, it was the bike for me.

I set my sights on a 2013/4 model with low miles. Nick's advice was to buy as new as possible to avoid issues down the line, but budgets had to be considered. Knowing what I was looking for made things very easy and I quickly saw around ten bikes to get a feel for what to look for and what to avoid. I spent some weekends on the road and chased a lot of dead ends. The bike seemed to really hold its value and there was very little between a used model and a new one (around £500), making a new one not only viable, but an attractive idea. However, I didn't want to be overly foolhardy. Taking a new bike into Africa just didn't seem sensible. Not only would I likely destroy it by dropping it repeatedly, it would also be very attractive to thieves. I covered most of the south of England in my search, but was not finding 'the one'.

Leaving *Autotrader* on my search setting and hitting the repeat every few hours of the day finally led me to her. She came up heavily modified, at quite a cost. That aside, she was nearly too good to be true. I called the owner, who said she was available and that I was the first to call. The hard work had paid off. I set an appointment and headed up to Peterborough, some three hours north, early the following Saturday. I had *the vibe* the whole drive. When the chap lifted the garage door it was like lightning hitting me. This was the one, no doubt. She was magnificent. I took the bike around the block and it was huge. Even bigger than I remembered in Wales. It was incredibly new, a 2015 model, and only eleven months old. I stood up on it and was so high I could have been in a truck. I could see right over the garden fences.

Her next stop was Nick's garage, where she would stay for two months being worked on. I set to work buying the world in bike modifications: crash protectors for the engine, 12v electrical supply, painfully expensive panniers, a top box, spare parts galore and pretty much every modification that can be done. All came to me and I would drive them to Nick's garage on a Saturday, arriving with coffees first thing. I would fit as much as I could myself, Nick giving advice along the way. I tried not to interrupt his full-time work too badly. Compared to some mundane jobs he got in, he loved a project or something a bit different. At one point my bike was sat opposite a bike from 1938; there was very little he couldn't do.

To date he had been a cantankerous, cranky old sort. Slowly but surely we started to become friends, and before I left he had become a dear trusted friend for life. He was never short on opinions. He had been in the motorbike game his whole life and used to work in the Triumph factory when they were still made in the UK. He also worked as sole importer of DID chains into the UK. There was nothing on a bike he could not fix. *Nothing.* His garage was possibly the dirtiest place I had ever been, heated with old engine oil in the winter, but it was never short on soul and great music. Nick always had a roll up cigarette hanging off his bottom lip as he told me what was what, and I learned the ropes. He sourced parts at trade discounts and kindly taught me the basics of changing oil and tyres, as well as a full check-up on the bike.

These lessons were invaluable in keeping us moving on the road – but more so for my confidence. We spent weeks building just the right toolkit for the bike, down to each spanner. Why take a full set when you didn't have half the bolts for the spanners? Anything unnecessary was removed. The bike was so key to everything I didn't quiver in its preparation. Nick was a true character and would be a constant source of information and support on the road ahead, a much-needed voice of reason for me. The man has a heart of gold.

Family & Friends (and myself)

Anyone who has done anything similar will attest that family are often in direct opposition to such an endeavour. *Especially mothers.* Mine was no exception, and took a lot of work. Unfortunately, the trip remained hard for people to process pre-departure and also while on the road. No one could understand what the impulse was and why I was undertaking such a trip. Conversely, for me it could not be clearer. People's lack of understanding was not part of my adventure. Obviously I love and care about my friends and family, and I am very grateful they care for me and love me. Their concerns and worries actually helped to arm me considerably in the preparation stages, which no doubt helped down the road. I had to take the time to explain in detail where I was going, what I was doing, and what steps I would take to protect myself. Everyone of course just thought about the worst (as you should do, from a technical perspective at least) and imagined me dying in a ditch alone.

Pleasant, but these things need to be considered, especially for a solo endeavour. Most people were upset about me doing it alone. Being an introvert, it was just how I liked to do things; it's natural for me. I also didn't know anyone who had a similar desire or budget to undertake such a trip. For me there was a romantic notion of riding off into the distance alone. I desperately wanted – *just once in my life* – to be somewhere so remote there was no trace of another human. I wondered if it could be done on land and I thought the Sahara was the most likely place, if at all possible.

Most friends thought it was great to follow my dreams, but thought I should obviously be careful. Family assumed the worst constantly. They understood my desire to travel; they just didn't get the destination.

'Why not South America? It's so much safer.'

'Why not North America? We are all here. You can visit us.'

'Why do you want to go there when they hate us?'

I had been to South America, and it's possible to cross the US in three days on beautiful tarmac – hardly an adventure to me after seeing it all so many times. Perhaps one day I could do it justice and try it off-road. The last question, however, was a good one which stuck with me. I'm sure many people can't tell you why they head to hostile lands. I felt compelled to see Africa. It called to me and I was simply answering that call. Not on a two-week packed safari, but to see it properly. Good and bad. This involved hostile lands. If travel was always pleasant, it wouldn't teach us much about ourselves or the world. I had no illusion that it would be 'beers on the beach' the whole way. Far from it. I knew it would be bloody hard work and I hoped I could rise to the challenge.

I was green, but determined. Great qualities for an adventurer, poor for a human. I had travelled a bit and seen some things, but nothing like this. I was certain I would fall; I was certain I would get ill. Ted Simon believes *the interruptions are the journey*' and I would surely have some of those. I foolishly believed I could navigate them all and somehow it would all work out OK. But you have to believe you can do it, otherwise you will never set off.

Before, and after the trip the most common question is, 'But why?' Sometimes, even in our most personal moments, we can't comprehend the influences of our actions. I cannot understand our world. I am searching and always will be, inwardly and outwardly. Descartes famously said, 'I think, therefore I am.' I add a further element: I move, therefore 'I think, therefore I am.'

It's annoying to be asked the same questions repeatedly, but if you listen it can be beneficial. Every time a worried relative threw out a random question two things could happen: one – I knew the answer and could allay their fears (and also build up my own confidence as well as theirs). Or two: there was something I had not considered and I needed to go away and work out what to do in that scenario, through the process becoming increasingly prepared. I absorbed every question anyone could throw at me, until I could answer them all. I would tell them at length how I would handle this or that scenario. After a few minutes into conversations people would say, 'Wow! You've really thought this over and done your homework.'

At which point I always thought, *It's fucking Africa! You don't just wake up one day and decide to go there. You need to be ready or it will unapologetically kill you.*

The trip clearly had risks, so I also had to get my affairs in order. Despite owning property and being middle-aged, I had nothing in place. A trip like this forces you to grow up. This was added to the endless 'to-do' lists, the very unglamorous side of it all. In time I would have a will and an accountant. I drafted my 'in the worst case scenario' letter for my executors and had those chats. Fun stuff.

Health was a major issue and there were extensive chats with travel clinics and my GP. Inoculations started six months out and continued right up until departure. I sourced a year's worth of Malarone anti-malarial medicine and all the necessary mosquito products. There was also camping gear, luggage, how to do laundry on the road, first aid, and a million other things to prepare. My sister is a nurse and kindly liberated some heavy-duty items for my kit. Amazon delivered the oddest things on a regular basis and the bills came in heavy. There are two types in this game: firstly those who prepare and likely have smoother trips. Secondly, those who wing it and have a lot more adventure, but also a lot more issues. Having been a boy scout as a younger man, I am a firm believer in being prepared.

Shooting the shit one day at my brother's house, he brought up the point of naming the bike. With everything on, it was low on my list and I was sure I would come up with something when we rode out. Despite owning it for a few months and giving it serious modifications, I had only ridden it a few times so far. I felt I had to know it to name it. My brother just threw out a name from a song by one of our favourite bands.

'I think you should call it "Gloria Lewis". That's an epic song and an awesome name.'

Without anything else in the mix, it stuck. He's normally full of shit, but it is a great song by a great band.

The Shakedown

All advice points to a 'shakedown' trip to test everything out before the big off, so I planned a small journey up to Scotland with my cousin. We set off early one morning, aiming for Edinburgh in a day from Hampshire. Nick worked bloody hard as always doing a final little prep for the trip, and I ran with the side panniers only. It wasn't a proper shakedown as only half the gear and baggage were packed on the bike. I was still purchasing a lot of it, but it would be better than nothing. It was my first proper run on 'Gloria' and she took some getting used to. She was not built for long boring straight runs like this. On the motorway we were keen to put in the miles, so kept around 90 mph most of the way. The sound was deafening – it was alien and uncomfortable. We made it fine, through some rain, and arrived early evening. From there we set off for the Isle of Mull through some great twisty Scottish roads. We joked the bike sounded like a machine gun as I slowly got used to the highly-strung low gears on it. It could go anywhere, but it was not smooth, at least not yet. In Oban I got a screw through the rear wheel, but thankfully caught it at a petrol station before I lost all pressure. My first lesson on the XT: being six foot tall, if your feet ever touch the ground flat, there is something wrong with the bike.

I had nothing with me in the way of tools at this stage. With the tyre totally flat, I struggled to push the bike around the corner to a bike shop which was soon closing. I rang and the kind owner Ali asked if I could be there in 15 minutes. Thus a desperate half-mile push down a busy rush-hour road in Oban ensued. The pannier hit my leg constantly. I had to walk on the kerb, with the bike still on the road to be able to keep ahold of it - it was so tall! It was a dead weight, and I almost lost it a few times, not a glamorous start to our life together. Covered in sweat and cursing vigorously, I finally rolled into Ali's garage. It was a nightmare and I hoped I would not have to do this in the African sun. Together we pulled the back wheel off and changed the tube out quickly. I was conscious of not taking up his time, but in the end we had a great long chat after the wheel was changed. He was interested in the journey and totally supported me. Much like Nick, he was an everyday guy who was sound. Travel is marked by the kindness of strangers and he was certainly one of them. Ali was a cool guy with whom I could have talked for hours over a few beers. I hope I can call in on him again one day and made a promise to e-mail him when I made Cape Town. If I ever did of course.

We returned happy but tired. I made some notes on the bike, and briefed Nick when I returned. I also briefed Glen, Nick's custom seat fabricator, who took the seat away to work on possibly the most important upgrade. I opted to go old school and had a black sheepskin fitted to the seat to ease the long days ahead in the saddle. I also had him stuff a couple hundred bucks into the foam in case of some emergency. Gloria went back into the garage for more works; there was always a long list of more things to do on her. I left her with Nick as I set off for a final lap of the US to check in and say goodbye to family before the proper off.

THE FINAL PREPARATION

'Be prepared'
Robert Baden-Powell

The last few months before departing are a whirlwind. Thankfully there is not a lot of time to worry or overthink things. It was a rabbit hole, and I was down it; there was no turning back. Everyone suddenly wants to catch up and say goodbye, there are a million things you must do, suddenly you have no time at all and you're off. It's fretful, but overall probably a good thing as it shuts down the mind from all the worry.

Visas are not a significant issue for West Africa, and in my research, I found the hardest visas to acquire are for Nigeria and Angola. I try to get a visa for Nigeria in London and despite £300 and providing the fourteen different requested documents to support my journey – they refuse me entry. I reside to try again in Ghana, hoping the rules are more relaxed there.

The money for the trip did not come through until April, so the plan backed up, and late April saw a flurry of spending. I was spending hundreds with all that was required: luggage, parts for the bike, insurance, medicine, clothing, bike gear and, of course, technology. I was highly uncomfortable. I had never spent so much money so quickly in my life and it did not feel natural. Of all the mountains to climb before departure – talking family around, exiting a full-time career, getting my affairs in order, etc. - this spending was the first time I seriously questioned my endeavour. I literally put my money where my mouth was and saw exactly how committed I was. Everything else had been fairly straightforward, but this was very scary.

Around half the bike's load would be for emergencies or problems. The other half would be a daily working load. The spare bedroom became ground zero and was loaded with all sorts of gear. On the surface it looked like two to three times what the bike could actually carry. Luggage was the first hurdle. Many go on about soft or hard luggage, so I'll skip that fascinating chat. I opted for hard luggage, as I was likely to drop the bike often and it would hold up better. It would also give me around 100 litres of secure lockable storage, which, being solo, I was keen on. A hard pannier was like a safe to me.

My main focus was having a bike fit for purpose, which I could drop without breaking anything. I couldn't say when or where this would happen, but I was sure it would. Crash protection was fitted all around the engine to stop flying stones from causing much damage while off-road, or any other random mishap I might cause. Several electrical items were also added to the bike, with a second fuse box. I turned up at Nick's garage and he talked me through doing things. The electrical work, however, was too complex, and he politely asked me to piss off while he did the hard part. I was more than happy with this arrangement. Under the seat was 'Spaghetti Junction' to me, and best avoided. While the bike gained some weight, it certainly gained what was needed to survive the road ahead and keep going. It looked strange having so many modifications on such a small-engined bike. It was tall enough, but very skinny so didn't have the typical appearance of an adventure bike. More Mad Max than something you would see in a glossy bike magazine. I was not quite sure about it – there was something threatening to it. I loved it.

Technology was another big expense and subject to burn time. I was keen on a GPS tracking digital camera which would track my location. It would add this information to every photo, making it easier to place where I was. Very handy when you intend on travelling for a year. A company called Spot had just released the 'Gen 3' tracker, which I thought was correct for the bike, but as it turned out it was better for me personally. I had fun testing it and was amazed how quickly it worked. It bypasses the need for mobile phone reception and goes straight to a satellite. So when I would be out of range I could still update family on my whereabouts, and, crucially, send word for help if needed. I thought I could simply have the tracker on me, and not bother with one for the bike. By the time we finished the bike, however, it was simply too valuable not to be tracked.

It would not have insurance on it, after all, so if it was stolen that was it. Not a situation I wanted to find myself in. Hence another tracker from Spot was sourced, this time the correct one for monitoring a vehicle, also by Spot – the 'Tracer' model. It was added in to the bike's electrical system, and placed in the air filter. Every time the bike moved, I now got an e-mail with precise GPS coordinates, which was perfect. If the bike was stolen, actually getting it back would be another matter, but at least I would have somewhere to start. My family could monitor both the bike and myself, and the tracker would also provide a useful tool in looking at the exact routes I took. In time it became addictive to look at every day as it sends a signal out every thirty minutes, drawing a clear picture of your movements. The application on my phone was a useful live map to show people when talking about the journey. People seemed to struggle to understand the trip in conversation, but instantly got it with a map. It was also very handy for chatting up ladies down the pub.

I was hearing more about bike and carjacking in South Africa and started to worry about this. I asked Nick one day in the garage.

'I've got a new one for you ...'

'Go on.'

'You know I like to challenge you ...'

'Yes.'

'What if someone pulls a gun on me at a traffic light and says, "Get off the bike!" Is there any way I can quickly shut the bike down or remove an essential part so it won't run?'

'Bloody hell ... let me have a think.'

He told me about a kill switch. Eventually I found a suitable machine from California which could do the trick and Nick fitted it. I had a handy small key fob with an amusing little antenna – like something out of a Bond movie for blowing things up. It worked well, up to 200 metres away and all. I now had the motorbike version of KITT in Night Rider. The bike had about eight keys for luggage and locks, so I chained these to me, including the remote, and had the ignition key on a detachable loop. Hence in the bike-jacking scenario I could just run and hit the switch. The bike would simply not start. Who knows what would actually go down in such a situation, but I reasoned it was better than nothing. These things are about confidence, and the technology certainly helped to build it up a lot.

My mother had her own addition as well, for that extra worry only mothers have. Originally she had wanted to supply me with a GPS watch tracker, but the Spot tracker was doing this job already. The next best thing was a satellite phone. To most people this is an utter extravagance. But for a solo traveller in trouble, it could save your life. I thought it was cool, my mother thought it was essential and got a bit of that confidence herself which I had from the other tracking devices. Satphones also have an SOS switch, like the Spot 3 tracker. A satphone also goes directly to satellites and does not need a cell tower or signal. As long as you are outdoors it works everywhere – ships, oil rigs, planes, deep Africa, etc. The most likely emergency scenario was me falling off and breaking a leg, or worse. With these two devices I could at least send up a signal of my exact location and initiate a rescue. (I also felt a bit like a spy, which was cool.)

Then came the decision on insurance, and a 'global rescue' policy. More boring but important solo traveller stuff to sort. The insurance was fairly straightforward, but expensive. Only I could be insured for off-road motorcycling around the world; no one would insure the bike itself across Africa.

As for 'global rescue', it's an emerging service, and anything but clear. There are a few key players, Spot partners with GEOS, who offer discounted policies with their devices. The satphone and Gen 3 tracker were compatible devices and used local government services – a bit like the NHS in the UK. Global Rescue was the firm touted by the overland websites and had the shiny brochures, but were ten times the price of GEOS. They were private contractors – often ex-services – so boast better rescue potential. Much like using private health care. That's the only way I could make sense of the difference between the two.

Both services are about the stage before the hospital. At the hospital your insurance picks up, but before this these firms get you there by whatever means, from whatever remote location quickly – in theory. That's all your policy covers. I had long e-mail discussions with both firms, and no one could adequately describe their fee structure or how a claim would actually work. It was fruitless and time-consuming stuff. I loved the concept, but the reality seemed messy. These services were pitched more at hikers in the US as opposed to overlanders in troubled faraway lands, from what I could tell. In the end I went for the cheaper GEOS and updated all my contact and next of kin info. Explaining this to my mother was another difficulty (parents and technology). However, she got the point that if something was to go seriously wrong she would hear from them and not from me, as I would likely be incapacitated. Another nice chat.

No one covered kidnapping. The only policies are corporate, for remote workers at prices I can only imagine. There was nothing for a person like me, on a trip like this. GEOS would not cover it; you are simply on your own. All advice was that if people had some idea where you are your chances of survival greatly increased. All the more reason for the trackers. At least if I got off an SOS as an abduction happened, it could greatly improve my chances of being found. I told myself that, at least. To complicate things further, these services are only good in 'green zones' as designated by the FCO. As are all insurance policies. If you are in a red zone and something happens – unless you are very important – you are on your own and it's all on you. If you get kidnapped somewhere you shouldn't be, your government will not support you. That's a position you never ever want to be. In the green, you will be rescued (if possible, of course).

The best insurance was the bike. It could keep me moving, it did not need a road, and if really necessary, it could be a weapon. It was my means of exploration, but also my means of escape should I need it. All the more reason I could service it and keep it going. People use the word 'solo' for a trip like this, but we would be a team. One does not exist without the other. If she packed up or crashed, I was likely flying home. If I came off or was kidnapped, I hated to think what would happen to her. I seriously doubted that she would ever make it back.

Keeping in the theme of paranoia, I also scanned all of my documents onto two encrypted flash drives. Everything I could imagine: passports, birth certificate, credit cards, health information, bike information and ownership documents, contacts etc. I called it my 'life drive' and put everything onto it. It's an identity theft's dream, of course, but it's heavily encoded with two 12 digit passwords. I reasoned there were far greater things to worry about.

Hundreds of other small things were considered, and ruled out. I had a hefty budget in my endeavour, and most people doing this on a shoestring would not consider half of these items, or the hassle. At the end of the day it's your trip, and you do it how you want to. With all the gear, I was of the mindset to get everything in one room, and then pare it all down. The best quote I know on the subject has to be: 'Put your money and clothes out on the floor ready to pack – then half the clothes, and double the money.'

You constantly consider what to do in endlessly different scenarios – a robbery, illness, an accident, imprisonment. You obviously can't prepare for everything, but you can certainly give yourself a fighting chance. Short of a bionic chip in my arm, I thought I had done a good job in preparing as much as I could.

At my leaving party, fate plays a cruel hand as I meet a lovely girl and think she's 'the one'. I never believed in 'lightning striking', but it did. The irony was not lost. Jo is the sister of one of the girls I work with, and also a big traveller. She's stunningly beautiful and I repeatedly kick myself. Another test of my intentions with the trip. We manage one date in Hyde Park, drinking champagne and getting to know each other before I leave. I have no idea how to make it work, but I'm convinced she is the one I will marry. It's another thought to endlessly process, albeit a pleasant one.

In the end I overload, and can't possibly take it all. I max out, and a few weeks before departure just give up on it all. If I don't have it already, can it really make that much of a difference? I've totally had enough of this shit. Mentally I have already left ... physically I am going.

TWO

'I GOT THE DEMONS IN ME'
London – Gibraltar

'Hell is empty, and all the devils are here.'
William Shakespeare

It's an early dinner in Cornwall, a small family affair. No fuss, just heartfelt goodbyes and perfect. I weave off on an overloaded bike into the dark, not to be seen again for some time, on to the dreary ferry terminal in Plymouth. There was a lot of fuss in the run-up, but in the actual final hour it's just me. I've been 'here' so many times it feels normal, but this time it certainly isn't. Fortunately the business of travel occupies my immediate attention, and I focus on the simple steps. I head to the bar on the boat for a drink, and chat with another biker over a beer.

'Africa? Really?'

'Yes.'

'Are you scared?'

It's the same chat I've had a thousand times before. Enough times to cut it short, and take a beer to my room to try and unwind. Despite being exhausted, sleep never really comes. My head is busy churning out the 'what ifs' as usual. Frustrating as it is, I'm happy to finally be leaving. So much talk, so much money and so much faff have led to this simple singular moment. It's impossible to really say when day one was, but at the same time, this is technically it.

I am full of worry. Setting off on a journey like this, it's only natural. There are so many things that can go wrong, your mind nearly melts down with the infinite scenarios of calamity and doom. Collectively I have come to term this river of negativity 'the demons'. The demons are terrorists, diseases, car crashes, prison cells, dirty food, filthy hotel rooms, unknown nasty-looking bugs, toxic animals that bite, cliff drops, guns in your face, an unfixable bike, contaminated water, rats in the kitchen and the like. The demons are mainly terrorists in the sand dunes waiting to get me. They're the ones I have no idea how to deal with. In the medical world general unease is termed 'malaise'. These demons are a mental malaise, which give a continual mild sense of

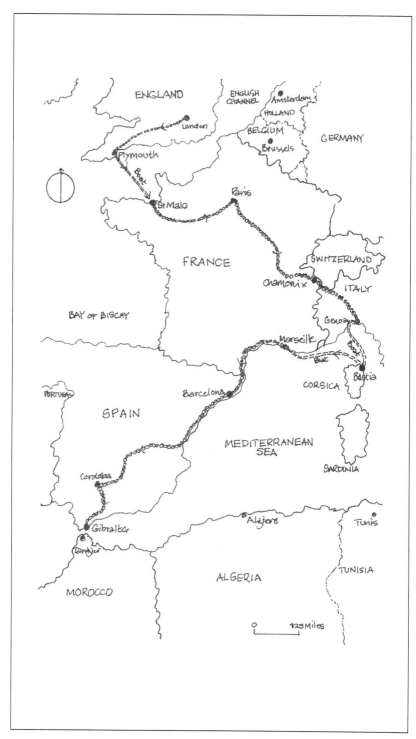

panic. One stage up from worry, one stage down from outright fear.

I'm heading to Corsica, visiting my extended family. It's more familiar ground and a pleasant stop-off on the way, making me wonder when it will all get real. Leaving the ferry is a circus: it all feels wrong, and I'm sure that I'm on the wrong road. Oddly, even this is familiar. The weather is good and once I'm properly under way I settle down, and just get on with it. I glance by Paris, but keep moving south-east across France. Despite wanting nothing but solitude for the last few months, I'm surprised to feel a touch bored. I have an issue at a toll booth as my credit card does not work. The cars stack up behind me. It's suddenly the end of the world and my anger flares up, but in the end it's fine. My emotions are so in flux it's easy to lose my temper. Why do people follow motorbikes into toll booths? This is just the preamble, the warning shot, and the road is slowly clearing my mind. Mile by mile it gets calmer, my mind becoming clearer.

In the morning the bike nearly snaps the centre stand as I roll off it. In the last minute rush to leave I had stupidly thrown everything on I could manage, hoping for the best. I have so much spare gear it's absurd, and I will have to do something about it at some point. It's really hard to know what is going to be used daily, what might be needed in an emergency, and what's just pointless. It will take some miles, but I hope to send a box home soon. It's absurd really, given how much time and money it took me to amass all of this 'essential' gear.

Back on the road the weather is good and I'm heading to one of my favourite places – Chamonix. It's distinctly European to round Lake Geneva on a beautiful day. The white sails are out on the water and the mountains frame a stunning view, all wonderfully affluent. On the way I pass hundreds of vineyards, with lots of famous wine names I've seen in fancy restaurants. In the sun, like today, it's simply superb. I typically head clockwise around the lake, but today I'm headed for Chamonix, so go the other way. The road up is a perfect warm-up to St Bernard's Pass.

Chamonix is a special place for me, and fitting to pass on my way. As my favourite place in the world, I want a picture of the bike in front of Mont Blanc. I used to live at the top of the valley, in a small hamlet called Le Tour. I pull in to take in the scenery and reflect on past memories. Moving the bike for a picture, on full lock steering, we promptly go over like a sack of shit. I'd wondered when the first drop would come, and it happens in a split second. Despite being highly embarrassed, I'm relieved it's out of the way within twenty-four hours of departing. One more thing out of the way. Two kind guys run over and help me get Gloria back up again. A motorbike at this weight is very top-heavy and its common to 'drop' the bike at slow speeds or when stopped. Traffic lights are the usual place, and perfect for maximum embarrassment. Thankfully the bike does not hit anything, as she could really do some damage when free-falling. We have her back up in seconds, nothing damaged but my pride.

Up and over the valley pass to Martigny on the Swiss side the road is fantastic. There is no real border, so I don't stop. I love Europe and how easy it is to travel here. I've done St Bernard's Pass several times before and I am excited to take Gloria over it. Previous bikes have all been two-cylinder sports tourers, so taking a single cylinder this loaded will definitely be a different story. It will be a good time to finally get to know the bike better. My first bike I had named 'St Bernard' in honour of this pass, but it never really stuck as a name and seemed a bit silly. The Swiss side starts nice and sweepy, but once you pass the first tunnel it's very technical and tight up the hill. It's work to get Gloria through it, but the cold temperature feels great as we push and my mind goes quiet as I focus.

She is great on the low end, but flat on the top. In first or second she races ahead, but in fourth or fifth gear she is lacking. You can't really blame her under the weight. We still happily duck and weave our way along. There are a few other bikers around, but no big groups. It's busy with tourists taking snaps at the top as usual. The Italian side of St Bernard's is pure class. Great surface, room to move, tight, tight bends, and straightish sections you can get your speed up on. Not one corner is the same, and some are highly technical. It's hard wearing on the bike. We both work hard, having a blast. After all the chat and planning, I'm finally out on an adventure. On the downside we met another biker on a wonderful-looking Triumph Tiger. He overtakes me with skill and ease, whip-turning while standing up. I try to keep up as he stands up on the pegs for miles on the lower mountain roads. It's inspiring to watch, and I hope I will be able to ride like that one day. Cocky bastard.

Around sixty miles from Genoa I pull in for the essentials – fuel and ice cream. While I had a blast over the mountains, Gloria looks sad and deflated. With a full load of fuel, my feet suddenly touch the ground fully again, just like in Scotland, and I instantly know something is off. The tyres are the first thing to check, but both have the right pressure. Perhaps it's the fuel. I poke and prod about, but don't have a clue. I have a non-refundable ticket for the ferry this evening, so need to move on. I decide to head for the port, on to Bastia, and work it out there. My instinct says something is wrong. The fear and doubt around the trip compounds the negative thoughtstream, as mild panic mellows to a nagging worry. In Genoa I ring Nick for a quick rundown, and he gives me some tests to do, which I promptly carry out. We think it's the main shock absorber, but can't be sure.

On one hand I'm furious to be having bike issues this early, but on the other hand I'm relieved this is happening in Europe, where I can get things done. I check the Yamaha dealer in Bastia and see they are open the next day, and I resolve to sort it then. As we drift out, I'm left wondering what exactly this trip is all about. So far it's been a lot of stress, worrying, expense and I don't feel connected to the trip at all. I hit the OK button on the tracker, and start the new daily routine.

My mind is still active, but fatigued. Moving all day and moving all night. My mind just carries on churning away without me playing an active part. I sit uncomfortably, just listening to the madness, trying to make any sense of it. The beer helps.

It's more confusion in the morning as we near Corse. The shore is near, but we are still an hour away, the boat creeping along slowly. The journey only takes four hours normally, but on a night crossing like this they stretch it out for ten hours, furthering the sense of a slow mental grind. For a moment I feel trapped in this steel cage. I have everything sorted to leave, only to learn I'm early and we still have thirty minutes to go. So I head out on deck to watch the sun rising over the hills of my ancestral home, resetting to a more soothing start to the day.

My great-grandfather was from Corsica. He left for the prosperity of the USA at the age of eight, most likely pushed by his parents due to poor potential on the island. He settled in Richmond, Virginia and started a new life there. Our family was disconnected for years. My grandfather reconnected with the family in the 1940s, and they were quite surprised to learn they had a big family now alive and well in the US. We have kept this connection going ever since, proud of our roots. My great-grandfather was one of four children. Two went to the US, and the other two remained in Corse, continuing life on the island. My cousin/aunt Marie was a descendant of the two who remained – the same generation as my mother – her children third or fourth cousins of mine. Being a small island, many people are related, and most people I meet are my extended 'cousins' somehow.

I first met Marie's daughter, Amandine, in London when she was visiting and we instantly bonded. On subsequent visits I met her older sister, Coralie, and we also had a great connection. They are the only two English speakers in the family so this clearly helps. On my first visit they immediately welcomed me into their beautiful home – practically handbuilt by their father Roland, just a few hundred metres from where my great-grandfather lived, on the very northern tip of the island in a region called Ersa. Marie and her husband Roland do not speak English, but are salt of the earth, very happy and welcoming. I can see my mother's eyes in Marie's, and it's a home away from home for me. I have always visited on the bike and they are used to it all, but like most of my family, they fear for me this time.

Arriving into Bastia is beautiful. Despite being born in the US, where I have no connection apart from family, I feel a real connection to this place – the physical land here and the European way of life. It's amusing to me that after my great-grandfather left for the 'New World' nearly a hundred years ago, I'm seeking to bring it back to the 'old world'.

Leaving the boat, it's the usual chaos. At 7 a.m. I am sweating before even getting on the bike. It's always an ugly race for some reason, with people jostling to get down the stairs and off the boat. I pull into a cafe opposite the port to order some breakfast as I wait for Coralie. There are some other bikers about, and we naturally all check each other out, nodding politely. As usual ,the other bikes look picture perfect all lined up. Bikes and luggage perfectly clean, properly loaded. Gloria is the odd one out, the misfit. People spend longer looking at her and shake their heads in disbelief. It fucks me off.

This is the most valuable bike I have ever owned and I think she's epic, but we still appear to be a bit of a joke, sloppily overloaded and top heavy. I feel a fraud at this point, having done nothing of note yet; it's all just chat at this stage. Their bikes are perfect for an afternoon exploring the island, going for coffees and posing for pretty pictures, but will not manage far off-road. Gloria does not need a road, and as a result I think she scares people a bit. She scares me a touch. She has a wild raw energy that people are not used to. She's not like a movie star in a pub, more like a fox napping in a field of sheep. It might get nasty. I feel like I'm calmly sitting here having a coffee with a lion on a leash. People want to talk with you, but they can't get over the lion being there. They want to stare at her, but not get too close or linger too long. Less a motorbike, more a weapon, she messes with their heads.

It's wonderful to see Coralie. As always, she greets me with a big smile and a hug. We have a good catch-up and eventually walk to the dealer close by, only a few doors up. 'Downtown' is fairly small here. In the shop she interprets for me. I take an instant disliking to the dealer; he's a miserable fuck. Everything is a bother and I'm another hassle. I don't even need to listen to the words he's saying, his body language says it all. We explain the situation, when he quickly dismisses me and the journey.

'We see this all the time. You guys come down thinking the bike can haul anything, and blow the shock – it's your fault, not Yamaha's.'

God forbid Yamaha actually produce a bike fit for task. More French scoffery continues to come out of the tosser. Without even seeing the bike, he says it's two weeks and one thousand euros to fix. Ouch. I ask for him to look over the bike at least, and go back to the cafe to bring her round. Thankfully, his tune changes instantly when he sees the bike. Familiar with the XT660, he can see the substantial modifications that have been done and acknowledges the work. The factory XT was not suitable for Africa, but he deems Gloria apparently is. Some good news from the miserable bastard at least. He advises unloading the bike and weighing everything out individually. Something I should have done to begin with. We discuss ordering and the process of fitting a new shock. It's all worst case scenario, but I feel in my bones that it will likely have to be done.

I kick myself for not considering this back home. Nick and I had discussed it, but after the engine it's the second most expensive piece on a bike. The bike is designed for two people to ride with luggage, so I dismissed it, incorrectly figuring that being solo it would all be fine. Nick also advises shedding some of the load. It's a trade-off with no perfection. I can either offload stuff I might need in an emergency and possibly struggle later when I don't have it. Or I can pony up and get the right shock, so I can carry the kitchen sink with me. Something else to think about. Losing one thousand euros and two weeks time is not ideal straight out of the gate and only two days in! However, I have money now and this won't always be the case. One week turning into two here is not a horrible thought. However, I know the anticipation of Africa will hang over me the whole time. I don't feel the trip really starts until I touch Africa. It's like going to the moon for me. I just have no idea what to expect. The shock is too big a decision to make right now, so I need time to think on it. For now its time to see the family and get into the hills.

We nip into the flower shop next door to the Yamaha dealer to pick up some flowers for Marie. Inside I meet a friend of Coralie's called Christine and stand around as they chat for a bit. I already have a bottle of bourbon for Roland (adding to the load on the poor bike). We head out of town heading north to Ersa along the coast. I quickly pass Coralie in her car, and settle into the road. It's only an hour drive but it's stunning. The first two-thirds are along the coast, and then the last third up into the hills proper. There is traffic but we float (or more likely bob) around it. The first section to Macinaggio warms me and the tyres up; the final section up into the hills is where it really happens. It's a cornering school. Thankfully the road is quiet as I overshoot the white line a couple of times. Even in her mixed state, riding Gloria this hard is soothing. You can really, really lean here – it's every bit as good as a racetrack. The warm wafts of eucalyptus and myrtle help calm me as I push hard up the hill. Through all the bullshit of departing I remember this is what I truly enjoy. The bike manages OK, but I can sense she does not enjoy the tarmac as much as I do. I look forward to seeing the bike off-road, in its natural environment. Right now it's like a fish out of water, and rides a bit like one.

I pull into the Gastmans' family home in Piazza as Roland is loading the truck, all smiles. I jump off to greet him as he points at the weight on the bike, shaking his head. He jokes in French about it, and although I cannot get the words, I get the meaning loud and clear. We have a humorous way of communicating: he does so in highly expressive French, and I in a more dialled-up English with excessive hand gestures. We follow each other's faces and movements to get the meaning. It works fine and it's good fun. Only 7% per cent of communication is in speech, after all. The other 93% is body language and intonation. I always try to follow the 93% and mostly do OK. This trip will sure test the practice. Marie comes out and there are sweaty hugs all round. It's wonderful to see them, as always. With all the planning, pushing, emotions and general blur of last few weeks I can feel myself let it all go here, and breathe out.

It's Notre Dame's birthday and, unsurprisingly, a national holiday in France. They really never do any bloody work. I quickly change and find we are heading out to a small gathering up in the hills to celebrate. I could really do with a nap, but off we go. I will be here for a while and can sleep later, after all. It's a little holiday before the trip really begins. I have a refreshing but brief cold mint cordial, and we all pile into Roland's truck, heading further up into the hills. The roads are as twisty as they come. I feel like I just swallowed some mouthwash as we snake around the cliffs. Five people in a truck, loaded with food, the sun blazing, heading for a religious festival in the hills of Corse. If only every incidental twist and turn ahead will be this pleasant.

We head towards San Florence, but turn off near Morsiglia, heading on to the top of the hill, at the stunning but low-key Notre-Dame des Grâces. The road tightens as we go, with sheer drops. Leaning out the window and looking over the edge I feel happy and alive. It's a very old small church at the top of the hills, with dramatic views to the sea below. The place is packed, and all the families are here. Men play pétanque, smoking and chatting away. The women also chat, but at a different speed, tending to the food as they talk. The kids run and play. It's all so very Corsican – it's beautiful, and not something you would ever discover in a Lonely Planet guidebook. The water is a blazing Mediterranean blue in the sun, and the soft breeze is slowly blowing the aroma of the flora through the air. It's foreign, yet familiar.

It's a jovial festival air and everyone is in good spirits. Everyone is drinking alcohol, but in the European way – no one is actually drunk. I'm introduced to lots of people, all of whom are somehow extended members of the family. I get introduced to Coralie's friend Christine the florist again. This time she is dressed informally and catches my eye. She is very French, attractive and definitely not related to me. She's good fun and we hit it off nicely. She has bold brown hair with fantastic brown eyes, big eyelashes and a great deep laugh. Very much a woman, very much French and, as they say, 'enchanting'. I am 'cousin à Londres' on a mad outrageous trip. Even in French it's easy to understand their facial expressions when they hear the destinations. I'm enjoying it all, but at the same time I'm ready to get away from this standard attitude of everyone to the trip. I have heard enough concern and questioning. It's the era of doing now, and I'm seeking to finally get some miles under my belt.

Before reaching West Africa this is great training for my French. I have a beer in hand before noon, eating delicious food, with no protection from the sun and not a care in the world. I just sit back and listen to them talking together, soaking up the vibe. The tourist. Best get used to the role – if that's ever possible when constantly out of place with no idea what's going on. I can't follow the words, but get the sentiments. Some jibes, some concerns, some encouragement and support. It's nice to just listen for a couple of hours. Good family banter, just a day in their lives. Coralie and Christine mention going to the beach and, as pleasant as this all is, it's an attractive idea. A budding holiday romance on day three? The tables turn as the miles burn. Just like the bike, you have to have gears. Get ready to go from heaven to hell five times a day. Just hold on the best you can. Although obviously there is no hell here; I'm sure it will soon appear on the horizon southwards.

Christine does not speak a word of English, but it makes her even more enchanting for me. Pour une surcharge française. In the short term at least. It's all things foreign, and I'm loving the fact that after so much preparation I am actually abroad now. She has a deep husky voice, which is momentarily mesmerising. I compliment her voice, using the word 'husky', which of course does not translate. They look up the word and the first thing she reads is 'chien' (dog). Smooth. Thankfully, this results in a lot of laughter. The joke keeps going all day, which is kind of a relief and kind of annoying. If you're going to put your foot in your mouth, you might as well bite the whole bloody thing off. We drift back to Piazza, and I ride the bike down to the girls' rented house for the summer season, around a mile further down the road in Poggio, to unpack.

It's a tiny village of around thirty houses; no one knows exactly how many there are. There are only four families here through the off season. A mixture of stunning restoration work and crumbling old buildings, nothing is square, stock or the same. It is a rabbit warren which spits in the face of cheap modern housing developments. Centuries of history, enticing and fascinating. Coralie and Amandine have rented an old house here for the summer. Its crooked, tatty, the walls are one foot thick and the roof is failing. It's throughly French and (fairly) enchanting. There are bedrooms everywhere, - even off other bedrooms. The toilet is the funniest part. It's on the landing of the stairs, and so tight a space you can't actually sit on the loo and close the door at the same time. Your knees sit over the door's threshold. I'm told the procedure is to announce 'la toilette' and close the door at the bottom of the stairs when you need a shit. Delightful.

It's not far off a commune. There are lizards in the shower. The kitchen is home to mice and everything is wrapped up tight, not that there is much food here. It's the perfect training ground for the road ahead, and I best get used to it. There is a nice terrace, complete with mismatching antique furniture. It looks down on the beach and the breeze is beautiful. A few hundred metres away we can also see the abandoned village of Cocinco, where my great-grandfather lived. There is only one key to their house, which is thrown into the flower bed opposite the front door. No one worries about anything here.

Down by the waterfront in Tollare we visit my cousin Marlene's restaurant for another beer. As we go for a dip I can't take my eyes off of Christine. She takes off her clothes, down to a tiny bikini. Wow. She pulls me in like gravity and I struggle not to be obvious, but my eyes clearly follow her into the water. Everyone can read this a mile away, of course, and as she is swimming they tell me I should marry her and settle here forever. A pleasant thought in the moment. I can't resist and follow her in. She is shuffling about in the water, worried about jellyfish as I joke that I'll sting her. Unfortunately it's lost in translation, but it makes me laugh out loud a lot. It feels like the first laugh I've had in years. Sun, beer and laughter soothe my tired mind. Maybe this is all going to be fine after all?

We head back to the house and out to dinner down in Macinaggio. Coralie drives like a lunatic, but I'm sat next to Christine, and focus on her. She has a lovely perfume on, and I let her know she certainly does not smell like a dog, to which the whole car bursts in to laughter. At last I'm letting go a bit and just enjoying the moment. The food is delicious, the company perfect. I get so lost in the moment, it's a sudden snap back to reality when I realise I've finally let go. For the first time in months I don't have a bloody 'to do' list. I have no idea what comes next, but right now I don't really care. Here and now it's simply about being in the moment and it's a great feeling.

We drive back up the hills, but after a few drinks the driving is even crazier. The hills are no longer enchanting, but frightening in the dark drunkenness. Back at the house we shuffle around as I try to get alone with Christine, but it doesn't happen. Her elusiveness just spurs me on. She puts on some insanely sexy pyjamas. Such a woman! She drifts out of grasp and into another bedroom for the night. Win some, lose some. We have a plan to meet up in Bastia in a few days and 'make party' as the French say. She also says she will wake me up at 8 a.m. for a swim, and I drift off to a deep sleep imagining just that. It's wonderfully quiet here, and as I let out a deep breath I slip into the best sleep for weeks.

Days go by like this … long, hot and lazy, with the girls at work, I hang around Amandine's boyfriend Perique, just chilling. Eventually I confront the bike issue. I weigh all the boxes, gear and myself one by one, making a list as I go. Overall I get 205 kilos. I check the max load of the bike and it's 190 kilos. It's all my fault. At this stage I only have four litres of water on it. For the Sahara I will go up to ten litres, and one litre of water equals one kilo, so it will get even heavier. I'm shocked to see the bike suit, gloves, helmet and boots almost weigh 10 kilos together on their own. 210 kg will be more the actual weight.

I can chance it and leave with this shock hoping for the best, but as the part takes a week to just reach Corsica, I expect it would take three weeks or longer to reach Africa, then hit import the tax, not to mention bureaucratic delays and bribery. At nine hundred euros that's not an import tax I want to work out, let alone pay. I weigh up my options, but it's another short list. It's frustrating, but again I am grateful this is happening here and I still have a healthy bank balance. I should have had her fully loaded for Scotland, then I could have found this out at home, but shit happens. I make the decision to bite the bullet, and go for it. The boy scout in me does not want to shed something I might need in an emergency. It's a choice of money or preparation.

I blast back to Bastia to order the shock. Nine hundred euros lighter, I'm in a funk at Christine's place checking boats and onward routes out. In the off season here there are not a lot of options. Hours slip by as I look at days, times and prices. People always see the glamour in travel, the adventure and the excitement, but never the graft that goes into it. This is the essential part which makes it all happen, but it's tedious work. I'm already worried about tiring the bike out with too many miles, which is absolutely ridiculous at this stage. I could ferry it to Nice or Marseille and ride the French coast (maybe stopping in the Pyrenees – an attractive idea). I could head south to Sardinia as intended, but the boat to Spain is only once a week, which would have me leaving even later than already anticipated. I could throw it all out the window and take a forty-hour ferry from Nice to Tangier, but that seems odd for some reason. I don't want to arrive cold like that. Even now late, I still want the anticipation to build naturally as I approach Africa. I think I need Spain to iron out the last bits, bond with Gloria properly before we do battle in Africa. It's all a boring headache, and hard to get back into the zone after chilling out having fun in the sun for so many days.

The trip will begin in Africa. I'm just treading water until then. Fun as it is, there is still a cloud over me until I reach the continent. The demons are more intermittent here in the sun, but still busy in the background. In frustration I throw Jo a text to see if she fancies a weekend in Tuscany, and, amazingly, she is up for it. The tables turn again. This brings a conflict in my mind over Jo and Christine, but I'm not sleeping with Christine and it's very early days with Jo – we've only had one date! I'm certain Jo is the girl I will marry and she's my long game. If things get more serious it will be a lot further along, and I will adapt. Right now I don't think I'm going to reach Africa, for fuck's sake, let alone get married. Just trying to enjoy the road as it happens. In my fucked-up logic it's all OK – as long as they never find out about each other of course …

We quickly throw together a plan, and I spring into action once again. After a week of downtime it's nice to have something firm (besides Christine) to focus on again. I unload unnecessary items from the bike, which appears to be most of it, and book a boat to Livorno for the weekend. Before I leave we have a big dinner in Bastia with some extended friends. It's a very international affair with an interesting and mixed crowd. A big outdoor table, surrounded with good-looking, successful young European people in the picture-perfect Mediterranean setting. Bar me, of course. Italian and German are being fluently interchanged along with French. Just getting my head around French, this is all hard to follow, but the beer greases the chat. I sit next to a pleasant family. The mother is called Diane and she speaks decent English, so we end up talking a lot.

I ask her where she is from. Diane grew up thinking she was French, but has recently found out she was born in Columbia and adopted as an infant. Understandably, it has blown her mind. She hopes to one day 'return' to Columbia with her son to show them her 'roots', which seems odd to me as she can't even remember being there as a child. I can tell Diane believes things make more sense now that she knows she is a not a native French person. She is clearly in question about her personality traits, wondering what came from where. How much is in her genes, and how much of her is from her surroundings and upbringing.

Diane is French, and thinks in French. She has always believed for some reason that she is different from everyone she knows. In her mind now it's the Columbian influence that makes her different from the average French person. Why can it not be that she is simply an individual? In reality, we are all different, regardless of our nationality. One of the only two things the entire human race has in common is how different we all are. The other is that we all inhabit planet Earth – for now. Paradoxically, we only seem to be comfortable when surrounded by familiarity. How much does nationalism guide us? Can we transcend culture? The powerful pull of 'normal' irons out so many unique character traits and holds us back from expressing our true thoughts, our uniqueness often rolled over into the idea of a common identity, born of weakness.

The weekend with Jo soon arrives, and despite no rain at all since I got here, there is handily a thunder storm as I set off for the ferry. Perique reminds me to take it easy, the only one up as I roll out early. On one corner I overcook it, hit the rear brakes and lock up on the rear wheel. I skid for around ten metres with my feet down to steady the load, right over the white line and into the oncoming lane. Thankfully there is no one around, and I have to remind myself to rein it in. It's my first big moment of the trip, but I'm sure there will be worse ahead. I question exactly what I'm doing. Things always sound so good in your mind: go to Italy for the weekend with a nice girl. You never imagine this scenario in your perfect idea. Late and stressed. Soaking wet from the rain, but also sweating in the heat and nearly crashing. For days I have been watching happy couples frolicking on romantic holidays here, having so much fun. It makes you morose as you sit there alone, trying not to watch. I want to be that guy, the guy with a stunner on his arm, sitting in a restaurant eating nice food and drinking champagne, laughing a lot. Not the loner in the corner people worry about.

Visions of the road ahead float across my mind as I sit on the boat staring out at the sea. I'm slowly building myself up to it. I have to trust myself to manage the difficulties I will face. I have to dial in my instinct to guide me constantly. Just the right joke, just the right money changing hands, just the right moment to bolt. The right moment to panic and the right moment to make the 'help – I'm in deep shit' call home. The patience not to lose my cool as I fall ill under a mosquito net in some dogshit hovel, miles from home, help and familiarity. I'm putting myself there. I want to feel far from home, a complete detachment. To see what most people will never see, feel what most people will never feel. I'm actively seeking 'another world'. It will not be kind, and likely not want me there. No one will understand, here or there – but I am going. Trust your instinct: principle number one. A mantra is on the way and, like pieces of a puzzle, I slowly put them together to help give me strength for when I will need it. One of the tenets will have to be 'I choose this'. One of my favourite quotes is by the Kenyan runner Paul Tergat, who said, 'Ask yourself, "Can I give more?" The answer is usually "'Yes.'"'

I see Hemingway in the hills of Spain during the war, drinking water from a stream with his leather hat as a cup. Do you think he gave a fuck about a water filter? I don't think so. Where is the line between being tough and being sensible? It's really not clear for me, but I guess I will find out. Who knows what the road ahead will bring? Thinking about it too much only fosters fear. Best to take it for what it is, when it comes, and not over-analyse it. Which is a lot easier said than done. The hardest part of anything is that first step. It's hard to explain the pull of making a trip. Conversely, if you hear the call of a trip in yourself, it's very easy to follow it. That's all I'm doing, and hoping for the best. It's clear to me that I will make this trip, there is no doubt. My mind still turns over endless worries about it, but you can't prepare for everything. They say you can prepare how you respond to things, but that could be psychobabble. I think you either have a disaster management mindframe built in, or you don't. People will always tell you to stick to the norm.

'Don't go there, it's not safe.'

'Don't do that, it's dangerous.'

'Don't open a restaurant, it's too much work.'

'Don't move there, it's too far away.'

'Don't marry that girl, she's bad news.'

Most of this advice is from people you love and trust, but at the same time you have to ignore it all and follow your instinct. When you reach a place no one thinks you should be, you are just about to achieve something great and break the mould set for you. Do something you shouldn't, and you'll be amazed what can happen. Don't be an idiot, though: know what you are getting into. When your family still supports you, despite you going against all their wishes, then you know you are loved. Safely in the fold we might never know the depth of our convictions, or the love of our family and friends. 'Calm seas never made a skilled sailor.'

It's the education of travel again. All we do is bitch about things, like expensive road tax. Try driving in Moldova or Mali; suddenly it's not so bad in the UK. Shower has weak pressure? Try not having running water at all. It's only through comparing and contrasting that we can understand what something really means. We have to displace ourselves to get that clarity. It always played on my mind that words are defined by other words. How is this possible? My mind is all over the place. I let it flow, and keep moving. Have a huge clear overriding goal and let it guide you, but don't sweat the bile that flows through your mind – it's just nerves talking. Africa is the overriding destination, but I can sense the subconscious trickle of madness in my mind will soon become a raging river.

We spend a lovely weekend walking, talking and eating well, staying in a beautiful hotel with a spa in Radda. For once I am 'that guy', frolicking with the beauty in the hot tub and laughing a lot. I savour it while I can. Soon enough I will again be that awkward solo guy in the corner that people wonder about. It's a lovely weekend overall, but it doesn't feel quite real with everything else going on in the bigger picture. Here I am living 'the life', like I have made the trip already, but I'm acutely aware I've done fuck all up to this point. I drop Jo at the airport, where we have a nice goodbye. Then it's Gloria and I bobbing away down the road in the darkness once again. Another overnight rocky boat ride with the demons. They grow bigger and busier the further south I head.

Back in Corse the new shock has arrived. After some pushing I get them to fit it in a timely manner (bloody French). Technically I'm now ready, but mentally I'm muddled. I want to do laundry, run and several other meaningless things, which all seem to be getting in the way. I'm inventing excuses as to why I am not ready. Facing another repack in my room, surrounded by all my stuff I feel like I could burst into tears. I'm desperate, emotional and frustrated. Nothing is clear except the doubt and fear, which is reaching grand proportions. Not having an exact plan or date to push on makes it even harder. Several times I just consider spending a year here. I need something to drive me forwards. I'm touchy about everything, and the smallest thing sets me off cursing and fuming.

It's time to get it together. I try to lose some weight off the bike again, but it's not happening. The new spring is rated to 220 kg so I should be OK. In the end nothing is right, everything is off, I'm a mess and there are a million reasons not to go. I can't keep going like this, and need to just push off. Amandine helps by making two small leather bags for the front of the bike to help hang the weight in the right place and distribute the load better. They are really distinctive and I like them a lot. It's very kind of her to make them so quickly. On a modern bike they give it some low-tech, old-school character. They are designed for tools, but not secure, so they end up holding emergency water. It does help put the weight lower down and stabilise the bike a touch. I also move my spanners into my tank bag, which helps put more weight on the front wheel. We have one final dinner in Amandine's place to celebrate Marie's birthday. It's a lovely evening, and a great end to my time there. They are truly wonderful people.

The next day I leave before everyone is up. Despite it being 6 a.m. I'm sweating within minutes of loading up the bike. My feet are near the ground again when I sit on the bike, and I don't understand why. I ride slowly down the mountain road, once again in the rain, over to Coralie's new place by her university near Corte. We have lunch there, sitting on the rocks by a stream, and it's an emotional goodbye. She will be my last friendly face for some time. From there it's a short blast to L'Île-Rousse and on to the overnight ferry to Marseille. It's never easy leaving Corse, especially now, and it's a bittersweet sunset on the deck of the boat as we pull out.

My head is all over the place as I ride out of Marseille, as is the bike. It feels like trying to learn how to ride it all over again on the new shock. She just seems off. The road out of the port seems wrong, and I drift into another melancholy mood. I keep thinking the spring will snap at any moment, and I will be thrown under a speeding truck to an instant death. I start to think of nothing but falling off, anything that will stop proceedings. In a tunnel, I feel it start to go over and almost throw it over. I imagine pulling out a big spanner and beating the living shit out of it. What would go first? The windscreen, the fuel tank, that's plastic – it should give and on and on … I think I hate Gloria. She doesn't seem to like me one bit either. I'm not falling in love with her like I expected to. She is the most expensive, newest bike I have ever had, and she's just shit right now. I'm constantly in the wrong gear, off with the balance and I feel like I just started riding a bike last week. The baggage looks like a child loaded it. At a petrol station I go to the loo and leave it with the keys in, hoping someone will steal her.

The small niggling worry of suspension becomes all-consuming, and I am in full hate mode by the time I skirt Barcelona. Why am I doing this trip? What's the point? Why am I spending so much bloody money on this stupid idea? Why am I not at home watching TV, eating and sleeping well? I am hate on wheels. Doubt nearly cripples me on the road, attacking my every thought – I cannot escape it. I must find a mechanic and get this sorted, but all

I really need to do is eat 400 miles. I don't even have a map of France, as this is supposed to be the easy part. It occurs to me I might die. In the moment I don't care; you just have to just say, 'Fuck it.' If those things happen then so be it. For now I decide to just ride it out.

I stop for a coffee after 100 miles and calm down a bit. I call 'the doctor' back in Andover to wish him a happy birthday. It's great to hear Nick's voice, and after two seconds of happy birthday we are into the business at hand. He says it's no big deal and just to get on with it – the bike will be fine. It's all I need to hear. I mention I'm in Montpellier and he says, 'You made it farther than I ever have, mate.' Instantly I snap back to the reality of what I am doing. I love that man. Perspective warms my heart, and I summon the emotion to continue. I plug in the tunes and say 'Fuck it'. The sun is shining, just keep going until you can't. Within an hour I'm singing along with Neil Young and having a good time again. Suicide to elation – five times a day. Dial it in.

I smile as the miles drift away in the sun. I strive for peace, but the most liberating emotion I have is when I tell the world to go fuck itself. Nothing feels more empowering or enlightening. So what if I'm doing something you don't understand or agree with. I'm not hurting or harming anyone, I'm paying my own way, so leave me alone and let me get on with it. This is my life and I'm living it. I don't care if it does not make sense to you – it doesn't need to. This emotion is like electricity, it powers me. I don't need your judgement. I appreciate the love of the family and the guidance, but we must live our own lives.

As I stop for lunch, a priest in the car park blesses the bike. I try not to lose my cool, but the smallest thing is setting me off, and it's mounting to a breaking point. I tuck into some salad and fruit as there won't be much of it downline. On the other side of Barcelona there is the biggest, dirtiest factory I have ever seen, like the Death Star. Shortly after, near Tarragon, the smell of the herb gently wafts across the road, and it's soothing. The suspension issue still nags away at me. I ride south to L'Ametlla de Mar, but thirty minutes out it pours so bad I have to pull off the road – soaked again. Another hotel room, another try to dry out the gear, another bad night's sleep. What am I doing again? I need to just get on with it and stop moaning. I'm fine really, but suffering very erratic mood swings approaching Africa.

The next's day ride to Cordoba is uplifting, and I am back in good spirits again. The scenery is stunning over the hills and the sun is out. I put on some music and just soak up the miles. The new Santana album. I saved it for the trip, along with a few others. It's good, but it's no Abraxas. What album can match that? I push on. In Europe 100 miles gets you a coffee. 250 miles gets you lunch and 500 miles gets you a beer. I learn the reserve tank as I go, pushing it a bit further every time, and seeing how far I can get on it. The further south I go, the more real the trip becomes. The long solitary stretches of tarmac slowly ease my wild thoughts. Gloria and I are not really talking today; we both stick to our own spaces. I stop for a pee and the wind down there is very pleasant. Au natural is always so much more satisfying. I run over what items I can send home. It's a short list. Cordoba finally appears, resplendent in the afternoon sun. The cobbled streets are not easy with the heavy bike, and I get stuck behind a horse and cart, of all things. In the hotel I take a load off and head into town for some beers and tapas. The next morning I take a brief run around to snap some pictures like a tourist and then gear up for the final pull to Gibraltar. It's only 150 'easy' miles, but my mind continues swirling approaching the coast.

Many overlanders have a mantra to help keep balanced in the mind. Some talk about it, some don't and I guess some don't care. I feel I will have one, and consider what it will be as I roll on. Dr Pat Garrod sums it up well with his weighty tome on the subject (the hilariously titled Bearback, well worth a read). His mantra is: 'We WILL survive, we WILL stay healthy, NEVER let your guard down.'

Simple, and to the point. I struggle to get mine into a bitesize form. It's an odd mixture of damage control, and stability should I get lost – mentally, that is. Dr Garrod was with his wife and I am solo, so perhaps I need a bit more. So far it contains the following thoughts in no particular order:

- Remember you chose to be here and worked hard to get here – appreciate it.

- Be tough – you're a human, with a great reserve of strength – shake it off.

- Think positive, focus on what has happened – not what could happen.

- Momentum is your friend – keep moving, keep learning, keep it fresh.

- Trust your instinct, don't listen to gossip and petty fear – everyone will tell you you're crazy.

- This, too, shall come to pass …

I'm unsure how to slim it down. I sure as hell won't remember all of that in a moment of crisis. They are all valid sentiments, but it needs to be catchier to remember in a pinch. They all sound noble enough, but the real meaning is more along these lines:

- Stop being a miserable bastard – you paid a lot of money for this!
- Stop moaning – if you fall, try to shake it off.
- Don't listen to the bullshit and don't bloody stop!
- When it goes wrong – get over it.
- If you feel scared – run!

Even that is too long. I have to be the most cautious 'adventurer' yet. Eventually the road drops down to the Malaga region, where money is growing on trees. Lots of flash holiday homes and golf courses. How quickly things are about to change across the water. I head to Gibraltar, dreaming of a Sunday roast. An English high street, where I can get the last bits I need before departing into the unknown, and the journey actually begins. On that note I start taking my Malarone.

It's amusing to wait at the barrier with everyone else, wondering what the hold-up is in Gibraltar. Then the childlike surprise of seeing a plane land just fifty metres away from you. A British Airways A319 touches down, and within less than a minute we are crossing the same stretch of tarmac. I have been here before, when I was younger, but can't remember much. It's a lot dirtier than I remember. The roads are annoying, with a one-way system across the whole downtown area. I break several traffic laws trying to find the hotel, but get away with it on a bike.

The hotel is a shithole and a complete rip-off. I try not to think about it and focus on the repack. Always stuff to do. All the bags go up three flights of stairs, and then some ruthless sorting begins. The big DSLR camera goes home, which seems sacrilege. The kettle goes. Which seems the most stupid thing to ever bring (thanks, Nick, for your infectious love of a cuppa). More straps and locks go home, more clothes, until I have about a box-worth. In the process everything gets reshuffled. I had an idea where everything was before, but now have to learn it all over again. It seems better organised as I'm getting more used to the gear I use the most now. I shed about ten kilos, which was a good effort. I finish late with no sign of a Sunday roast at all, but I do get a pie and chips with a pint of Guinness, which works just fine.

I was hoping for some sense of normality here, but I don't find it. I get into bed as horrible scratching noises start. My first 'visitor' appears as I'm about to drift off and then more come, one by one. It's too much for me. My nemesis is cockroaches; they just unsettle me. Give me mosquitos any day. I chase some around the room, trying to squish them with my shoe, but they are quick bastards. They are massive. I put up the mosquito net as some kind of (mostly mental) protection. It doesn't keep out the demons. Between the two it's impossible to drift off. For £5 in Mali, I would expect this – but for £70 in 'England' I'm raging, making sleep impossible.

I wake up angry and out of it after only an hour or so of crappy sleep. It's going to be a hard day, no matter what. I'm not sure I can get it all done, and have not even booked a boat yet. Running around the island sorting things, someone goes into the back of Gloria on a roundabout. A stupid Spanish builder, probably drunk. I vent at him, but he's clueless. Thankfully he hits the pannier without the fuel on the back of it (could have been a game changer if he'd hit that one). His headlight was already broken and taped up, so it didn't make much difference to him.

I find 'Pitstop Mechanics' on the other side of the island, and they can help with the shock. It's great news to hear. They are busy, though, and want me to come back after lunch. I decide then and there to go to Africa tomorrow. I head back to my hotel, venting more at reception as I pass. I book a lovely-looking hotel on the Spanish side, near the port for under £40, and breathe out. Another excuse – maybe. Peace of mind – definitely. Back at Pitstop, I pull in fully loaded so they can inspect the shock. I set the side stand down but my boot coming back up raises it back up again, unknowingly. Thinking it's down, I drop the bike spectacularly in the garage. Immediately they all jump to help us back up again. We fell onto one of the mechanics at work and I'm desperate to make sure he is OK, but the boss just shouts, 'Fuck him, is the bike OK?' We all have a good laugh. Thankfully the chap is fine. Great start, dumbarse. Also thankfully, Gloria is fine. Another scratch, another drop – she's breaking in nicely.

The guys are wonderful. They check the shock. Yamaha had simply installed it at zero and given me the manual with an adjustment tool. The tool does not actually reach the shock, so it's impossible to adjust it with it, as I had feebly been trying. The guys advise just taking a screwdriver and hammer to it as they do with other bikes. I would have never done that myself on something I paid 900 euros for! It's the confidence a good mechanic gives you. The guy is there working on it for half an hour as I talk to the others about the trip. These guys remind me of Nick and I feel at home. Give me a real mechanic like this any day, not these showroom-type wankers who just fit only stock factory parts and never really get their hands dirty (Yamaha Bastia). The kind who can't do anything which is not in the manual or recommended by the manufacturer. Gloria seems to appreciate the attention and we bond a bit further. If a bike is like a horse and follows the rider's instinct, it's no wonder she is confused. I'm certainly confused approaching Africa, but we both mellow in such good care.

I take her out for a spin, and she is back to her normal top-heavy, floaty self. A nightmare on these streets, but in the dusty ruts of Africa she will be solid. My mood surges ahead with positivity for the first time in days; it's just what I need to get my shit together. I get back to the garage and officially bless the bike 'ready for Africa' , making a cross sign over her as they all laugh. Privately I bless myself ready for Africa. It's a moment. You must have confidence in your machine; it's truly astounding what it does to your mood. Scotland was more of a run on Gloria, but these three thousand miles are the actual shakedown. We have a quick photo, and I leave with five new friends wishing me well on my way. The owner, Arron, does not even charge me. I would not advise heading to Gibraltar – it's a shithole – but if you do find yourself there and need a good mechanic, look no further. These guys are seriously capable and truly hospitable!

Back over the border in Spain proper the hotel is wonderful. I set to some last-minute faffing ... always more faffing to do. The room is delightful, not a pest in site. I settle in for a good meal and a kip before blasting off into space tomorrow ...

Finally.

THREE

TOUCHDOWN
Morocco – Dakar

'Watching the coast as it slips by the ship is like thinking about an enigma.
There it is before you, smiling, frowning, inviting, grand, mean, insipid, or
savage, and always mute with an air of whispering "Come and find out. "'
Joseph Conrad – Heart of Darkness

Sitting at the docks, I'm early. The second vehicle in line on an empty lifeless
dock. A few fixers shuffle about sizing me up, but passing by. The sun rises as
huge birds scour the docks half-heartedly. It's game day – equally calm and
tense. After all the fanfare, expense and the efforts, I'm finally on the starting
line. Life's biggest moments you face alone.

The hour approaches and passes, but there is no boat and no explanation.
The only thing clear is that we are not leaving on time. Eventually a boat
arrives, and we dutifully shuffle on board. The miserable customs man sees us
one by one on a table in the bar. He does not like my new passport because
it's new. He wonders if it's real, so he tries to tear into it. Handily he stamps
page forty-six with my immigration number for Morocco. Why start at the
beginning? I have what I need and set about updating my 'fiches' as we wait
to depart. The ease of Europe in the past, now it's time for serious paperwork,
and seriousness in general.

Fiches (or forms to us), are the key to a smooth journey on the Western
Atlantic route (along with avoiding kidnapping). A fiche is a short summary
of you and the bike, including name, address, occupation, registration, engine
number, etc. You get three to an A4 page and tear them off in advance. At any
checkpoint you present your passport and a fiche to the authority. They check
it matches your passport, keep the fiche and hand you back your passport,
waving you on. In theory at least. Without a fiche he will take your passport
into his hut/office/tent, and will have to copy all of these details down by
hand.

If they dislike you, then you could be there for some time answering a
series of inane questions. I use the word 'he' not in a sexist way; 'they' really are
only ever men here. The women are mysteriously absent. With a checkpoint

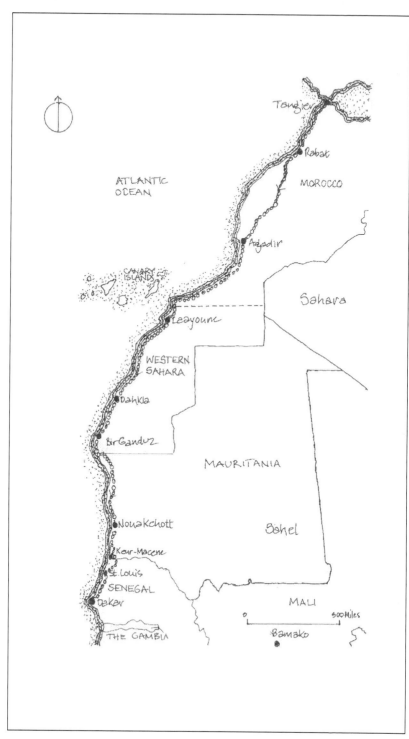

approximately every thirty miles, you need to speed up the process to make any decent distance in a day. I will go on to leave a paper breadcrumb trail the whole way south to Dakar. What anyone does with these bits of paper I have no idea, the other side probably becoming a shopping list. If indeed they do any shopping.

I sit on the deck watching Europe disappear, trying to summon some emotion, but failing. My mind is firmly focused ahead. Africa appears in no time, and I remember Ted Simon's thoughts at this moment on his trip: 'For me this ferry crossing to Africa represented a decisive leap into the unknown, a voyage of no return.'

I have been to Tangier before, but that's only dipping your toe in the water of North Africa. Now I'm about to dive in head first, and hopefully swim to the other side. Then I was greeted in Tangier port by a rabid growling dog. Now I pull into the massive new Tangier Med port, some thirty miles north-east of Tangier proper. It's an impressive stack of concrete. Back on the car deck, I sit on the bike watching land and sky blur past through a small opening at the top of the ramp as the boat positions itself. A pinhead of detailed rocky hillside flies by too quickly to read, a blurry light at the end of a tunnel – in many ways. I can't tell if the world is moving around me or I around it. T minus ten and counting …

I don't feel a sense of touchdown, too busy trying to follow the clear lines and signs. Despite a lot of agents around, no one actually seems to be working. The signs have been put there by someone who designed the place. The people who run it, however, had different ideas, and use it in a totally different way. The numbers on the stages say 1,2,3 by design. In reality they go 3, 2,1, so you have to go to the end to start, and work your way back to the start to actually finish. Welcome to Africa.

I begin the bike import and start filling out forms. A little man with dirty hands and wide eyes grabs everything and points at random things for me to open. I comply as he gives a brief uninterested look, and runs away somewhere with all the paperwork. As I'm waiting, another officer wanders over to 'make conversation' with me. *Red flag.* He speaks very good English and wants to chat, the bike clearly not blending in. After the 'where did you come from/ going to' chats he goes further:

'Who is your favourite band?'

'Led Zeppelin, you?'

'Dire Straits.'

Good answer I think.

'Favourite song?' I venture to keep the chat moving.

'Sultans of Swing', you?'

'Down by the Waterline' – that intro is amazing. Also a big fan of 'Tunnel of Love … I love that part 'And girl it looks so pretty to me, like a Spanish city when we were young'…

He smiles as we chat a bit more. It's the dance, of course. He couldn't care less about what music I like. He's just reading me. The subtext is 'what are you doing' and my response is 'nothing I shouldn't be doing'. He doesn't need to look into my bags, just my eyes. If he see's a flash of fear, he will dig deeper and deeper until it goes away – or he finds its cause. He knows what he's up to, but so do I. We shake hands as equals and part with a smile. Little man returns with my paperwork and I am free to go. Just the right amount of humour, chat, concern, seriousness and mostly calm. Sharpen that instinct. The dance will get more complicated down line. Despite all this, my heart is beating in excitement on this moment of the trip. I'm really here now – it's really happening, and it's hard to take in.

The road is perfectly paved and the view wide as I pull away. The wind picks up and out of nowhere it's the worst wind I've ever ridden through in my life. Either it keeps the demons at bay, or is actually them finally becoming physically present as I touch Africa. My emotional pot is now boiling over as the mild fear becomes acute. You are here now, big boy, no more chat. I can feel the safety net receding with every mile south. The bike and I are all over the road in the wind. Negative thoughts stream across my mind: sickness, kidnapping, robbery, theft, crashing. Solitary suffering. I'd like to say it's all in your head and just shrug it off. It is, of course, but your head controls your body. In truth, I'm shitting myself at the enormity of it all right now, and it's impossible to just 'shrug it off'.

I pull in for something to eat to try and calm down. As I get back on the bike I check my pockets as always to make sure my passport and wallet are zippered shut. I brush against something in the front pocket of the jacket and, unsure of what it is, I pull it out. Mild fear sets in as I remember. In a moment of kindness Coralie gave me a cloth bag of myrtle from Corse to smell when I felt homesick. Touching. It is a dried herb and looks like another famous herb. *Fuck!* Not something I should be crossing borders with. It's bloody ridiculous, but my nerves are stretched to the limit and the smallest thing instantly becomes huge. Feeling supremely ungrateful, I ditch it. Must be careful that sharpened instinct does not cut you.

The wind continues to distract as we fight it out. South of Tangier the road gets busier. Cars stop anywhere on the motorway to pick up passengers, as people use their cars as taxis. Lorries use the central reservation as a rest stop, and park up in the middle of the highway. Actual traffic is light, but things happening around the road increase by the mile. People milling about, animals around, and rubbish blowing by quickly in the wind. It helps me focus a bit and forget the demons, for a while at least.

With the sun still up, I pull into Rabat. First impression is a massive security presence; there are people in uniform everywhere. Like ninjas, they just appear out of thin air. Our lot could learn a thing from the police here. I check in and park up Gloria, giving her a loving tap of thanks. Maybe there is hope for us yet. I get the 'foreign eye' on the street, as every man stares at me until I look at him, and then he looks away, never making eye contact. It's maddening. As for the women, you're lucky to see them, let alone make eye contact. I walk the streets looking for some food, finally feeling 'abroad'. Most joints are playing a football match on the TV and filled with men smoking and talking. They all stop what they are doing and look up at me when I walk in the doorway. No women to be seen at all, not inviting in the slightest.

I'm in Rabat for a couple days sorting visas. It's tedious and hot work in the heat. I start with a visa for Mauritania but do not get far. I turn up at the embassy and there is no queue, no guard, no nothing. Not even a seat. I sit on the kerb for a while and watch nothing happen on an empty street for an undetermined time. A German couple turns up. He looks like he just stepped off a tractor, and she is wearing a monk's robe and also pregnant, I think. So the madness begins. Not even the Westerners are normal anymore. We chat in broken tongues, and they confirm there has been a technical issue for a few days and they are not currently issuing visas here. An official magically appears out of nowhere and confirms the system is broken and that you can get one on the border. At least I tried. I have better success with the visas for Mali and Burkina Faso. I duck my head into the Ghana embassy, but they are having none of it. My proper visa hassles officially start with Ghana.

For reasons unknown some countries only grant visas to citizens or official residents of the country in question. For instance, as an English citizen on a tourist visa in Morocco, you cannot apply for a Ghanian visa. Why? No idea, that's just the way it is. Some countries don't have this rule. Why? No idea. How do you find this information out? Talk to people on the street or lose hours in boring forums on the internet, hoping the information there is still up to date. It's frustrating when you believe tourism is a positive thing for a country, which I do. A lot of countries (Nigeria, Angola) do not want tourists, and some (Burma) view them with outright suspicion. Coming from the ease of Europe it's all an epic drag, and expensive. Before you arrive in a country you already really hate it (e.g. Nigeria).

As part of the border-easing process, I had bought a carton of cigarettes. Now and then I had one. At most one a day, and only after getting off the bike if it had been a difficult day. I needed one today, so head to my balcony and close the door behind me to keep the bugs out. The door instantly locks behind me. I'm on the third story as mild panic sets in and I realise the full implications of my situation. Thankfully I have my phone, but once connected it's £2 a minute and the receptionist cannot understand the predicament at all.

'You're outside the hotel and can't get in? The door is open, sir, I am here!'

To make matters infinitely worse, I had thrown the deadbolt on the hotel door, so they could not even access the room with a master key. Fuck. I eye up climbing down the balconies, but it's highly treacherous. Some kids opposite speak English and kindly go to reception to help them understand the frankly utterly ridiculous situation.

Eventually a doorman just kicks down the hotel room door about an hour later, the frame shattering all over the room, along with my pride. I file it under my 'why does shit like this only happen to me?' file.

The landscape starts to change subtly, as heavy wind continues to blow stuff all over the road. The north of Morocco is highly cultivated and worked, but this slowly decreases as you head south and it gets more barren. A dust storm obscures the sun for most of the day, but it's still hot. A light brown dust blows everywhere, and you cannot escape it. Gloria and I soon look like we've been on the road for weeks. Rocks break down into dust in the relentless sun and heat. The number of crashed cars on the side of the road slowly increases, and dead animals are scattered around in various states of decomposing.

My mind switches back and forth between the landscape and the road ahead. On the Western Atlantic route a key source of information is *Sahara Overlanders* by Chris Scott. He has an encyclopaedic knowledge and experience of the region. Back in England I had read it, but re-reading the website here has a new relevance. There is even a 'kidnapping summary' page, with up-to-date details. What I read, I did not want to know, but of course I should know. On the road I'm travelling three Spanish aid workers had been kidnapped in 2009. Terrorist groups seize foreigners – travellers or workers – to hold them for ransom.

Often the press doesn't cover these cases; they are not high profile and are always drawn-out ordeals. They either end with the poor people being murdered, or a private individual paying out to get them free. The Western governments do not want the second fact openly discussed. They cannot directly bargain with terrorists, but often go through local intermediaries to try and secure their citizens. It's messy, complex and causes great stress to the kidnapped person's family at home. Not to mention the poor person being held.

Algeria, Mauritania and Northern Mali are all interested in forming a breakaway independent Muslim country. Northern Mali has already tried, calling it 'Azawad'. The Sahel itself is the equivalent of the Wild West, stretching from this side of Africa right to the other side eastwards in Sudan. A belt of unforgiving rocky land, just south of the Sahara desert, it's an intriguing part of the world. The place where adventure movies could be brought to life – except its real here. The inhospitable bareness is wedded to an active criminal underworld. At least that's what we are led to believe. Borders don't exist in the desert when you don't use the roads. Criminal nomads wander easily. Police forces are underfunded and cannot patrol such vast lands. On the face of it nothing is happening here, and I see nothing but sand. People follow simple routines to stay alive, as they have done for thousands of years.

Danger is in the wind, though, and if you are in the wrong place at the wrong time it can be fatal. It's not a direct threat, more a general sense of intimidation. These vast beautiful open stretches of sand have a wild sense of lawlessness. Growing up watching spaghetti Westerns on the television, I'm suddenly in the set. Outlaws are not going to ride around the corner on a horse with a shotgun, however. Instead it would be a Touareg with an AK47 on a camel. John Wayne would not make an appearance to save anyone. Without a gun, I feel like the poor old man with some valuable cargo, soon to be robbed and shot dead. If you ever find yourself seeking a lawless wild badlands, this is the place.

The demons have a landscape now. Like swimming in shark-infested waters. People I cannot understand or communicate with want to harm me for being there and, even worse, for who I am. Mauritania will be my first 'red zone', where in theory no one will come and get me should the worst happen. Cheery thought.

Agadir is an odd place. A final outpost before the desert really starts, one last hurrah before emptiness and conflict. The bright neon lights and pumping club music clash with the rest of Morocco I have just passed through. I wander the streets having a nose about and reason it's less Las Vegas, and more like it's poor cousin, Reno. Westerners are everywhere, busy 'making holidays' and it's a surreal sight having come overland. So much of this world you can't absorb with the fly in-fly out ritual.

Southwards, the checkpoints steadily increase and the routines become more aggressive. A fiche and the occasional cigarette help. I also start to belt out a hearty *As-Salaam-Alaikum* as loud as I can each time, and tap my heart before any other words are exchanged. They duly respond. I think it helps, but their poker faces give little away. They are always very busy relaxing in their hut, hiding from the sun a full-time job. You are only ever a supreme annoyance. Everything is barked in abrasive French. After hearing the same questions several times you learn them:

'Why are you here?'
'What is your profession?'
'Is that a camera?'
'Are you a journalist?'

It seems it will be their head if they let you though and something happens down the line. Any foreigner from any country simply equals suspicion here, and is naturally an enemy. Each town has a grand entrance – a huge decorative feature in a desert of nothing. It sticks out miles away and is always a straight line of paved road with street lights and flagpoles leading into the town. The cops typically hold this spot as the gatekeepers to the city. No one uses the sidewalks. Odder still, the sidewalk only exists on this stretch; further into town proper there isn't one. It appears like it's built to impress the foreigners which they do not want to visit. The street lights have no electricity or lightbulbs. The ragged flags flap in the wind – if they have flags at all. It's all over the top, given the town it leads to is so poor. I dub them *'avenues of intimidation'* as they just give you the fear, which is probably the point. There are no bypasses here. By getting hit at the entrance and at the exit, passing one town takes over an hour.

The road steers away from the coast further south and heads inland. The temperature rises as the landscape becomes more desolate. I rarely see people and those I do see look shifty. They are always crossing the road and never actually using it. They come from the vast open left and go to the sparse vacant right. I have no idea what they are doing. They do not use any roads or leave any tracks in the wind; it's all wonderfully mysterious. As I approach the 'border' with Western Sahara I expect an increase in checkpoints and general hassle given the current land dispute between Morocco and Western Sahara. Thankfully there is nothing but a small town called Tah, with no checkpoint at all. Like they want to play it down and be sure you know you are still in Morocco. The current conflict between the countries seems to be in a stalemate. This side of the 'Burg' (a giant sand dune) is 'Moroccan', and the other side remains Western Sahara. I stay in Laayoone, or as they say, El-Aaiún. With an active military base there comes even more extensive security, checkpoints and distrust.

The town itself is beautiful and I feel like I catch a glimpse into another world. It's hugely build up and decorative, which I did not expect. There is a lovely main square, with a giant fountain lit up at night. The buildings are unlike any construction I have seen before. They do not see a lot of non-Muslims or foreigners and do not trust them. Walking in the city at night, a woman actually shields her children from me as I walk past. Restaurants are worse than the north, and totally uninviting. Being solo, it's hard to walk into a room of intimidating men and make enquires about the food. The waiters want you to leave and are very unhelpful, much like when a homeless person wanders into a restaurant in the West. I retreat to my hotel room for tuna on crackers. All the formalities, dangers, bike practicalities and heat leave me with very little when I get off the bike.

Being culturally adventurous requires energy and determination. I just want to be still, alone and away from prying eyes when I stop. The 'now and then' cigarette becomes a daily thing. It helps curb hunger, stops the vibration in my hands and dulls the sensory overload. The body works hard to push the bike, but the mind also works hard processing what it is sees. I'm fine with breakfast and lunch coming off the bike. It's dry, bland and unexciting, but it keeps me going and is safe. I need a proper dinner, however, but in a lot of these places I feel very unwelcomed, making meals alone in public difficult. In the desert on the bike I'm loving it, but I come to dread dinnertime. There is only so much attention I can take everyday. It's too much for me to have fifty people watch every time I take a bite of food that I'm not sure about.

I've yet to find a rhythm in all of this. Riding the bike is primary, but rest is also key. Where and how to get food I am comfortable with is also important. At one stage I go six cold meals in a row off the bike and get quite low. 'The fear' is constantly present and I'm just desperate not to get ill here, so don't take chances. I often find myself in a blurry confusion, where it's hard to make clear rational decisions. I'm disappointed in myself. Operating in this zone of reduced mental balance, everything appears a hazard and the smallest thing becomes the biggest worry. I resolve that I will be fine if I keep moving, so doggedly push on. I develop a navigational system of fallbacks which helps. If I can have a few options available I can take it as it comes. If I make it to X by noon, I will proceed to Y. It takes time to learn the road and my average travel times, as well as dealing with psychological swings and energy levels. The age-old traveller's mantra comes through time and time again, be it sleep, clean food, petrol, water, anything – 'Get it while you can.' This is the Sahara desert, after all. There are moments of pure elation at making it this far. One minute it's amazing, one minute deadly; the scenery changes but the mental loop remains. I am here, and that accomplishment feels wonderful, but it's all a bit foggy.

The Sahara is enchanting, like the surface of the moon. The land has a rhythm. Standing on the edge of the earth as it falls into the sea while looking back to the depths of the desert is truly mystical. It helps balance out the road and quiet the demons in my mind. You may die here – but who gets to see this? I dreamed of literally riding off into the sunset, and here I am doing just that. The view stretches to the horizon in all directions, with nothing moving and no signs of humanity at all. It's an incredible feeling.

I've never had a GPS before, but figured I should have one for the trip. I call it 'the box' and never really get on with it. I reckoned that out here it could be the difference between life and death, however. Here now, it simply says, 'Head straight for 500 miles'. There are no other roads. Bloody useful that. I'm now working in GPS co-ordinates, and note petrol station locations and hotels as numbers. With Gloria holding 23 litres, I can get 250 miles easily and never have any real worrying moments. Petrol and water are the only two things I never really struggle to find. Hospitality, clean food, feeling secure, comfort and good sleep are intermittent.

I pull off the road for a rest in Dakhla. Time off the bike is great for the body and time off for the mind helps me process everything. While planning back home it all seemed 'desert'. Being here it's fascinating to see the many stages. It's far from a plain flat desert. Morocco was a teaser, Western Sahara the real deal and I have no idea what to expect from Mauritania. The land just seems to stretch on forever.

Further down the road Bir Gandouz is known solely for the Hotel Barbas, and a petrol station. Straight out of an Indiana Jones movie. The main courtyard lobby is covered with a military-style netting that flaps in the hot wind, as all walks of life gather under it in the central open plan lobby. I park in the lobby, right next to tables where people are eating and no one bats an eyelid. One table is on a religious crusade, one a treasure hunt, another planning a robbery. All sorts of shady characters. I can imagine in the Dakar Rally days this place was a big hang-out.

The annual rally was cancelled in 2008, and from 2009 now runs through South America, but sneakily still holds the name 'Dakar'. It was moved for security reasons, mainly terrorist attacks on competitors and support staff in Mauritania. Now it thrives with over 500 competitors in South America bringing in millions of dollars to the local economies of Peru, Bolivia and Argentina. Cynics would shove it in Africa's face and say, 'See what you're missing out on due to your lack of control?' However, your typical African here doesn't give a shit, as nothing makes much of a difference here.

Dinner is served in a tagine bowl on a dirty piece of thick cardboard. The UN show up for something and add to the crazy vibe. It's a real life Mos Eisley cantina – ready to kick off at any second, and then instantly settle again as it happens all the time. Hot food sets me up for sleep in a basic room, and

I leave the madness just outside the paper-thin door. For the first time I get a cockroach on the inside of the mosquito net. The demons chase me though the night again. I wish I could say it was a pleasant midnight interlude, but it certainly wasn't.

In the morning I head for coffee in the lobby, trying to hit the border before it opens. The waiter's just arrived and as he switches on the lights the cockroaches scram off the service counter. He literally wafts one off the bar before he places down my coffee cup. Solid start to the day. The sun casts a beautiful glow as it comes up over the rocky sand dunes, the sand in the wind occasionally blocking out the light. The road is empty, desolate and eerie. The rocks are another unique wind-mangled mess in the half-light. I keep a steady clip and press hard to make the border in time, another surreal personal moment in an unforgettable landscape. The early twilight and moving dark red hues create a mysterious mood. I can't see anyone else at all as I throttle the corners and lean the bike over. We might just be starting to bond.

The lorry tailback stretches out for miles, the only sign there is a border ahead. I arrive ten minutes before the gates open and relax before the stampede. It's somewhat ordered here as you get penned in with a gate at the front and one at the rear exit. Once in, you go through about six steps, with no discernible order. Many people don't have the correct paperwork and people are trying their luck, creating tension. In amongst this they are building here, so workmen push wheelbarrows and shovels about. Men sit down on the job and stare blankly at you while they smoke their cigarettes. The only directions are from other travellers or heavy-handed officials, pointing and chastising the place in line. We shuffle about, like temporary prisoners having a chat in breaktime. Everything is barked at you and everyone stares at me – the odd one out. It's frustrating and confusing, but eventually I get through the steps and make my way to the exit before one final check.

'Did you see the guy before me?'
'Yes.'
'Where is your ticket?'
'He didn't give me one.'
'Back!'

This happens at every stage. Two steps forward and one back. It's like each officer in the process has never met or talked to any of the other officers before. They only know their one stage, and run it by the rules as if the entire universe rests on them doing it by the book. No one considers the whole process from start to finish. It's completely binary, and there is no room for grey – it does not compute. You can only be a 1 or a 0 here, nothing else. Still, there is some kind of calm pandemonium to it. Finally I'm cleared. Having thought a lot about no man's land, I now face one.

No man's land is a fascinating idea. A piece of land with no owner, no sovereignty – a small but wild lawless place near our doorsteps. Could the no man's lands of the world form a union? I feel like I'm going into another world yet again; it happens a few times a day here. Surprisingly, it's fresh black tarmac. It runs for about one kilometre and abruptly stops. There are no signs, the tarmac an arrow pointing to nothing. I look out to nothing, just an open view of sand, rock and small hills. I catch sight of a lorry in the distance, driven by a drunkard, zig-zagging its way across open land. The surface is sand, gravel and some natural stone. I head for the direction of the lorry, and hope for the best, trying to avoid deep sand where I can. I focus on trying to keep the bike upright, thrashing around for about four kilometres. I look up onto the hillside, and see the same UN trucks from Hotel Barbas last night. Soldiers behind sandbags, with a fifty-calibre machine gun pointed in my general direction. Comforting. Further along I see two white posts in the distance, and conclude it must be the spot. There is more sand, but I open her up and we reach the concrete ramp out of the sand into to the unpromised land of Mauritania. It's a small victory to tackle it without dropping the bike.

I stop at five 'soldiers' with machine guns at the top. They have no uniform and look more like bandits. One kindly pulls down his face scarf so I can read his face. I have to wait for 'visa man'. One of the soldiers talks with me a bit in loose languages, keen to study the bike. He asks my team, I say Chelsea and his face lights up. I pretend to know what I'm talking about and make a friend. Soon I attract a fixer, but the friend stays in the chat to make sure he doesn't mess me about. With an hour time change, I'm stuck for at least an hour waiting for 9 a.m. More people from the border start arriving and milling about. Visa man eventually shows up and instantly gets mobbed by the crowd, a bit like a pop star arriving. He reminds me of the Imp from *Game of Thrones*. Mock him on his walk to work, and you are fucked. He has that look as he circles the room and makes eye contact with anyone – *'Are you looking at me? Go on, laugh … make a joke.'*

Eventually the visa comes, as the fixer tries it on with the usual methods. At one stage he jumps ahead with my passport and bike registration to get the import stage started. I'm wary, but it's a small closed border again. Sure enough, I get stopped moving forward, and challenged for my papers.

'Muhammad has them.'

'Muhammad who?'

'Um, I don't know. He works here. He's been here all morning.' I realise how stupid I sound.

'Muhammad who? Everyone is called Muhammad!'

'He was just here.'

'Wait there and do not move!'

I have a small panic at the foolishness of the situation. On the positive side it's a stolen moment to scoff some dry bread. You are never supposed to let go of any documents to anyone, of course, but it's easier said than done. Muhammad soon reappears, inquisitively asking why I am waiting. I point to the guard and he shouts to him in French. The guard's eyes light up and they exchange long hand shakes, hugs and pats on the back and have a long friendly chat.

'This is Tall Mohammad. Why didn't you say, my friend?'

Borders. Five hours later, sometime around noon, I'm spat out the other side – officially in Mauritania, apprehensively staring at the first 'red zone' as hundreds of bandit-looking types are staring at me. I pull in for fuel, but there is no petrol. People appear to be nodding as they do the head to toe on me so many times, looking me over. I stop to get some supplies and the docile crowd quickly stands up and walks towards me with their wares. One chap even runs to be the first hawker to reach me. I get the feeling I will be mobbed and instinctively pull out. *Run.* They all frown as I pass at speed. I'm sure it's harmless street-selling, but it was the first time people have reacted like that. Won't be the last either. In the confused hot blur the stupid needless fear is magnified a thousand times.

The sun and temperature are impossible. It's over 40C and I think the tyres are going to melt. I put my head down and push inland. The sand turns from a normal 'sand' colour to a beautiful light red. The hills disappear, and it's an inhospitable flat, brutally hot desert. The dwellings are crude, made out of rubbish, the plastic edges flapping away in the hot wind. I lift the visor and for the first time ever regret it. It's like a hot hammer to the face and I instantly snap it shut again. An old train runs alongside the road, totally surreal in this setting. I get low on petrol as it nudges 48C. I'm riding a motorbike in a large oven. I stop to ask some people in a village about fuel and they are really helpful and nice. Surprisingly bubbly in the heat. Without lunch it all blurs a bit, but in a red zone I'm not hanging around. I find fuel at Station Inn Boamatou. The forecourt is sand, a joy on an overloaded bike. It's a rest stop for tour buses, so there are people everywhere. Street hawkers selling who knows what abound. Gloria and I get swarmed as we pump fuel. Two feet away one guy smokes and another uses his mobile phone. By the time the tank is full fifty people surround us. No one seems to give a shit about anything except the bike.

The day starts to drag on as I reach the outskirts of Nouakchott. The town starts miles out, with the biggest avenue of intimidation yet. In the desert proper there were no real checkpoints. I wasn't sure if this was a good thing or not, but didn't stop to find out. I get lost in town trying to find the hotel. Most of the streets are sand, so it's hard work. I stop for fuel, and the attendant asks if I am going to Senegal. He sneaks a picture of the bike with his mobile and goes to take one of my face as I stop him angrily.

'What was that for?'

'I'll tell my friend to look out for you down the road – you're headed to Rosso, right?'

'Yes.'

I wasn't going for Rosso, but he didn't need to know that. Quickly you pick up on these little tricks.

'Are you alone?'

'No, my friends got here earlier. I had a flat tyre and am catching them up.'

'How many of there are you?'

'Ten.'

I quickly adapt to give a constant flow of misdirection if asked anything here. It's instinctive to throw them off the scent and remain totally unpredictable in my movements. At the hotel I research the route ahead one more time. The maps start getting confusing here, so you also have to use Google Earth to double-check the reality of the road. Often the paper map says one thing, the GPS another and the actual road another again. Sometimes there can be seven roads coming off one junction, with no signs. The only sealed road is the N2 to Senegal, passing through Rosso. Rosso is either the top border experience in Africa, or the gates of hell, depending on your disposition. It sounded like hell to me, so I planned to bypass it. The main hassle at Rosso is apparently theft from bikes while they are not attended, making it tricky solo. It's also well known for general madness, bribery and stress. There is a smaller border called Diama, through Diawling National Park, which involves around forty miles of off-roading. Most people avoid it as it can be a nightmare in the rain, but its time for Gloria to step up.

The road to Diama is not on Google Maps, but is on the satellite image. This is often the case for West Africa, where roads are being quickly built by the Chinese to get at the natural resources. Often of poor quality, lasting only a few years before they sadly fall apart, there is no money to maintain them. The locals are left with no resources, and no roads either. Of course the Chinese are not the only ones at it; we did more than our share of exploitation here. Outside of Nouakchott the road continues to deteriorate. The main 'highway' south is one lane on either side – a 'B' road in England. At one stage it just stops and the way forward verges off the side of the road on to red clay for ten miles, the dust overwhelming and visibility poor. Cars and lorries steer for the same evenish patches of land in a high-speed death dance. It would be fascinating to sit and watch, if you were not working so hard to stay out of their way and not get killed. I'm extremely happy with my bike choice at this stage. Gloria is the ultimate all-rounder.

The landscape starts to change rapidly. In a few places the red sand gives way to red clay dirt, and then, like an old friend, brown dirt appears again in places. The first dirt I've seen since Spain. There is even a tree here and there. Past Keur-Macene and into the park this increases, passing into green subtropical lands. Unlike the subtle slow changes of the Sahara landscape, this is much quicker. In just one ride I go from desert to jungle. I stop and ask an old boy sitting by the side of the road the way. He simply smiles and kindly points. I turn for the off-road section and it goes totally quiet. The mud and clay road is mostly dry, and I breathe a huge sigh of relief. Finally alone, I feel an enormous weight lift with no one staring at me. Finally free. Up on the pegs and hammering it through the rough dirt tracks right at the edge of the Senegal River.

Huge birds sit at the river's edge and giant lizards run away from the bike, along with the ugliest wild boars I have ever seen. It's finally an adventure. There are a couple of slides on the back wheel, but we stay upright and chip on. After the past few turbulent days this is simple old-school fun and I'm shouting like a ten-year-old. The track continues along the water's edge the entire time. At some stages it gets boggy, but nothing too difficult. Halfway I come across a truck which is stuck in the mud as another truck tries to pull it out. A few guys are pushing and sweating profusely. It looks like the first truck had been there for some time. I offer assistance, and we have a brief chat. They have been without provisions and only want water, so I give them a bottle of mine. Now and then I see a minibus coming at me full speed, trying to stay moving on the muddy track, but I'm mostly alone.

Sooner than expected, I pitch up to Diama. Thankfully, it's the sleepy border described. No one is crossing. Nothing is happening at all, in fact. The bike is not an issue here. Sadly, as I nearly enter 'black Africa' the bribes begin. It's a known factor on every crossing south. Each stage of the border has a bribe. They ask for it and you can either dispute it and wait it out, or pay up. If you contest it, they will eventually let you pass hours later, after a lot of tut-tutting and aggression. Or you can simply pay and go. The last beer I had was in Rabat, so I'm keen to get to my hotel, just thirty minutes on the other side of the border. I know what my approach is.

Ten euros here, five dollars there, five bucks to lift the barrier on the bridge and over to the other side ... another five to get the barrier lifted on the Senegal side, ten euros for immigration, ten dollars for customs and off you go. Forty-five euros in forty-five minutes, or free in ten hours, with lots of anger and waiting about. Your choice. It's less 'time is money' (a shit way of seeing the world) and more I simply didn't want to fight. It's exhausting. Today at least. Sure enough, I have a massive row with customs on the Senegal side. They really do not like anyone who talks back. Nothing is ever clear in these unique places. Any questions at all, no matter how innocently asked, seem declarations of aggression towards the officials.

Magically, I am suddenly in the tropics. All the faces are a dark shade of black. Glorious beautiful smiling shapely women! They walk the streets half-clothed and it's a wonderful sight after the Muslim countries of the North. How women brighten our world! There is also an army of new bugs and pests. Things the size of golf balls swarm through the air everywhere, causing me to duck a few times as I ride along. Senegal is also a return to a green zone. Women, safety and beer – at least, that's what I've prepared myself for mentally. It's not what I find, however. Here the weight of African sociology and economics finally kicks in. Everything sparks an endless string of thoughts, with an explosion of people and activity on the streets. The road means people, and everything is happening on or around it. More stalls are set up at the roadside. The dwellings are simply on the side of the road, daily life happening right on the road.

It's work to take it all in. I struggle to find the hotel again, as it's across a field of sand. I pass kids playing football next to a giant burning pile of rubbish. The whole setting is an urban landscape I have never seen the likes of. The hotel is basic, and the water stinks. It's taken directly from the river and I think I might get dirtier using it. I keep my mouth clamped shut as the sulphur-smelling sticky liquid runs over my face. Odd bugs are all over the room. The restaurant is open to the air, now that I am firmly in a malaria zone. The beer is cold and plentiful. From the bar I can see Gloria having a rest herself and happily think, those bastards aren't laughing now, are they, girl?

Leaving Saint-Louis, it's only 150 miles south to Dakar, but it will take all day. I roll through Saint-Louis in the early morning, instantly shaken by what I see. Like most people, I have seen documentaries about Africa – pictures, TV and talked to people from 'there'. Now 'here', however, it's done nothing to prepare me for seeing it in real life. You have to see it yourself to understand. The poverty and filth is unprecedented. You can get your head around a village without running water or electricity. When you see one hundred of them in one day, however, it makes you question everything. If the Sahara was the peak of this leg, Saint-Louis is the trough. Skirting the fringes, I see things I wish I had never seen.

There is filthy standing water everywhere, like the river has flooded. There are no drains, so the sewage and the river water are one. The smells go from burning rubbish to sewage, rotten flesh and back to burning rubbish. The river runs along the road on one side, with rough dilapidated buildings and vacant lots on the other. In the river children play, where ten feet from them a man is taking a piss in the water. Another ten feet on a woman is doing her washing. Another ten feet on there is a dead bloated cow rotting away, swollen in the sun and crawling with maggots. Ten feet further and another group of children are playing. This pattern repeats with small variations for over a mile.

Open sewage runs across the road and into the river. On the other side skinny goats and chickens feed on piles of rotten rubbish. I can't tell if buildings are being built, or just falling down. People also scour the rubbish for anything of value or sustenance. At this moment, if you ask me to describe this part of Africa in one word I would only muster 'hopeless'. They all stop what they are doing and stare at me. How can they ever understand a journey like mine? I have money and I am using it for something non-essential. It doesn't translate. My trip of a lifetime instantly seems totally absurd. Every direction I look the images are too hard to absorb. The conflict in my mind grows by the metre, my idea of the world changing by the minute. Like a child with a bad nightmare I'm shit-scared – except this is real.

The Sahara had intimidated me, but Senegal shakes me to my core. I've never seen poverty and filth like this. I cannot process how people can live like this. It shuts me down and I can't think, nearly frozen in shock. All the streams of thought which have been so active go deathly quiet. At no stage do I have the urge to get the camera out. In this moment, I do not want to remember what I'm seeing, but know I will. I put my eyes forward and roll on. Like a car crash, I don't want to look, but I can't help it. Is that a dead human over there? Maybe: who knows?

The air is heavy and it's hard to move. Here it is. Everything happening in slow motion. My body is pumping fear instead of blood. I am humbled, blown away, crying inside with the sight. The maggots are in my mind now, eating away at me. *'If you gaze long enough into the abyss, it will gaze into thee.'* The kid who played with fire is now getting burned. How does such a place exist? What the hell am I doing here?

I roll out of Saint-Louis haunted. Green landscapes help calm me down and the road is endlessly distracting, demanding all my concentration. Reflecting on Saint-Louis, I think it was the arsehole of the world. I challenge anyone who thinks they know the world to walk those streets and not feel their mind turn upside down. In one filthy sweep, it challenges every assumption I have about our way of life. I grow disappointed that I cannot appreciate the reality I am in. As a well-travelled adult I pride myself on getting in step with whatever culture I'm in, but this is a whole new level and I am lost. Like a child going abroad for the first time. I can only think - you don't know shit, boy. It always upsets me when people don't want to go places because they do not want to see horrible things there. As if they don't see it, it's not happening. I think that's shit. All the more reason you should see it if it upsets you. Change the world then. Try at least. I have to admit to myself, though, I don't think what I've just seen can be saved. Trying to understand Africa has begun. This is possibly the world's greatest conundrum, with millions of suffering lives on the scales.

I consider what we can learn from Africans. Watch a TV show on hoarding or 'doomsday preparation' in this light and you see how utterly absurd and excessive our culture is. Happy people are on the streets here, laughing and chatting – filthy, in the same clothes for a month. They have no idea what a running shower is like – how can they miss one? They have no idea what a supermarket looks like; you just get your goods at a shack down the road – if you are lucky. Sometimes they have things, sometimes they don't. There might of be tinned tuna, but there are not fifty varieties of it. Houses are shacks. They don't have windows or doors. They are the size of a double bed and several people live in there. There is no bed, no sheets and no pillows.

Mainly they live outside. They cook on fires in front of their homes, mostly maize foodstuffs. Not 'dishes', for they do not have dishes or cutlery. They eat by hand, directly from the pan the food is cooked in, not on a table but in the centre of the floor. I think of a kitchen cabinet showroom back home, and I cannot reconcile the thoughts. The efforts we go to to be comfortable, thinking they are normal. I understand people are different, but this gulf is so wide I cannot mentally cross it. Am I actually still here on earth? I've never seen so much nothing before. I have been to Australia, South America and beyond, literally to the other side of the planet. Yet in this moment, only 3,000 miles from home, I have never been this far away from 'home'.

There is a never-ending African village along the side of the road the whole way. I dub it 'NAV'. It's thick, slow going and requires all of my attention. With a maximum daily range of 200 miles, not only is it physically tough, but mentally it requires stamina. I have all the gear, a golden bike, the determination and money to make this trip happen. However, I do not have anywhere in my brain ready to file these images and thoughts away. They fester on my consciousness, clouding my vision. They stack up in my mind, getting heavier by the mile. Just like the liver processes units of alcohol, the brain needs to process disturbing things. My mind nearly shuts down by the time I reach Dakar, sick with some kind of mind poisoning.

Near Dakar, the sight of a motorway is a shock, even if only for a brief blast into Dakar on an elevated stretch. Either side of the road is more conflicting chaos to absorb as I get deeper and deeper into an urban hell. I have a week in Dakar to chase more visas, give Gloria some TLC and process what I've seen so far. I stay two nights in a crappy hotel, and then do some research which leads me to La Villa 126. Sylvie and Gil, the French expat owners there, breathe hospitality. Once there I am back into comfort and some sense of normality. I'm spooked, and several times I simply decide to call it a day and head home. I sleep a lot, and think about the world. I can feel 'my world' rapidly changing. It's exhausting and I lounge about for a few days trying to process it all. Time slows, and I find myself staring at the wall, trying to adjust. Saint-Louis was just a small taste of the road ahead and it sits with me for days.

Unloading Gloria, we whiz around town like we are on air. It's a refreshing change. The Ghanian embassy is first and they need my passport for a few days. Despite a lot of hassle, they eventually grant me a visa. At this stage I am racked with doubt and unsure if I want to go on. Nigeria remains a huge obstacle and the visa game is driving me mad. I don't want to admit I'm scared, but it's true. I'm scared to go out there on my own again. I think Saint-Louis will stick with me forever and I have no desire to see more versions of it. I've come all this way and I will kick myself if I don't continue, but I really have no urge right now. The doubt is crippling. I rethink everything – not just the trip, but my understanding of the world.

There is an odd knee-jerk reaction for me, which bizarrely manifests itself in a complete reaffirmation of all things English. I want to be the guy in the pub, laughing and joking with his mates, and staring at the odd uncomfortable foreigner that no one can understand. I want to be understood, and understand the world I wake up in. I think I want to marry Jo, have kids, settle and never venture back into this cruel fucking world again. I takes days to calm down and normalise. It takes a lot of beer and sleep. Sylvie and her girls look after me like royalty. The food is wonderful and restorative. Gloria gets some needed attention. She is safely parked next to Gil's bike, and I have a garage to work on her, crucially out of sight.

I strip the tyres and put on the off-road tyres I've carried thus far, literally a load off. Then comes the oil, and a new filter. I have an amusing moment when I ask the security guard Etienne what to do with the spent oil. He merely grabs it and says, 'I'll take that.' *Phuf* – it's gone – into his own moped likely.

The heat is intense and even out of the sun my clothes are soaked through in minutes working like this. It's hard to see working on the bike I sweat so profusely into my eyes. As I do it some local guys are working on an air conditioner in the garage next to me. When they arrive both wheels are off the bike and parts are everywhere. They stop in their tracks.

'What's wrong?'

'Nothing.'

'What are you doing?'

'It's called "maintenance".'

Clearly something that does't happen here. Most machines are on their last legs as parts are impossible to come by. They are busy with a blowtorch on a freon tank. I have to look the other way, fearing they will blow us up any second, and all this fretting will be in vain. There is no concept of safety here whatsoever. I meet a friend of my boss's, Cedric, a French expat who works in corporate security here in Africa. He specialises in bringing executives from Europe to tour their various 'industrial interests' in Africa. He reviews all my preparation and asks if I have a weapon, to which I say no. He says, 'Do you want a 9mm? Might be a good idea. We can go to the market now and get you one for 800 euros.'

'Um, no thanks. I think I'm OK.'

He says the best thing with my plans is that I am solo with no fixed plan, which has to be a first. No one has ever said that. Apparently, with a fixed itinerary, people can leak this information. The bad guys will know your movements and you are liable to risk. We have a beer and chat about life in Africa. It's great to talk with an expat who lives here and enjoys it.

Often in the night after a power cut the locals walk the streets banging pans and making a din. It happens daily. You never see them, just hear them. I ask Sylvie about this and she doesn't know why they do it. She goes on to tell me many stories about life in Dakar which are all fascinating. Sad as it all is to hear, it's also cathartic to talk about Africa with someone. When you roll around with all this shit in your head and no one to talk to it gets heavy. Daily chats and a cup of tea with Sylvie help me no end in processing this new reality I find myself in.

After a few lazy days, I start to feel a lot more myself again. I research the road to Ghana and make a basic plan. I try the Nigerian embassy in Dakar, but they drop the 'non-resident' line on me. Nigeria accounts for one-fifth of Africa's entire population and scares the shit out of me. I don't want to go at all, especially when they make you jump through so many hoops to do so. The visa application in the UK was a dead end – fourteen documents and over £200 later. I was going to try my luck in Accra, but I felt it was going to be a fruitless. I consider skipping it, and somehow going around it.

Cue days of research online. Boats to San Tome, boats to Libreville, planes to Kinshasa – all dead ends or megabucks. Angola is also a troublesome visa country, so I wonder if I can fly to Namibia and pick up the trail from there. It's an attractive thought, and one of those that once I had thought it, I couldn't unthink it. I was short-changing the whole idea of London to Cape Town, but I was not inspired at this stage to go further. Every source of information is bad. Local advice is to totally avoid doing Nigeria alone. I'd just thrown caution to the wind in Mauritania, but didn't feel I'd be so lucky trying it twice.

For me this part of Africa is bloody hard work for very low inspiration. Of course, I'm not giving the centre of Africa the justice it deserves. However, I can look over ten pictures of ten rural African villages, in ten different countries and not see any real differences. The land changes, and I'm sure it's beautiful, but the way of life doesn't really change in a way I can appreciate. It's all hand-to-mouth, dirty and very uncomfortable for a Westerner. I'm used to the depth of culture and variation you would see in Europe, but these parts of Africa just don't have that for me. Maybe you would see the differences if you spent some time 'in the huts' but I have no interest in doing so. I'm far too cowardly for that; they simply freeze me with fear. I'm convinced that inside of them is disease, drama and danger. It's hard enough to watch life outside the huts. I'm dazed by what I have seen, and disappointed in myself that I cannot summon the gumption to continue. It's disheartening after the huge build-up to the trip. I'm disappointed in myself with all these irrational fears I can't seem to control.

I update friends and family and spook several of them by accident in the process. My uncle drops me a note saying, 'Are you OK? What happens if it fucks up there? Do I need to be ready to come and get you?' I run through the worst case scenarios myself for him and it helps us both a lot. With all the distractions in the last few days I had forgotten all of the preparation I had done. All the worst cases are mostly covered, but it's the step before that which worries me. The thought of contracting dysentery and being on the toilet dehydrated for a week in some filthy hovel terrifies me. If I can keep moving I will be OK. If I stop, I'm sure it will invite some drama.

My uncle goes further, which amuses me.

'You know you should be careful, criticising these Muslim countries. They could be monitoring your e-mails and communication.'

'Um, they can't even keep the power on down here for longer than a couple hours. I don't think that's an issue.'

I'm finally packing the bike up again before leaving town tomorrow when I notice a rear flat tyre. Fuck. These streets are covered in broken glass and it must be a slow puncture. It's 10 p.m. and pitch dark outside, but still 35+ C. I know if I tackle this now it will take an hour and my clothes will be soaked through. I consider staying another day as Gil wanders by.

'Can you get the tyre off? If so, just give it to Etienne and he can ride it into town and get it fixed …'

Within a minute the tyre is off and disappears down the road on Etienne's moped between his feet. Twenty minutes later it's back, fixed. Two dollars. I give him five bucks and he is over the moon. Show me where in London you can get that done at 10 p.m. I have breakfast with Sylvie and Gil the next day before I leave. They have become dear friends and they want me to keep them updated with my progress. If I have any issues in Senegal I am to call them immediately. It's a great comfort; they are my first real connection and lovely people. I can't thank them enough for helping me over the initial shock of Africa. Sylvie also gives me a delicious cake which lasts for days on the bike, a real bonus!

I leave Dakar more stable mentally and physically rested, but still deeply afraid of what's ahead.

FOUR

GLORY GET YOUR GUN
Dakar – Accra

'The depth of darkness to which you can descend and still live is an
exact measure of the height to which you can aspire to reach.'
Pliny the Elder

Busy waving goodbye to my friends at La Villa 126, I nearly stack it on the first corner. After a week of being fully unloaded, school is in session once again to manage the kitchen sink on the back of the bike. After a brief blast out of Dakar on the motorway, it's back to NAV. Despite the slow chaotic progress, Gloria and I are developing more of a rhythm now. The villages become more familiar as I start to spot the patterns.

We develop tactics to navigate the terrain. There are two ways to handle potholes: firstly to gun it and take the hits. This keeps your speed, but leaves you liable to punctures. Second is a more reserved pace of around 50-60 mph, trying to snake around them. This slows you down, but avoids punctures. Both likely net out the same speed overall, one with just potentially more hassle factor. I mostly go with the second option. The day starts that way at least, but later in the day the first method starts to creep in as I get anxious to get off the bike. The ceaseless attention gets worse the further I travel inland. No one else wears any kind of protective gear at all, and I assume I must look like an alien in mine. I imagine if I crash, I'll be swarmed by crowds, all trying to get a look at an alien that fell from the sky. If my guts are hanging out, they'll be looking to see if green blood pumps out of me. They stare at Gloria like they have never seen a motorbike, or at times never even seen the wheel before.

Locals blow the checkpoints unless actively pulled in, so I follow suit. I learn to creep in neutral behind a truck approaching a road block, using it as a shield. At the last minute I drop her into second gear, pop out from behind the side of the truck and wave at the police as I swiftly pass. They jump upright in surprise and naturally wave back. Once I have that wave, I look forward only and pull off sharply. I call it 'ghosting' and it works well. The more I do it, the more my confidence grows. The apathy becomes overwhelming.

The trucks are a subculture in themselves. They have a driver – more like

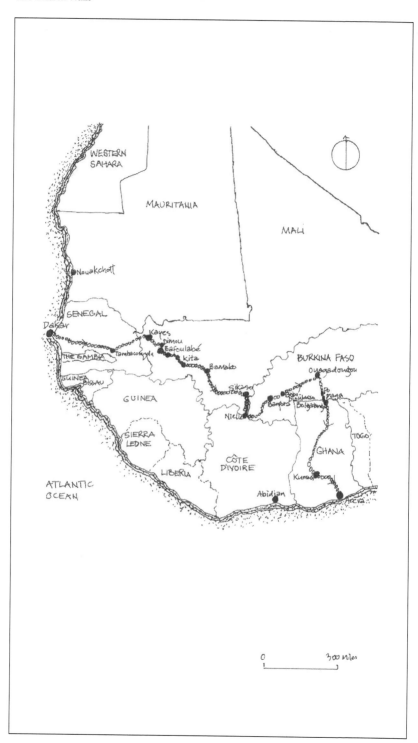

a captain – with a whole crew, usually four or five people. The captain has two older 'seconds' who do the important mundane and heavy stuff. Then there are two 'runts' around 10-12 years old, who do the lighter daily graft. There is space in the cab, so they all can cram in there. You often see the wide-eyed runts staring down in amazement as you pass the truck. Collectively they look after the load, but their main purpose is to keep the truck moving. They are a bit like a pit crew in Formula 1, in extreme slow motion. I estimate they get one flat tyre every 100 miles – they use the first option on tackling potholes, hitting them head on. Then the whole crew springs to life, and everyone has a clear role.

The typically slow Africans, suddenly working quickly to change out the tyre, then throw it on the back with the other 'spares'. They often have a stack of ten wheels on the back for just this purpose, further weighing down the crippling loads they are carrying. All of the tyres are worn and scrubbed, and there was not a new tyre to be seen anywhere in the whole of West Africa. I didn't see anything remotely new in this area, to be fair. With so much time spent on the road I observe more truck life and their bizarre subculture. When stopped at a border or when they often broke down, the whole crew lives under the truck. They carry out their daily life there. I would often see them cooking, praying, bathing, playing cards and sleeping. There is often extra cargo stashed on or around any free space on the truck. Bags of potatoes over the wheel arches or bags of carrots or coal in the space around the spare tyres on the back. No journey is wasted, which is respectable. At the same time they are working the truck too hard and it breaks down as a result. They approach it one journey at a time, as opposed to looking to the future.

Mornings become a comfort zone, a quiet moment alone. Rising for a coffee at 4 a.m. in the room gives me peace. With the bike loaded, I catch sunrise as I roll out. The first two hours of the day are always the best, a refreshing sense of tranquillity after the madness from the day before. The road is quiet, and I enjoy the views, covering big distances. The sense of freedom soothes me, and a sense of routine helps keep me steady. The light is special in the morning. Being on a calm African street is rare; every time feels like a special experience. To observe without being observed. My eyes learn new colours and hues which I have never seen before. It's not becoming *normal*, social scenes still have a huge impact, but it all slowly becomes more familiar. Some days you just roll with it, taking it as it comes. Some days you feel like the Africans have removed your brain and are playing football with it. I continue to see many things I have never seen before every day.

Approaching Kidira on the eastern edge of Senegal, near the border with Mali on the River Faléme, nothing is clear. Eventually, after a few laps of the busy streets, I find Immigration. I pull up to a line of over five hundred sweaty people with a sense of dread. All of them watch the white man sweating, with no idea what to do. Fortunately, there is an official overseeing proceedings who barks for my passport. He ushers me into a dark room (there is no electricity). Someone stamps the passport, and off I go again. I walk back out feeling guilty, looking at the pleading hot faces. I have no idea what the queue is about, but feel terrible thinking I'm a rich white tourist getting preferential treatment. I later find out the queue is for those without paperwork, coming from Mali into Senegal. It's often the case: if you have your paperwork in order you can usually get through quickly and smoothly. However, you never know until you know. Crossing a border is partly a rush, and partly a glimpse into the peak of inhuman bureaucracy.

The bridge to Mali is the only concrete structure for miles. I am waved through the barriers, and told to find customs further up the road. The bridge is packed with trucks, tail to tail on both sides of the road, with only one lane in the middle moving towards Mali. There is not much space, and the bridge has seen better days. I slowly roll up the road, taking it all in. The trucks parked on the sides have been there for days, truck culture in full swing beneath them, the camps well established. The road remains elevated after the bridge, but either side the ground falls sharply away to a row of huts and bustling activity beneath. Between the huts and the raised road is a stream of sewage and rubbish. People walk down by the huts, mopeds sloppily whiz between pedestrians. Watching all of this, the truck before me slows and unexpectedly stops. Quickly I understand I should be down below with the mopeds. Immediately I turn around to check my exit as another truck is twenty feet away, creeping up behind me. I'm instantly boxed in. Panic strikes. A lorry to the front, back, left and right – all stopped. A box less than twenty foot square leaves me trapped.

The crews just stare at me, like at a frightened caged animal. Twenty pairs of peering eyes watch every move I make under the noon sun. I put the side stand down and try to look calm. I pretend to ignore them, but my eyes are doing a constant circuit of everything, watching for any signs of increased energy or movement. I hold the best 'what the fuck are you looking at' face I can muster to anyone who makes direct eye contact and they look away when I look directly at them. They stare away at this uncommon sight. Being a border, there are the usual shady types, spitting, eating, smoking – a bunch of filthy-looking criminals. My mind immediately assumes the worst in everyone. I try to keep my cool. I've not had lunch, but I'm not about to break out the wet wipes and make a crisp sandwich with this audience. Outwardly I busy myself with the bike. Inwardly I just try to keep my composure. This is the most vulnerable I've felt on the trip so far. Any one of them can rob me and there will be nothing I can do about it. We sit like this for two difficult hours. There is no explanation, and I can't leave the bike to see what the hold-up is. Nothing to do but sit. The trucks feel like a car crusher slowly squeezing in on me under the stifling sun.

I run every scenario over in my mind. I examine the gaps between the trucks, but they are too small to fit through, and have a nasty drop-off down to the river of sewage. I could run if I had to, but I expect Gloria would be picked dry in seconds. She is my only ally right now and I might kill someone if they try to touch her. It's a clear battle line. I will defend us with whatever I have: my fists, a spanner from the tank bag, even the bike pinning someone against a truck. They are my soldiers ready for war. We're clearly outnumbered, but have everything to lose. I feel like a general about to go into battle shouting 'Hold, hold, hold!' Waiting to give the call to lash out and charge, but the provocation never comes and I sit here like a lion backed into a corner, claws out, ready to pounce and fight for my life. As usual here, the only real battle is in my mind.

Instead, the sun bakes us all and we grow lazy. They stare on, I stare back. Street hawkers wander between the trucks, selling all kinds of goods I've never seen before and don't want. Everyone passing stops to have a look at the bike. Many try to chat, but I don't encourage it. I have a spanner out, working on tightening a bolt, which doesn't really need tightening. Holding it, pondering the meaning of life, I'm alerted when the truck in front miraculously moves. Deliriously I reason it must be a modern day staff, and somehow I had parted the mechanical seas. The African sun at noon is like a full moon for us. In just thirty minutes of direct exposure, you'll be jabbering at the skies like a madman.

I hold back a bit longer, keeping at least forty feet in front of me this time in case I need to bolt forward. Eventually things start to move freely again, and once again I keep as much distance around me as possible. People often ask about what weapons you are carrying; the bike itself is by far the most powerful one. She certainly scares people. It would be a short-lived display of power, but a big one. I would rather Gloria goes out like that under my control than gets stolen. Eventually I hit customs and it's the usual madness. No one knows what's going on, but everyone is shouting about something. Every room is chock-full of hot, filthy and tired people who just stare at you. It's pandemonium, but it's also normal now. I focus on the business at hand, showing them how the carnet works and stamping it myself. I smile as I take a moment to reset before entering a new country. Destiny would have never delivered me here. It's madness, but it's my madness, and I made it happen.

After such a busy border, outside of Diboli the road goes eerily quiet. There is nothing. If I thought Senegal was poor, Mali is another level below it. The potholes become big enough to swallow cars and break lorry axles. The land is burnt and black. The trees fight for life in the sand and everything is desiccated and dying. Anything that lives seems born to a slow torturous death here in this unforgiving oven. The hot wind is desolate, intermittent and the demons ride it like jellyfish. Transferring from pandemonium to silence makes it all the more stark. My mind starts to drift. There is no 'wildlife' here, just a hard life of wild. Over the horizon and out of sight, I can sense a pot of West African magic simmering away.

Approaching Kayes the temperature rises over 45C. One of the hottest places in Africa, apparently due to the copper mines surrounding it. The town is more poor hectic dusty chaos, the heat totally sapping. Things are once again as they seem – harsh, bleak and highly unmysterious. The hotel has the word 'palace' in it, but is not any form of a palace at all.

The demons are frantically busy again here in Mali. Mauritania was number one for danger, and Mali is number two. Northern Mali a strict red zone. So from here I work out a route south which will involve a lot of off-road. I'm intimidated, but excited to get away from the NAV. There is a clean motorway heading east, but it's off-limits as it's all in the red zone. The old road to Timbuktu, long loved by overlanders, is a strict no-go currently. People still do it, of course, but no one I had heard of has done it solo for years. I'm sure they are out there – there is always someone more hardcore than you. Certainly tougher than my childish scared self right now. I don't feel I have anything to prove, however. I'm happy to have made it this far.

Mali features in the news often, and is currently the deadliest place to serve in the UN. They really, really hate Westerners. My route would head along the River Senegal again, through Bafoulabé, Manantali and Kita on the way to the capital, Bamako. Rolling out through the city centre is the usual madness. It's here I realise I prefer the country to the cities in Africa. You can get what you need in the cities, but they also take what they need from you. The city feels wilder than the wild.

I make good progress as I head to Diamou, the road still busy with people, but it has a good surface. The landscape opens up and the road becomes more interesting. I feel something pleasant finally nudging my brain, rousing me to wake from active slumber. Finally, something beautiful in West Africa to observe. The river sweeps across the landscape; it is the landscape. Like the US, there are mountains and buttes in the far-off distance. It's beautiful and I stop for a few pictures here and there. Past Diamou the road gets quieter and it's mostly just me for once. I sit on a bridge over the river and take a look around. Apart from the water, nothing is moving. I breathe steady and calm in the stillness, a novel feeling here. Unpressured and unobserved, my eyes look up to truly see the landscape for the first time in ages. Like I just magically landed here from another realm.

The map is not the territory, as usual. The roads seem to do their own thing, refusing to be properly recorded. Like the people here, they retain a sense of anarchy. From Diamou to Bafoulabé the first 'new road' unexpectedly appears and instead of the off-road I had anticipated, I'm averaging 70 mph on a newly sealed road. Opening the bike up in this setting feels wonderful.

Bafoulabé means 'meeting of two rivers' and is the confluence of the Bafing and Bakoy rivers, which become the River Senegal, 600 miles from Saint-Louis at this point. 600 miles of Africans washing their laundry, pans, themselves, as well as going to the loo, dead and decaying animals, discarded scraps of voodoo, and who knows what else into it. No wonder Saint-Louis is such a shithole – it literally is the arsehole of Mali and Senegal. It's quiet and pleasant here, though. I catch a boat across the water and into the town. The boat has seen better days, there is no infrastructure at all, just a boat which lands and lets down a steel ramp to a banked hill of mud. Thankfully it's dry today. Waiting to board with me are some locals on foot, one truck, two cows and around two hundred goats. We all board as I snap a few pictures. No point trying to hide being a tourist here – it's clear as day.

People swarm the bike, oddly fascinated by the paper map in the tank bag most of all. It's the most low tech item I think I'm carrying, but it appears they have never seen a map of their own country like this. I try not to fret as they happily touch everything. The animals are not happy as they are whipped and shoved into place. They are savaged with sticks or dragged along with ropes around their necks, and it's sad to watch. I am the only one on the boat who pays. The man charmingly counts using his fingers and says 'one, two, five, three, five', twice to make sure I have understood. Their teeth look as though they have been eating dynamite. Women bathe naked in the water by the shore, making the child in me smile, as it's just like *National Geographic* pictures I saw as a kid.

I check the map at 10 a.m. as this is where I planned to be by nightfall. Solid start. The road goes over an old railway bridge across another arm of the river. An old man stops me and tries to extort a fee, but I feign I can't understand and he lets me go. I think at this pace I could make Bamako by this evening. The road skirts the river further, but I still don't see much wildlife apart from birds. I reach Manantali before lunch and weigh up my options. This is supposed to be night two. I look for fuel, but strike out. I finish Sylvie's cake as I ponder it. There is no one else here. I thought I might see another overlander or two, but it's just me as usual. If I make Bamako today, I will be ahead of schedule and have a complete day off the bike relaxing. It's an attractive thought, so I go for it. In a rush I'm off again.

After expecting three days of off-roading, I finally get a real taste. It's a basic track with mostly red clay, gravel, and some rough blockwork under the rivers to stop erosion. Without the blockwork the road would wash away in the rainy season. The brush grows thick on either side, and I imagine a hippo just wandering out in front of me. I don't see any, but feel the presence of animals all around. With the off-road tyres Gloria is a wonder and finally doing what she was born to do. A bull out of the china shop. Ten miles takes over thirty minutes, and I'm covered in sweat. I have no idea where the energy is coming from, but I take what I can and just push it. In rain this would be an all-day journey, but today it's sunny and dry. We stop for a picture or to spot a river crossing here and there. Gloria tears it up as trees and thorns thrash about us, catching my jacket often. The road just drops a foot here and there; it's basically a dry clay river bed. All the gear holds up and does what it should. I'm not sure I will make it out the other side, but I'm smiling ear to ear – it's simply superb!

There is not a single 'built' building, just occasional groupings of huts. The few people that see us have jaw-dropping stares, far more pronounced than the normal reaction we get. It's the most remote location on the trip so far, and the most dangerous riding yet. I'm likely 500 miles from the nearest hospital, but I feel comfortable, in control for once. The bike is a phenomenal machine, taking it all in its stride. It's a boxing match and we're raging twelve rounds without being knocked down once. There are plenty of punches, but we don't go down, thankfully. The golden rule rings true: when in doubt, speed up. The faster I go and hold it, the quicker my confidence grows. It's a great feeling to really be doing this. I'm here and now – totally in the moment. After days of worry and overthinking, I am finally thinking of nothing else but the piste.

Over halfway on the track I'm shattered and running on the last bar of fuel. The road improves a touch, and I absolutely hammer it to try and make up time. Stood on the pegs in full attack mode, I'm cheered on by some locals as I hit 60 mph with the back end all over the place. Their faces light up like Christmas as their fists punch the air. It feels incredible to let Gloria roll open full speed in this terrain. At the next round of drops I soon regret it, however, as they nearly throw me off the back like a rodeo. I've not slept well in days, carrying a 'no coffee headache', dehydrated, hungry, sweating profusely and simply having the time of my life! None of that shit matters now – only the ride.

The road is a big boulder as I freely swing my giant sledgehammer to break it down, a huge escape from all the woes. Near 4 p.m. we re-emerge on the outskirts of Kita, firmly in the reserve tank, wet through with sweat and heavily worked. As I fuel I check the map again. Struggling, I drink a litre of Coca-Cola. Within minutes I'm blasting off again into the stratosphere, like I've just done a gram of cocaine. Fast and loose, dangerous and quick. It's a joy to forget all the shit, fighting the dying light instead of the demons.

On a mission, with no confusion, a day off is a wonderful motivator. If anyone is in my way, Gloria is a big gun I wave in their face. I'm not shy with her anymore, not embarrassed, and I use her to make people jump out of the way. Deep down I sadistically enjoy it. If they are going to stare at me regardless, I might as well give them something to look at. It's sad in a way, but I'm just venting after all the endless attention. Childish, but very real. I also really want to get there. I can't believe I'm this close.

The fun doesn't last forever. I can see the sun starting to drop in the sky, and I panic I won't make Bamako by dark. I push harder and faster into the falling light, the classic recipe for an accident. I reach Kati as darkness takes over completely, still ten miles out from Bamako centre. Ten miles of hardcore

NAV, in the dark. The pleasant rushing abruptly stops, and the flushing begins. Being ahead of schedule, I have no accommodation booked. I reach out to my English brother who books me a room in a nice hotel. He kindly sends the coordinates, but they are unrecognised in the box. Pushing hard into a capital city, with no idea where I am going, in the dark, it all blurs again, more than ever before. Although it's only ten miles, I have to earn every single metre.

Kati is a transport hub, and just a small taste of what's ahead. A bus stop with thirty buses, except there is no station. Like a dusty football pitch with no order, and crazy shit going on everywhere. The road disappears into an unreadable mess, the way forward indiscernible. Dust is like fog blowing across the road. It blocks your vision, makes you choke and gets in your eyes. You follow a bus, only to have it pull in sharply and abruptly stop. When you go to get around that one, another bus nearly takes you out as it flies past. People are everywhere, and I can't see through the dust or hear through the horns. All the vehicles are careening around the place in aggressive unreadable paths. There are no street lights, only half the vehicles actually have lights, the others just moving around in the dark. It's an orchestra of close calls.

The road from Kati to Bamako is down a long overpopulated hill to the city below. Yet again I feel like I am descending into hell – this time with the lights off. Saint-Louis was the first circle of Dante's Inferno; this is more like the seventh circle – the circle of violence. I get stuck behind a full bus with no windows or lights. I don't think its engine is even running, it's just coasting down the steep hill and trying not to slow or stop. My upgraded HID headlight light kit comes into its own and thankfully saves the day. It's brighter than anything on the road and people stop in their tracks wondering what this alien object is hurtling towards them. In a backward sense, speed is my friend, so I push very hard.

I'm choking on dust and trying to wipe it out of my eyes so I can see in this pitch dark, while struggling to keep the bike upright. The mopeds are so light they can cut and dart. Getting Gloria to dance like that under the weight is a Herculean effort. She rubs shoulders with a few people in the process and I'm thankful for the steel panniers. Looking in any direction leaves me reeling in a sensory overload. At any hold-up the traffic and crowd of people just swarm around us like water hitting a dam, building pressure quickly and about to burst. Everyone spreads out as far as possible, trying to touch the starting line. Charging again until the next hold-up, where the pressure builds once more.

There is little order. It's a dark hurried hot chaos, the stuff of nightmares. Everyone stares at everything, especially me. My mind sees only two outcomes: either I will die tonight, or reach my destination. Either way, I will stop this bike and get off it, now my only priority. Hopelessly exhausted and lost, I pull into a petrol station and kill the lights. I disappear in a dark unlit corner like a spy. For a brief moment it works and I stare out at this truly foreign scene, dazed. It doesn't work for long, however, and soon a crowd forms around me. The noise, dust and stares suffocate me. For some reason I pretend I know what I am doing, keeping up appearances like an actor, but in reality I have no idea. I cannot find the hotel on any map source I have, and have no idea what to do. I have nothing in me and am horribly lost in all senses. I have lost track of time and am not really with it, not really here. It's the blurriest moment of the whole trip. My body has given all it had today; there is nothing left. I am in the third person.

Somehow I remember the old trick and flag a taxi to lead me to the hotel. He is dubious, but in the end I thankfully find the words. It's a good ten minutes out of town. I was miles off. I hug him when we get there, even through he really stinks. So do I at this stage. Finally some rest and comfort – it's a Radisson. It's *that* Radisson. The one which terrorists attacked in 2015 and killed twenty-three people. I'm pulled apart at security. I'm in no mood for it and have my first 'moment' as a Western tourist and completely throw the toys out of my pram. I have a lot of toys, and a very big pram.

They want to see in every bag I have. It's 9.30 p.m. and I need to stop and eat something besides dried goods. Oddly, I'm still jacked on the Coca-Cola, so let everyone have an earful, like a five-year-old having a fit. I reach my room and order some food, trying to compute all I have seen and done. It's too much. It's all a messy blur and I try to get a grip, but fail. I'm elated, angry, frightened, jacked-up, fatigued, alive, dead and just done. The madness is no longer around me, it's in me, pumping though my veins. It's one of the best days, and one of the worst days. I was not an observer of the landscape today, I was a part of it, completely in it. It was raw. It was African.

The next day I walk down to Gloria and it feels like returning to the scene of a crime. She is in a right state, much like myself. She looks her very worst and at that moment she wins me over completely. What a performance.

Abused and ridden hard, she fires first time – every time. My leather gloves were so wet with sweat for hours they stained my fingertips blue, also with a white sweat salt line on the wrist. It's disgusting, but I earned that bloody line. Gloria is covered in clay dust and tree branches. This is a journey of a lifetime for us both and we talk often now. If she is working well the whole world is open before us, full of positive possibility. If she has the smallest issue, I am searching for a razor blade, ready to leave this cruel world of misery behind. Our rhythm has developed as the world changes around us. We dance our dance and in turn the world puts on a show for us. My world is turning up and down like a washing machine, but she is here with me the whole way, the only constant.

I talk to locals often, but they are locals, and for the first time I admit to myself it would be great to have another Westerner to talk with about all I've seen. To have a beer and shoot the shit about Africa in general. Another outsider seeing it for the first time with their own eyes like I am, but Gloria is all I have. As such, she is no simple machine to me, but has a complete personality of her own, which I get to know more by the day.

When my brother named her *Gloria Lewis* after the Kyuss song, I wasn't keen, but couldn't think of anything better. (*"If you're gonna ride, baby, ride the wild horse."*) It soon became *Gloria* for short, and I was still not very keen. Yesterday I found myself shouting at the top of my lungs, 'Come on, Glory!' It describes her perfectly, and is her final name. Often I console with her at the end of a long day. 'Well done, girl, amazing effort.' Always with a pat on the underside of the fuel tank, and a little stroke of her fairing. We are still working each other out, but yesterday was huge for us.

Back in my room I think of home and Jo, admitting I'm ready to settle. The idea feels right just now. My world is upside down here and I desperately need stability. Drifting far on the road has me drifting far in the mind, rootless and vulnerable. Outside the hotel room I feel under attack. At home you only think of travel, yet on the road your mind is constantly on home. Is it simply the grass is always greener? I make a note to *'remember these days'* in my room, which has me in tears;

Remember these days. Remember your longing for rain and sitting by the fire. Of comfort and security. When and if it comes, do not fight it. Embrace it. Remember you were only a few hours from home, but so hopelessly far away. Remember this fear, deep inside your stomach, clouding your thoughts. Remember waking up in the night with the demons. Never forget what you have seen. Never forget this emotion. Never forget how lucky you are, simply to be born in a nice part of the world. Remember how unbelievably different and harsh this world can be. Savour your security, don't loathe it. Relish your money, don't chastise it. Embrace the structure of Western society, don't fight it. It's not perfect, but it's better than pure chaos. Be THANKFUL for what you have. Life did not make sense, but now it does. Remember this when it ceases to make sense in the future.

The day off passes by in a second, and I'm back on the street being stared at once again all too soon. People obviously stop to look as it's not something they see every day. Not a lot happens here. Kids often wave. Of all the people it's the young boys who react the most. They hear the engine, stop, and when they catch sight of the bike, their eyes light up in wonder. They often try to run alongside you waving like mad.

The scenes and the conversations are the same mile after mile, the endless repetition not inspiring. I can only assume this is what its like to be a celebrity. It must be bloody exhausting to have an endless parade of people walk up to you like they know you and just start talking. It's flattering, but you just want to blend in and go about your business. You never can. It's easier to brush it off on the streets, but when the police stop you, regardless of your mood, you have to engage. Just a few times I want to lash out and scream.

I try to reset everyday. The mornings are slow and easy. I chat a bit. As the day wears on I get tired and the chat dries up. In the evening it gets sharp, on a need-to-use only basis. There is only so much I can give before I run dry. I shouldn't really be making a trip like this. Bit late now. I know I am introverted and I'm fine with that. Not much choice. I have learned how to deal with it at home. My friends and family around me understand it. I had never added it up for this trip, however, and considered what the daily experience would be like. It's draining. Hotel rooms are a refuge for me, although an expensive one. I have days where my body needs to rest, but I also need to be out of sight of people to restore my energy. These environments are a total overload.

Instead of embracing interesting strangers, I am pushing them away. I hate people getting near the bike, but it's a pointless fight – I cannot stop it. I have to admit to myself that Africa is not what I expected, or hoped for. It's a lot less 'adventure' and a lot more just trying to stay sane and alive.

One day I might remember this as high adventure and living 'the life'. Whatever the fuck 'the life' is anyways. The fear is oppressive and, worse still, it's all in my head. I'm fighting myself. It's a barrier to being in the moment fully. I thought the trip would have a few singular life-testing moments of risk and jeopardy. Something you might see in an Indiana Jones movie, and remember fondly for life. Having to jump over a canyon or outrun dangerous bandits. The reality of it is nothing of the sort. Sadly, it's just a constant haze of worry and confusion for me. Maybe I'm doing it totally wrong. There is no one to consult with. Finding north in all the madness is impossible. It's not the stuff of Hollywood movies by any stretch. A violent revolution is happening in my mind every day, but outwardly all you see is a weary and rude traveller grumbling away, trying to find some comfort and normality. It's not a bunch of short snappy stories to recount to beauties in the pub over cold beers – it's difficult, confusing and often scary.

I head south for Sikasso, near where there are lots of bad reports on the Burkina Faso and Mali border. Everyone in Dakar advised me not to cross there, hence I scooped up a visa for the Ivory Coast. I plan a detour south, then cut back north into Burkina. Vehicle jackings are rife apparently. You can never tell if it's an exaggeration or reality. In a comfortable environment I'd take my chances, but not so much here. On weaker days you assume it's the truth. Glory is the vehicle of choice to smuggle drugs in the area; she's a rock star of a bike, that can go anywhere with plenty of room for cargo. 'They' tell me she is very attractive to these bandits. Trying to cross two African borders in one day is lunacy, but the distances are small, so I go for it.

The borders here start to look more like Glastonbury than the entrance to a country. Military tents, surrounded by trees. One poor bloke always on duty, while the rest of the soldiers sleep on the floor, still in uniform, covered in flies. They never have a pen, but always need you to fill something out.

Everywhere has 'the book', where all your details are religiously entered – the book of pointlessness. I am convinced no one ever looks in it. They have stacks of them on a shelf, covered in crap and dog-eared from so much wear. They don't have much here but the bureaucracy, so they really cling to it. The latest new field I'm being asked for is my phone number. What the hell do they need that for? They don't even have a phone, let alone power. I make up a new one every time as a small unseen act of protest. I meet their pointlessness with my own petty affront. If there are any fields which are not facts related to my documents (name/age/address) I constantly make up new stuff. I have several different lives in the world's books of pointlessness. It's important to have small victories in your battle for sanity.

Crossing out of Mali and into Ivory Coast is fine. I have a quick run through, but not long enough to do it any real justice. They have just moved from red to green status on the FCO and are enjoying some peacetime prosperity. I hope it lasts for them. It's litter-free and pleasant, but much like the rest of rural West Africa. The road is in a bad state, but quiet, so I make good time. I have an amusing stop by the military, where they all want a picture with the bike thinking I'm some kind of a celebrity. They catch me at a good moment and we have a round of pictures on their phones. For a moment I consider asking to hold one of their AK47s for a picture, but think better of it. They are even jovial on the exit border itself as I leave, making me regret I didn't see more of the place. They seem like fun people. No man's land is huge between these borders, with all kinds of activity in the trees. Trucks turn off the road headed into the woods to be obscured by the trees as illicit things are being shifted about. Odd noises come from out of sight as questionable sorts walk about in hazy states with steely eyes. The usual shady shit. Everyone looks high. I have no idea what is going on, nor do I want to find out, so push on.

Arriving in Burkina things sour immediately. I catch a shitty customs agent, who wants to see everything and has me strip down the bike. It's lunchtime again, under the noon sun, and suddenly I'm in no mood for fucking about. Neither is he. He points, I open. Stuff spills out on the road. The locals watch as I display the contents of all of my bags. It's like watching Christmas for them, except they don't get any presents. They can't believe their eyes. All activity stops as everyone watches on; well over a hundred people gawp as I hit red.

'Why are your bags so full?' he asks.

Fuck me – a full bag! Can you imagine? What am I supposed to do – pack them empty? Have you ever seen an African catch an international flight? Really?

'I'm just doing my job.'

Yep, got to put on a good show for the locals, right? I'm fishing shit out of the bags and just throwing it on the road.

'In this bag is a tent.'

'Show me.'

'Here, see,' I say as I unpack it, 'these are pegs that go in the ground.' I hand him one, bang one against my head, hold it up to him. 'A peg. This is a stove. You use it to eat food. Do you eat food?'

'What about this bag?'

'That's a sleeping bag. You use it to sleep in.'

'Show me.'

It's an acute moment of cultural awkwardness. People look at the medicine in my bag and it's probably more than the local clinic has stocked. If they even have a clinic. The tools in my pannier are more tools than they have ever seen, let alone the local garage has. If, of course, they have one of those. I have more clothes in my bag than they own. My tent probably keeps the rain out better than their shack does. I have no idea what they are all thinking as they look upon this scene.

I pull out in a childlike huff, looking for a lunch spot on the side of the road, putting it all down to being 'hangry'.

I constantly look for a quiet shaded spot for a piss or a quick bite. As I eat every passing car has to toot or flash their lights, every bike has to wave. I don't know what this incessant habit is all about. I'm sure its good-natured, but it's really annoying. I'm trying to piss, for fuck's sake. *Yes, I see you and I hear you … was there something you wanted to say? No? You're just letting me know you saw me as well? Well … that's nice.* They all want acknowledgement. An individual event is no big deal, but repeated a hundred times as I eat my lunch every day, it drives me insane.

I pull into Bobo-Dioulasso long before the sun sets, getting horribly lost again. The side streets of Bobo are worse than the off-roading in Mali. It's mostly sand and has rubbish/sewage streams between the dwellings. The ground is uneven with lots of little hills. Thankfully, the noisy exhaust is a clear heads-up to any pedestrians. After Mali I'm riding more confidently than ever before on Glory. She isn't taking any shit either; we're running ragged and mean. It's another struggle through security to get into my hotel. They want to make sure I have not carried a bomb all this way to blow the place up. I tell them I did consider blowing up my own hotel, but then wasn't sure where I would sleep that night. They didn't laugh, but they never do.

I cross into Ghana at Paga, and it's the usual circus. I'm excited to get back to a green zone again. Why, I still don't know, as it doesn't seem to make any difference. When alone out here, stuff like this crowds your mind. As far as I can tell the risk factor is always high everywhere. Outside the green zone is fuel for the demons. In reality, everyone I've talked to has been welcoming and friendly. Over thousands of miles in West Africa I never once felt genuinely threatened. I was worried on the bridge in Mali, but nothing happened. The people in Mauritania and Mali were really nice. Maybe I was just a lucky one. I do feel the whole region certainly has the potential to ignite at any time. You just need to be ready for it, if that is at all possible.

The border guard in Ghana asks, 'How are you?'

'So happy to hear that in English, my friend. I'm well, thanks!'

It's a huge boost to hear English again. English on the surface anyway; it sounds more like Caribbean accents. French has been giving me a headache. The road in Ghana is much like the rest of the roads in West Africa, except I can understand the jeers now.

'Hey, white boy – nice bike, man!'

'Hey, look at this crazy fool, that's not a bike – it's a house!'

Following the pattern I set for myself, I get hopelessly lost in Bolgatanga. After an hour of sweating, cursing, and frustration I pull into 'Mama's Place', which is part of the Afrikids social development work in Northern Ghana. The girls working here are all orphans from the local area and very welcoming. My first dinner is 'gizzard' spaghetti bolognese. I assume it's chicken, but who knows? It's chewy, spicy and hot, however, and does the job just fine. The digs are basic, but through Afrikids I have a small support network here so relax a touch. The net is up, and I'm out in no time. The next day the 'gizzard' has an explosive exit and takes the entire contents of my stomach, but thankfully it's isolated. In the end my journal just has a string of words, which all elicit a different response in me. A sigh, a moan, a recoil like something has been thrown at me, a shrug of the shoulders or a hot flash of anger. I'm here, but still feel like I'm not really me.

Afrikids is a children's rights organisation set up by Georgie Fineburg as part of her university dissertation. She has done an amazing job setting up

African-run businesses in Northern Ghana, centred around children's rights. Their official mission is '*To ensure that every child in Ghana is afforded his/her rights as outlined in the United Nations Convention on the Rights of the Child, and to do this by building the capacity and resources of local people, organisations and initiatives in such a way that they will be able to continue their efforts independently and sustainably in the future.*'

Unlike most developmental aid, the goal of Afrikids was to establish African-run businesses in Ghana and cease to exist by 2019. Given the typical Oxfam style of constant giving, this seemed much more tangible to me. Through a friend I had helped Afrikids in 2008/9 as they planned to build a hotel in Northern Ghana. I had hospitality experience and was very interested to learn about social development, so happily pitched in, learning what I could. I was pleasantly surprised that my skillset could be of use in this field. Due to the Ebola outbreak in West Africa, sadly this hotel was never built, but they did go on to build a conference centre.

I had all the enthusiasm for the project back then, but over time got confused as to what the point was. We gave a lot of advice to Ghana, and they ignored most of it. Being in Africa now it made a lot more sense, but back then it just drove me mad. Everyone was a volunteer, so nothing happened fast. Nothing seemed to ever really happen, and I just found it frustrating, drifting away from the project. I kept in touch with some of the team over the years and, as I approached Ghana, I expressed an interest in seeing the team down there. Afrikids kindly helped me with my Ghanian visa. I was keen to check the operation on the ground and help if I could to show my appreciation. While I didn't understand how it all worked, I still believed in what they were trying to do.

Every time you turn a corner in Bolgatanga, you see something with the Afrikids' logo on it. They have done a wonderful amount of work to help the children of northern Ghana. My first day of 'work' was on a Monday, and for the first time in months I found myself in an office. It was an African one, and another interesting glimpse into the culture here. I worked with Sandra and Ray, who were really cool and welcoming. I helped work on their conference centre just outside town, trying to drive business to it. I gave some advice, but I don't know how much was of value. It felt slightly fruitless, like before, but they seemed to appreciate it. The way they work together is totally different to the West.

Most people talk to everyone while travelling, but that's not really my style. I hate small talk and prefer to have a good deep conversation with one person, rather than lots of superficial small ones with hundreds of people. I spend so much time alone, however, the questions in my mind just back up. Ray is a character, and we have several long chats about life in West Africa over my week there. Like in Dakar, it's great to have someone who can answer them all at length. My knowledge of life in West Africa grows enormously during my time in 'Bolga' and Ray becomes a good friend.

With a bit of downtime, I am able to collect my thoughts and plan. After a lot of deliberation I make the decision to skip Nigeria and the whole central African stretch. It's a tough and conversely easy decision. I feel I have danced around some potential dangers, but Nigeria feels like real danger to me. I know it's all in my head, but it's firmly there. I can't remove it. Travelling solo is just different. Most people travel as a couple or in a group, providing a huge safety net. One to watch the gear, one to do the bidding. One to tend to the other when one is sick. Someone to have a beer, a laugh and chat over the things you see to stay balanced. A sane person to talk to. Being solo, my thoughts are bottled up until they become so heavy I can't hold them. I never thought this would be my challenge here.

I'm finding a new respect for real explorers. The likes of Rory Stewart walking across Afghanistan, or Tim Butcher walking the Congo river. Most people of course talk about Ewan Macgregor and Charlie Boorman. They did a trip around the world in four months and 19k miles. They did it with a support crew sorting visas and providing one of the biggest travelling envelopes I can imagine. I'm not sure that really counts. When you read the book they just pine for home and their families, which when I read it I thought was all a bit soppy. Yet here I sit pining for Jo and having a family at home. I'm neither the weakest nor the strongest out here, but this is not easy going stuff alone. To reach Cape Town overground you have to *really* want to go through all that. When I'm honest with myself, I just don't want it that bad.

My research on shipping the bike leads only to air freight. Wherever I tried to go in Namibia or Angola the flights all connect through Jo'burg. Someone advises I just fly there and ride out the rest of the miles. I like the idea. That way I can ride north to Victoria Falls, then across the Caprivi strip, and into the top of Namibia, essentially connecting with where I would have exited from Angola. Mile for mile I would go over the original route distance, and do more miles than London-Cape Town, around 11,000 in total. I doesn't feel like I'm 'cheating' as much this way. That's what I told myself anyways. I thought I could do the central stretch but the point was – I didn't want to. I felt it would just be more visa bullshit, more filth and more ceaseless attention. I hadn't taken into account the staring and how I would find it so bloody draining. Had it been 2,000 miles of sparsely populated desolate landscapes, I would have been a lot more inclined to do it.

Financially, it's a similar cost when you factor in all the hotels, petrol, bribes and bloody visa costs. I go for the idea and start to line up shippers out of Accra and learn a whole new language of air freight. Jo unexpectedly quits her job of ten years and is planning to do a trip across Africa herself. It's not entirely on my behalf by any means, but she is starting it with meeting me in Accra for a week of proper R&R. All this does wonders to finally lift my mood. As a result, my last few weeks in West Africa are a lot more relaxed after I have abandoned the idea of central Africa. A huge weight is lifted off me. The demons quieten down, and I can focus on making the most of the moments I am here, like I should have been doing the whole time.

I spend some quality time with Sandra, Ray and the Mama's Place girls. They are really nice people and we chat about everything. Before leaving I have some CFA I need to change. I try the banks, but get the cold shoulder.

'We don't change CFA.'

'The border is ten miles from here.'

'We don't change CFA.'

'Of course, why would you?'

The routine is old by now. People do one thing, and one thing only. Outside of these parameters, you are met with questioning looks. Other options are never proposed, it's just a straight shootdown. Ray 'knows a guy' in the lorry park in town who can change money. The 'lorry park' is the local transport hub deep in town, and basically a dirt field surrounded by shacks. Buses and lorries come and go as street sellers do their thing in filthy chaotic madness. Ray drives us to a particular spot. He goes to great lengths to get his truck as close as possible to the place in question, squeezing through the bikes and other vehicles around. I'm used to staying at the edges and being ready to split, but he takes us deep into the heart of things.

We get out and walk into a place, I'm sure what exactly type of place (nothing is ever just a one thing type of place, it always does a few things). I'm stood there with a pocket full of cash, feeling shifty as everyone looks like they want to kill me. All kinds of shit is going down. I can't take it all in. You see something odd and start staring, and all of a sudden a loud noise happens. You shift your attention to somewhere else. Keep repeating this until you have spun

360 degrees, then start all over again. The people all move and the sense of the scene you thought you had shifts. Like a circus with no audience or focus. You never get the lay of the land, unless you sit there for hours, which I am not going to do.

In the establishment someone is serving a sandwich of what looks like meatballs, with no sense of hygiene at all. It looks like red vomit in bread to me. A shady character shouts at Ray.

'You want to change money?'

Ray won't have him, though, and asks for a certain individual. No one else will do. A guy shuffles in from the dark back room and Ray greets him with a big long sweaty handshake and comments that he's put on weight. *Great start, Ray.* 'Fat Boy' has a wedge of dirty cash in his hand around four inches thick. He can barely hold it; he is definitely the money man. We exchange a long sweaty handshake and the crowd gathers to watch the white man be uncomfortable. At this stage, I can't remember the last white face I saw and think it was back in Dakar. We use his old Nokia mobile calculator to do the maths. I have 121,500 CFA and he offers just over 800 cedi. The Forex check I did today said 808 cedis, so I'm more than happy with this. Ray, however, digs in, trying for a better deal. He's key to this exchange, after all. It's part of the culture; it's not 'my' deal, it's 'our' deal. We haggle a bit and joke about. My bills are clean, his are filthy. He counts mine, and hands me 500 cedi, then says he will be back and walks off.

We sit there for an awkward five minutes as the whole gaff stares at us. *Deeply uncomfortable.* I'm hoping that if they rob me, maybe at least they will let me live. It's dark now and the bugs are out, most of which I have never seen before. They are trying to get in my ear, or savagely bite my neck. They take turns dive-bombing at me, all buzzing around my head. Only me, of course; they seem to leave everyone else alone. I'm trying to keep my cool, and not worry about the cash or the bugs, but it's far from the case on both counts. Fat Boy is nowhere to be seen, and the room he entered into has no lights; it's just pitch dark. What the fuck is he doing back there? Ray is cool and just chatting away, so I follow his lead. If he panics, I will completely freak out and start running around like a headless chicken, shouting about demons or some stupid crazy shit. Fortunately, after what seems a very long time, Fat Boy returns and simply hands over the remaining cash with no drama. Another round of dirty sweat shakes and we're off again. Watched every step of the way, we back out and pull away – just another day here.

We head to a bar for a beer. The ladies know Ray well, and are very welcoming as we settle into big bottles of cold lager. He likes the look of the fish, but we have a curry waiting at Mama's Place for us. The fish is identical to the sandwich ... no plates, pans, nothing. It gets seasoned on a wooden bench and put in a metal grill, then held over an open flame to cook, the heat coming from half an old oil drum, fuelled by scrap wood and who knows what. No sinks, no soap, no utensils, no washing – the grill rack is simply cleaned by the fire. The fish is only handled by hand, before and after cooking; no utensils are used. A restaurant with no running water or soap. The food is served right on the table by the waiter's hand (who knows when that was last cleaned). The table is only ever cleaned by a broom going over it, and rain. No napkin, no plate.

Dogs, chickens and pigs wander around between the tables of the bar, doing their thing, a farmyard in the city. Most Africans tend to live with their animals. When they slaughter them, they fry or dry them, a bit like beef jerky, to preserve them. They taste like old boot straps. The people don't have fridges. Millions of people slaughtering their own meal, with no clean water, no education on hygiene and certainly no soap. Why do all the diseases spread here first? We have a nice final meal at Mama's Place with the girls, and it's time to hit the road again after a pleasant educational stay. I'd like to think my work at Afrikids helps somehow, but I don't know. I offer my support going forward, but I don't hear from the team in Ghana again, which is a shame. I ride down through Kumasi and spend a night there before heading on to Accra.

I'm in Accra for a few days before Jo arrives, and busy myself with shipping the bike. Leads online are scarce, but the minute I show up in 'Cargo City' I'm nearly mauled by people who want to ship the bike for me. It's all new to me, hard work in the heat and yet another version of what I expect hell could be like. I try to learn the new lingo fast and make some good connections. Moto Freight out of the UK give me some fantastic advice which really helps. If you ever need a shipper out/returning to the UK, look no further. Here, however, I have to deal with these cowboys, and it's another big insight into African culture. In the end I go with Conship, but regret it. They have no sense of urgency and take forever to do the smallest thing. Boxing Glory is like caging a wild animal. We have a quiet chat and I talk her through everything that is going to happen. It will be the first time we are apart since we set off.

Jo arrives, and thankfully this time it's very easy to spot each other in a crowd of five hundred black faces. It's more like a football match than an international arrivals hall at the airport. We head for Labadi Beach Hotel, arguably the best hotel in Accra, for five nights of luxury. It's great to see her, but I'm back in Cargo City dealing with the bike in the morning as she sits by the pool. I've never known such disorganisation and incompetence. I was aiming to send Glory out a week before me to know that she definitely leaves before I do. However, frustratingly, in the end she leaves on the very flight before mine. For the first time the tracker is invaluable.

'We tried to load the bike on a flight last night but it was refused.'

'No you didn't. It hasn't moved in four days.'

I sweat, push, pack, bribe, sweet-talk and chase nearly everyone in the cargo area to get it done. I make lots of friends in the process and also have a lot of fun somehow. It's probably the upcoming changes which have me in high spirits. That and there are some real characters here. Jo definitely helps as I can confide in her and talk about everything. It's a surprising how simply venting about it all makes it more manageable. I practically load Glory onto the plane myself in the end. It's a steep, stressful and expensive education. The time with Jo is lovely.

Flying out is emotional, and I feel a sense of relief just stepping onto a plane as it's something familiar.

Bring on South Africa.

I'm still me, but different now. West Africa very nearly broke my mind. Fuck.

FIVE

WHERE THE SUN DON'T SHINE
Reflections on West Africa

'Science may have found a cure for most evils, but it has found no
remedy for the worst of them all – the apathy of human beings.'
Helen Keller

The Road

After spending so much time on the road, most of my observations are
from the back of a motorbike. Hardly the most insightful viewpoint to see a
culture. That said, most of life happens here on or around the road here. The
road itself was a variety of surfaces and conditions, the vehicles not roadworthy
back home and the driving standards hugely different. There are very few
signs in West Africa. Locals do not really travel, more commute between
the same places over great distances. I saw several cars without their axles
aligned, moving strangely on the road, and clearly the result of accidents. I call
it 'crabbing'. With a car this effect is mildly amusing. With a bus it's terrifying,
as they take up the whole width of the lane, line to line, often going over it and
into your lane, at speed.

I asked Ray about this in our chats and was surprised by his answer.
West Africa is where all the European and US insurance write-offs end up.
If you total your car in an accident, and the insurance company buys it, they
send the wreck here. Labour is cheap here, so ten people go at the car. If the
frame was separated, they weld it back on. If some of the panels are smashed
in they beat them back out and try to match the colour with inferior paint.
Serious wrecks are brought back to life. Like magic a 2010 BMW 5 series rolls
out into West Africa. The airbags are gone and the exhaust is gone (hence the
noxious smoke). Often the axles will not line up. But it's a 2010 BMW! The air
conditioning even works a bit! This is a 'clean' vehicle here, and gets a good
price, with no safety checks or emission standards at all.

When this vehicle crashes, none of its original safety features work. People
may live or not. Then, if possible, the vehicle will go through this process all
over again. Then it's 'dirty', and even cheaper to buy. A whole market is at
work – the underside of capitalism. When trucks or buses crash or break down

here, they get worked on in the same spot, right there on the road. I've seen a crew removing the entire engine of a bus on several occasions. Like open-heart surgery – the ground black with spilt oil, debris everywhere. The bus is pushed off the road and either burned or made into several homes for people, right on the side of the road. A whole family happily living in one cargo bay of it.

You can judge the poverty of a country by how severely they strip the cars, like some kind of mechanical vultures. In the end they burn the wreck and leave it there to sit forever, another addition to the already bleak landscape. It leads you to think the driving is bad here. If we just pushed every wrecked car to the side of the road at home and left it, people would likely say the same of us. We just clear up our mess. Getting parts for these vehicles is impossible, so they use ingenuity to keep them going, but eventually run them into the ground. The import tax on shipping car parts into these countries is prohibitively expensive, so no one does it, making life hard for locals. The write-offs only get in as they have a very low value.

Safety is not on the agenda. Cars have ten people in them, when they are clearly only designed for five. No one wears a seat belt. No one wears helmets on bikes. Its normal to see a family of five on a motorbike, with infants being carried inside a jacket, and no safety gear of any kind. The gear is not for sale, and even if it was they don't have the money to buy it. With poor road safety standards, life quickly becomes cheap. Death by driving here is a daily fact of life. Burkina Faso saw over five thousand deaths by road accident in 2013, approximately fourteen people a day. That's the recorded number; the actual is likely higher. It's roughly the size of the UK, where we see nearly five per day. These are not fair comparisons as the rate of vehicle ownership in Burkina is much lower than the UK. If they had the same amount of vehicles on the road, the number would be staggering. *The Economist* had the following:

> 'Africa is the least safe place for a road user, with 26.9 fatalities for every 100,000 people in 2013 compared with 9.3 in Europe—which has ten times more cars as a share of its population. And Africa's safety record has worsened since 2007, the only region to do so. Of the ten nations with the highest death rates, eight are African. The WHO recommends legislative standards for key risk factors: speed in urban areas, drink-driving, helmets for motorcycle users, and wearing seat belts and child restraints. African countries fail on nearly all counts.'*

The signs on the side of the road I do see are confusing. Adult literacy is below 50% in West Africa, so you can argue signs are not important. Another marker of the poverty level is paint. The poorer the country, the less paint they use. Sounds obvious, but you don't really think about it until you realise you have not seen a painted wall for hundreds of miles. Buildings only have the colour from the material they are made with. Billboards are very rare. The only advertising is for mobile phone and satellite TV companies. They pay to paint the side of a shop, driving custom through awareness.

In Mali I saw a sign that marked a project from the University of Denmark, an agricultural scheme gifted to the people of Mali. The sign was written in English, from a Dutch-speaking country to a French-speaking country, which made no sense. At the Diama border in the immigration building there is a metal detector that everyone has to walk through. It's not plugged in. On the side is a sign that says, 'A gift from the people of Japan'. Yet again, neither country involved can technically read that sign. More to the point, it cost a lot of money to buy and deliver, yet it was not being used. More aid money wasted. One of my favourites was an old truck which had rolled and been abandoned, the parts stripped long ago, and the cab burned out. You could just make out the logo on some of the panels on the back of the truck. Fifty metres down the road, you could see the same logo on the panels for a shack. They certainly make use of everything they can, when it suits them.

I saw an ambulance in Morocco, but not again until 3,000 miles later in Ghana. Accidents are daily and people just swarm over them immediately. Riding the bike in such dangerous environments is bloody exhausting, but unlike so many other times here, I feel a degree of control. I came up riding a 125cc on the Euston Road in London to work every day and it was the best training ground I could have cut my teeth on. Snake or be snaked, both there and here. Over and undertaking – whatever it takes. If you aren't afraid to get gritty on the road, over time the lack of rules becomes liberating. Watching other bikes was also fascinating. I was being cruel with weight on Glory, but after seeing some of what they transport on bikes in Africa I'm not so sure. I've seen the following:

A family of five heading to school/work, (looking at me like the nutter). Three full-grown men in suits having a heated business conversation and waving their arms around and shouting. Ten chickens (some looked alive, but couldn't really move). A basket with ten lambs in it (alive). Various tools, building materials, pieces of wood – causing the bike to be five foot wide. Often metal rebar (for reinforcing concrete) is carried on a bike. One chap on the back clutches an arm full of rebar, which is dragging on the ground twenty feet behind them, throwing sparks as they go and a trail of destruction. I saw a full 8X4 foot sheet of plywood on the back luggage rack of a bike. How the guy kept the bike upright, I have no idea. A man with a complete wooden door frame around him, including the door (open). A man holding a bicycle off the back (several times). Various bushes of green plants, often in baskets the size of small cars (causing the bike to weave in and out). Once even a small tree being dragged down the road by a moped. Tyres for cars and other bikes, even including lorry tyres. Items of furniture, including a three-seater couch. Amongst many other random things. How the springs hold up, I don't know. It seems the philosophy is to run it until it dies.

Somewhere in rural Ghana I got delayed in a traffic jam. Two lorries in a stand-off at a junction arguing. In this little traffic jam street hawkers are out in force, working hard. Several things get shoved in your face: a bathroom scale, all boxed-up and ready to go. Ten rolls of toilet paper. A bag of salt, batteries, toys, a broom, sweets. They don't need a supermarket with all this. I guess this is how most Africans do their shopping. It's the poor, selling to the working class. They haggle over everything, prolonging the transactions.

This is every corner of West Africa. We can do a weekly shop at home in around 30-60 minutes. At this rate it would take two days and involve talking to over two hundred people to do the same thing. It's exhausting just to think about it. My all-time favourite is the chicken sellers. Kids standing at the side of the road and frantically waving the poor live chicken in the air at me. I always think, *What the fuck am I gonna do with that, kid?* Here no one would bat an eyelid if I strapped two to the back, still alive, and carried on down the road. Anything goes here.

The People

People are people, I guess. They drive me mad at home as well. They do it in a very different way in West Africa. You can't help but notice the chronic apathy. The heat must play a part. Africa is consistently portrayed in a negative light, but I try to imagine the same circumstances in a Western society. I believe we would have similar issues. I am not a sociologist or an economist, and even I can see there is a chronic lack of education and economic activity here. Riding through village after village, with one hundred people in the shade sleeping in the middle of the day, only makes you wonder or angry, often both. The culture is so different, on such a massive scale it repeatedly shocks the system. Most who have work seem to do it with the minimal effort, making the simple task of doing the job even harder. The sense of lethargy is paralysing.

In Bolgatanga I go to buy a sim card – a relatively simple procedure. Finding the right place is a struggle and involves talking to over twenty people. There are then fourteen handshakes and seven shoulder touches before I even get to the right place (yes, I counted). Imagine all those hands have not been washed in a week, and the handshakes are long and lingering. They love to touch, which as a human is a really positive thing. With the poor hygiene, however, it's really no wonder disease spreads so fast here. Is that education, cultural habits or apathy? Hygiene is not a feature here. It's hard work as a Westerner, and can be hugely unsettling. You have to consider, how would you keep clean with no running water? It's impossible.

Clothes are washed in a river, but then left to dry next to the road and soon covered in dust. In the likes of Burkina or Mali the act of bathing did not appear to happen. Conversely, in Ghana, people took care in their appearance and often I could smell heavy wafts of perfume or deodorant. It struck me as odd how people cared for their appearance and could be so well turned-out, but would exit a crumbling shack covered in litter. How do they care for their own appearance, and not where they live?

People here are always in groups and rarely alone. If you are on the street, you're in the conversation. It's kind of infectious and fun, but also intrusive and annoying. It's like they are all actors on a giant stage, trying to grab the limelight – an introvert's nightmare. Coming from the UK, with a sense of social etiquette, it's difficult to adjust to this public free-for-all. We have a variety of subtle words and gestures we use to avoid interactions, but there is no subtle here. Words need to be shouted loudly and clearly to get the point across. Being on the street for a couple hours has me retreating to a hotel room swiftly. I wonder what would happen if you put one of these African extroverts on one of our streets alone in the UK, with no idea what was what. Would they think and feel what I was feeling now? Walking on the street in Africa, I feel like I am at a house party, where everyone is invited and all have something to shout about. Great fun when you're in the mood, but quickly exhausting. It's hell when you're not in the mood.

Once inside the correct place for the sim card, I start the procedure with the lady behind the desk. She is talking to a friend as she serves me. Not the slightest bit interested in me, the customer. The friend is breast-feeding her child and sat next to the clerk, behind the desk. I have no idea if she works there or not. I assume not. The clerk talks to me out of the corner of her mouth, never making eye contact with me. I ask for clarification.

'Are you sure?'

She instantly turns to face me with a challenging, 'Yes, why would I not be?'

I think, maybe that scrunched-up 'I don't give a fuck' look on your face, love? No one cares about anything customer-orientated, body language betraying everyone. At home many people in customer service don't care for their job either, but they never thrust the fact in people's faces (as they would soon be fired). They gloss over and keep the facade. There is no front here at all; they openly just don't give a fuck. No one running the business seems to even notice, let alone care. It's hard not to take it badly. Harder still to not return in suit. You end up getting angry, or speaking in a derogatory tone to compensate when it's not a behaviour you typically exhibit.

The attention Glory and I got was a burden for me. I obviously understood we were not a common sight, but I didn't enjoy being treated like a circus freak show. Stopping anywhere drew a crowd immediately. Minus the arms outstretched, it reminded me of a zombie movie. I know that sounds harsh, but it was a real feeling when I stopped and people crowded around the bike. They didn't know why they came, but they walked towards me nonetheless to stop in front of me, just staring, like moths to a flame. I know it's 90% the bike, but fuck, it's unsettling. My brother-in-law often jokes, 'Africans will come to the opening of a crisp packet'. It's true.

Of all the elements in a journey like this – fear, poor sleep, poor diet, long hours, hot temperatures, difficult environments, navigation problems etc., the constant attention was easily the top factor stressing me out. I can't handle it. I was not ready for it, and although other travellers had warned me of it, I did not heed this well enough to realise it could be this oppressive. I'm used to being the guy in the corner, watching proceedings and learning about cultures with quiet observation. Here I'm on centre stage, local life stopping whenever I enter the scene, making quiet observation impossible.

A glimpse into the business world was fascinating to see West Africans in the work environment together. In the offices of Conship and Afrikids I got a sense of how different it is from us.

- The Phone – all calls are answered, all the time. If you are in a meeting it is acceptable to take personal calls. The number of calls you receive in a day is a sign of importance. The more you get, the more important you are.

- Being 'in business' usually means you have several business interests you are working on. It's perfectly acceptable to cross-promote these business interests. For example, at your full-time employment you can work on your personal side business(es) openly. The more side businesses you have, the more successful you are seen as being.

- Body language is difficult, and the way they talk to each other is not respectful. People sit in meetings checking their Facebook account openly, not listening and not even trying to be subtle. They slouch in meetings and have body language which says, 'I'm not interested – at all – please fuck off' throughout the meetings. When talking with each other they bark orders. I never heard the word 'please' in an office here. The ruder you are to your colleagues, the more important you are seen as being.

- Air conditioning is a sign of status – the more important you are, the colder your office, even if it's deeply uncomfortable to sit in.

- They never reach the point. This is the hardest to deal with. African speech is overloaded with ambiguity. Popular phrases are misused constantly. When you throw in Western business 'buzzwords' tangents seriously abound. It's impossible to hold a topic of conversation and ever reach a point.

The boundaries of work and personal life totally overlap. It can take days to schedule a meeting, let alone have it. At the appointed time a plethora of reasons come up when people cannot attend. A sick child, a cement delivery at home, a meeting elsewhere, a personal emergency, a sporting event on TV etc. It's culturally normal here, and massively unproductive. I found working in a French office difficult enough with short hours and long lunches, but this was a whole new level. Business development obviously follows this pace and new initiatives never start. Trying to insert any sense of urgency is futile. If you are a checklist person, this place will drive you insane.

The Conship office was the hardest for me. Nothing was ever completely done. Everything was a maddening 'work in progress'. You never got a straight answer to anything. It was always, 'I'll call someone and check, then come back to you asap.

No one ever called back. I started to think they are all cowboys, but in reality I think everyone in business in West Africa has an element of cowboy in them. Working in such a turbulent and inconsistent environment you probably have to adapt and be a bit wide to cover things. My insurance papers 'were done, just needed updating and would be sent tomorrow morning'. The bike was 'ready, but just waiting on paperwork'. *Maddening.*

Everyone loved the banter. It's infectious and fun. They always wanted to show you something, a picture of a family member or something from their side business. In the West, we start meetings with 'how are you' and have five minutes of preamble before we get into the business at hand. Here the preamble is the entire meeting, the business rarely discussed at all. Throw out a difficult question, and it will go unanswered. The language is so bloated with incorrectly-used popular phrases and Western business buzzwords that it's hard to follow the point. It's a toxic mix of our crap and their crap coming together to form a river of bile. That will never reach the sea.

Buying an airline ticket to Johannesburg was another insight into businesses here. Online you can make a reservation for a flight, but not pay. You have to do that in a bank – in cash. Airline tickets are over your daily withdrawn limit, so a simple task becomes a big hassle. When I booked, I was given 72 hours to pay and confirm my reservation, only a week before the flight. If I did not do it in the allotted time, the reservation was cancelled. Either they are overselling flights or they are running them empty. I've never heard of such a backwards system. I've never bought goods from a company that makes it nearly impossible to pay them. In the West such a business would quickly fail. Here it's the norm. (On that note, South African Air is shit.)

At work, Africans seem miserable and disengaged. On the street, in their own time, they come to life, and love the banter with friends. I know we can be the same, but I found it extreme here. I can't reconcile living in these conditions. Lack of money seems to be the top cause of strife, yet people are not inclined to work hard in an effort to gain a better quality of life. It's a fundamental difference to everything in the West. Even if there are no paid jobs to do, you can still make your environment more comfortable to be in. The word that it all boils down to for me is *apathy*. Apathy is expressed as 'absence of passion'. In 1950 US novelist John Dos Passos wrote:

'Apathy is one of the characteristic responses of any living organism when it is subjected to stimuli too intense or too complicated to cope with. The cure for apathy is comprehension.'

The life here is too intense and complicated to cope with. For someone with no education, work experience or world travel, could they understand it? The root of apathy is defined as 'state of indifference towards events and things which lie outside one's control'.

Who does in fact control West Africa? Who drives it forward? No one seems to know. Because in reality no one does drive it forward. It's frozen in crippling poverty and anarchy. Everything is reactive here, and nothing is proactive. Unlike the West, there is no strategic vision of a future to work towards, no overriding goal or common vision. The only common cultural identity is merely to survive. Despite all this, there seems a deep sense of happiness and enjoyment of life. For a Western mind it's truly difficult to process. There is a lot we can learn from people simply enjoying every day. In having nothing, and not seeking to acquire anything more, they can be happy.

It took many miles to work out it's a liberation – of sorts. I see a filthy wild anarchy, yet I also see people simply enjoying being alive. People with huge personalities who laugh a lot. In the Western mind, it's a struggle to see happiness without order. They are conflicting elements working hand in hand. It's hard to describe, but I've seen it with my own eyes and felt it.

The Scenery

The landscape of West Africa is sadly clouded with rubbish. It's everywhere. In the city, in the countryside, in the rivers, beaches and fields. People drive around and just throw it out the window without a care. It's hard to watch, and hard to be around. Living on a farm for years, we occasionally had people fly-tip at the entrance to a field and it would put me into a rage. We had a recycling centre just a mile away. Here it's the culture. Most towns have a burning rubbish heap at one end of the town, constantly soldering away. They still just throw rubbish anywhere. I can't think of a bigger way to say, 'I don't care.'

The Sahara was the most striking landscape for me, the sense of space enormous. The desert is the same size as the USA. The more space around me, the more comfortable I feel. In the tight city environments I am very uncomfortable; it's a complete sensory overload. I will dream of the Sahara and irredentist land claims of sand for years to come as I found it deeply mystic. I sought to forget most urban landscapes I saw.

Further south in West Africa proper the land is tropical and dense. Natural flora grows well in the wild, but cultivated crops struggle. The soil is not suitable for farming, and no one does it large scale. That takes organisation and agreement, which doesn't happen. There are patches of crops here and there, usually where people live. If they own the land, or just occupy it and work is unclear. I expect it was the latter. On the one hand it looks like making the most of everything, on the other it looks like chaos.

The dwellings are primitive and ranged greatly. They all are always in a half finished state, the only common theme being no regard for appearance, or often even structure. It's hard to imagine living in a house with no windows or a door. Wild plants are harvested, mostly fruit and some herbs, to be sold at local markets. Often on the side of the road hawkers are selling fruit and vegetables. It's strange to pass fifty stalls all selling the exact same thing, all on the same spot. I have no idea how anyone can make any money at all, and I doubt they do.

Final Thoughts

West Africa is about the people. It has few sights and little tourism. It's not really about the landscape, although it has some nice parts. The people are mostly lovely. The way they live, however, is so unfamiliar for me I was deeply uncomfortable. It was beyond 'foreign' and into 'alien'. There is a filth here that simply doesn't wash away. On the surface you can of course wash it off. Over time part of that filth stained my mind and is forever in me now. So much of Western society I dislike – the rampant consumerism, the 'perfect life' ideal marketing creates and this flippant 'iGeneration'.

Compared to this chaos however, I felt it was better – at least more comfortable. It was not an easy realisation. I was disgusted and disheartened at my weakness. It was the first wall in my life I found myself unable to scale. I found it hard to get in step with reality here, but perhaps that would come over time. It's always a trade-off; nothing is perfect. With big populations in the West, organisation can seem over the top. However, it's better than this anarchy; I'll take our comfort and security over this any day.

To most people this is obvious, but I had to see it for myself. It's not something I could have absorbed from a book, or watching television. Not even reading a story like this, or speaking to someone first hand brings you very close. Nothing is more clear than when you stand in front of it, breathing it in. A society that values human life, over this 'unvaluing' of it, is preferable to me, even if our social contract is overbearing at times. Human life carries so little weight in West Africa. You live or die; the system is not a system to protect you. There is no system, making us banging on about 'inalienable rights' sound absurd. It's genuinely *wild*, has always been so, and likely always will be. The common perception is that this is down to poverty and poor education. It's not that simple: attitude is also a key component. I could not escape the overriding sense that people simply didn't give a fuck.

It's so raw on this scale, too big to turn the tide, and also not our place to do so. Africans also feel it's too big to turn, so don't bother trying. Clean citizens with good infrastructure does not mean happy citizens, but it does mean comfortable and secure citizens. If you can get over all of that, then West Africa opens up as an exciting place to be, where rules do not matter. Many expats live in such a world, and fair play to them.

People tell tall tales about the Wild West in the early United States, but West Africa is the modern day real-deal Wild West. If someone commits a crime like murder mob justice instantly ensues, long before the police can be present. There is no need for a court. The street is the jury and justice is fast. I saw several people being dragged off by angry mobs. As a politics student, I had read about anarchy and 'spontaneous order'. I had first seen it in the favelas of Brazil, but it's on an unprecedented scale here. In Brazil at least the drugs are delivering money to invest in the community. It carries a certain hard romanticism to it. In Africa there is no income at all. The entire continent largely has no rule of law. There are no 'systems' in place for anything, as there are no institutions to facilitate them, once again adding to the overall sense of 'nothingness'.

I was told if you had money in Africa you would be OK. It only applies to an emergency in West Africa. Money can get you out of trouble, but rarely could it buy you luxury. It's simply not there to be bought. I had a striking sense of nothingness for the first time in my travels. Hearing 'West Africa is the most underdeveloped part of the world' did not mean much to me before I got there. Seeing it first-hand, it was driven home forcefully for me. I had never seen so much nothing mile for mile. It was hard to process. Wild land I can understand, but a heavily populated busy nothing was totally new to me. In the West we carry a sense of place. We arrive somewhere to a sign, a landmark, a building. Here there was nothing to 'mark the spot' in a town, hence you never really arrive, you just kind of drift around. I've seen bigger signs for McDonalds in rural Missouri than the signs I saw for major cities in

West Africa.

This disadvantaged part of the world is largely silent in the global dialogue, so we forget it exists. Apart from looking at a map, I was scarcely aware of its existence. Standing in it now I am forced to learn it's face, it's mannerisms and its identity. It bears no resemblance to anything I have ever seen before, and as a result both scares me and humbles me.

People are grouped around the country, seemingly rooted in nothing – no structures or landmarks but the natural earth. It reinforces how highly fake and conditioned our Western world is. 'Places' tend to be somewhere we have built large structures and changed the landscape radically. It's fascinating when these features and concepts are removed. It added to my confusion. I realised our obsession with concrete and cleanliness for the first time; it defines us. It provides a structure against the elements, but also against the chaos of pure wild freedom.

I could not believe I was still on Earth, let alone only three thousand miles from home. West Africa hit so hard, I often rationalised it was another planet.

––––––––––––

Weighing it all up on a personal level, it's unsatisfying to admit I did not enjoy it. A journey of a lifetime was hard both mentally and physically. I did not appreciate the mental weight involved. After putting so much effort in, it was sad. I'm deflated and confused, as so far it's all been a mental battle. Worst of all, I am fighting myself, and I know it. I often thought the fiches I left behind were small pieces of my soul, torn off and left to melt in the sun. There was just a sameness to it all. It was totally uninspiring for me. Always the same responses from everyone I talked to, the same stares. In Asia they often joke it's 'Same, same, but different'. Here it's 'Same, same, and same'.

But I was here. I'd made these thoughts first-hand, and not tried to learn this in a book. This was something I had done, not 'going to do one day'. There is a sense of accomplishment in that, however retarded.

People often portray West Africa as hopeless, but there is a lot to learn here. The apathy is nearly matched by the adversity and ingenuity of African people. If you ask them about their economic opportunities you will get a negative answer. If you asked them about their favourite song, however, they will come to life. They are not miserable out on the streets – far from it, they are full of positivity, life and character. They would slouch at work, then dance like mad on the streets when off work. They appear happy to be alive and live firmly in the moment. Their bonds with each other are deep and healthy. If ever in genuine need, I was always met with kindness. Despite a tide of concern, not once did anyone step to me or try to rob me. I clearly have more money than most people here, but not once did I truly fear for my safety.

Our culture can indeed learn a lot from West Africans. Obviously the crystal-clear fact that we really don't need all this shit we keep buying. 'Brands' have no real weight, and so much of our consumer culture is like a cancer. It's pointless, a sure sign of excess. Try and drive a Rolls Royce through Mali, motherfucker. How flash do you feel now? Do you see how absurd you are? Our food needs to feed us, and keep us heathy, but it does not need to be a statement about who we are. The clothes we wear can be about quality, but again, cannot represent who we are. West Africa can teach us it should be our thoughts and actions that should express our character, not our modern trappings. We should worry less about what people think of us, and more about having an enriching life which makes us happy. A good chat with good friends every day should be more important than owning a nice car. We don't live forever, and need to live more while we can. We need to appreciate what we have – we are infinitely lucky. When you ask yourself, 'What shall I have for dinner?', be grateful the question is not, 'Is there dinner?'

Only people with full stomachs and roofs over their heads can covet Gucci handbags, and can think in abstract theories to define how they 'feel'. For those with empty stomachs, such things are utterly irrelevant. Is it any coincidence that through the enlightenment, humans became comfortable for the first time, and we found ourselves depressed? Sigmund Freud in Africa might have been too busy trying to find his dinner to be fleshing out his theory of personality. On a personal level, I realise my own fear is my little iteration of imperialism and it disgusts me. The enemy is familiarity and righteousness; it makes you soft and afraid, which drives division. Gil Scott was almost right – 'home is where the hate is' – *born*. Our acquired love of vanilla creates wars, and it runs deep.

The whole experience here turned my world upside down. It's painful to know it's still there, even though I am not. It will always be with me going forward. Nothing is fundamentally wrong with life here – it's just the way it is. It's hugely unsettling for me, but will obviously carry on without my judgement. People here seem happy; they just live wildly differently from us. It undermined my understanding of the world, making me afraid. That doesn't make either culture right or wrong; they are what they are.

The issue was my inability to adapt. Incorporating their point of view into everything I look at now is very difficult, two realities that don't really blend. The gulf is not even polar – as the poles are on the same planet. I cannot see things through the eyes of a West African. I've not lived their lives. I do have an idea now about how their minds work, what reality looks like on the ground. I can filter thoughts along these lines to try and see what they would think of something. Every time I take this vantage point it destroys everything we hold dear and shows it to be absurd. Once you have seen it, it's hard to 'unsee' it. Walking the streets of London in this mindset, everything I see is fake.

When I look at the world my perspective is wider now. I understand more. Which despite all the pissing and moaning along the way, is exactly why I came here.

*https://www.economist.com/blogs/graphicdetail/2015/10/daily-chart-10

SIX

SONG OF THE OPEN ROAD
South Africa – Victoria Falls

'Anxiety is the dizziness of freedom.'
Kierkegaard

The plane feels like a spacecraft, carrying me from another galaxy. Being on a plane is familiar; toilets have soap, people smile when they serve you, everything is clean, and no one is staring at me. Viewing central Africa from above, behind a thick plate of glass, is surreal. It occurs to me for the first time that in a plane you can see the world below, but you're not really in it, not really *'seeing'* it. It is a version of a spacecraft, taking you outside the immediate atmosphere on the ground, disconnecting you from it.

I'm relieved to be skipping two thousand miles of filthy chaos, and also sad it's not something I would have 'done'. I didn't want to do it, I wanted to have done it. Landing in Johannesburg its back to 'civilisation' again, comparatively at least, more like life back in the UK. Walking into the terminal to see five coffee places is a reverse culture shock, a first for me. It's never been odd to arrive in a familiar place before now. What I thought was normal previously is now fantastically over the top. Life was so pared back to nothing in West Africa, that now when it's built back up again so quickly it appears filled with absurdity. I don't use the word 'civilisation' as I don't like it. It stinks of imperialism; they go hand in hand. Fitting thoughts as I arrive in South Africa, the epicentre of the African black/white divide. Just when I thought I was getting a grip, the fundamental dimensions change once again. It's not like home at all.

To do the bike shipment I needed a large amount of cash. I left Ghana with excess currency, nearly 400 US dollars. I thought I would simply sort it at the airport before leaving. I arrived, cleared security and was told money-changing is only before security – which I could not go back to now. Africa is unnecessarily frustrating like this, every single day. I resolved to get it done in Johannesburg. On arrival here, however, despite there being ten different currency exchange places, they all met the Ghanian bills with the familiar

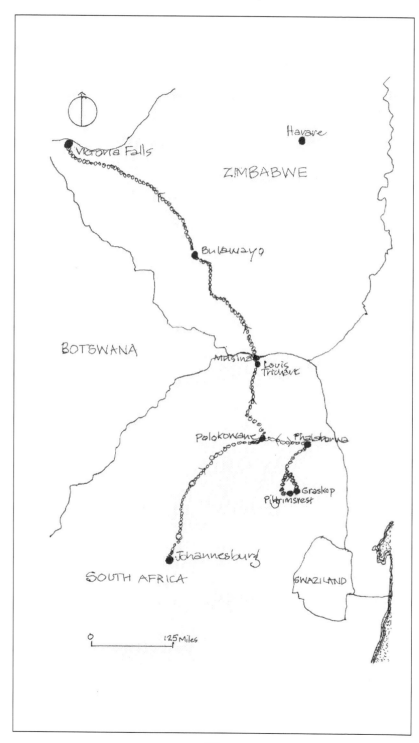

screwed-up face of confusion. A facial expression I was getting to know very well. A manager is fetched every time and I wait, only to hear 'no'. Ghana is a closed currency. I should have known this, of course, but no one informs you of these things. I will now carry these notes all the way home, and even there will not be able to change them. I could think of no better souvenir - they sum up Africa beautifully on every level.

The new sensation of reverse culture shock continues on the street. In the hotel I am happy, everything is perfect. The bed is nice, the room is big enough, the sheets and pillows are pleasant, the staff warm and welcoming. I sit on the bed looking around in a sublime euphoric comfort, totally at peace. Eventually my little bubble bursts. The room is entirely average on all counts. Anything was up from the standards I have just come from, my expectations the lowest they have ever been. After weeks of having my arse kicked, it's wonderful to have a small advantage in the game. Maybe now I can get on with the proper business of travel and relax the sense of simply trying to stay alive. It's a welcome change, and just what I'd hoped for.

Glory is also here, so the next day I fetch back to the airport to try and collect her, going headlong into more epic pointless African bureaucracy. Conship knew an importer here, who they told me could handle the shipment for me. I was pretty sure I could do this myself as I had technically done it several times before. It was my first time by air, however, so I let them talk me into using an importer. I might as well have walked into Kwik-Fit and asked if my brakes needed replacing. Their name was put on the air waybill. Two days later – before the bike had even left Accra – they conveniently declined the job. At that stage I did not know how it all worked, so didn't catch the error. On trying to collect the bike, it quickly dawned on me that it was addressed to them, and not me. Several calls later, someone from the importer is at the cargo office with me and it looks like it will take all day to jump through the hoops.

'Walter' is actually a nice chap, slightly chubby, sweaty but very helpful and kind. That's not his real name. Black people in South Africa always have a few names, from what I can gather. At least two – their real name – typically difficult for English speakers to pronounce, and a more 'made up' name for English speakers to use. Often they have more. Life seems to exist on several levels here. Everyone speaks two or three languages, interchanging them mid-sentence, and South Africa has eleven officially recognised languages. A wonderfully complex social structure, with a historically sinister undertone. A proper African name is something like *Itumeleng*, or *Nkosazana*. Words in local languages like Xhosa, Zulu or Shona, which in these cases mean 'Joy' and 'Princess'. Either white people cannot pronounce these names, or choose not to. I couldn't work out which. So black people also have an English name which is far easier to pronounce (like Walter, or worse, John). I'm not sure exactly why this is, but it's what happens. Through South Africa (and later East Africa) the chat would go:

'Hi, my name is Stephen.'

'Really? What's your real name?'

'Tsholofelo.'

'OK, I'll try and call you that.'

I try, but sadly mostly fail. Story of my life. Proving why they have dual names, I guess. A single exchange is easier, but when you meet five African guys at the same time, who all give you a local name, it's hopeless. I sadly revert to calling them John.

Walter and I battle all day to try and import the bike. At one stage we are in the office of another company which is trying to take over the import for us (and add $200), seeking to take advantage of the situation. I put my foot down, and proceed to customs directly for an official answer with Walter in tow. A kind customs lady gets very upset when she hears the story. She takes it all out on poor Walter and gives him both barrels.

'You bloody lot trying to scare tourists into our country! This man has all his paperwork in order and understands the process. Why are you getting in his way and taking up his time? You are giving South Africa a bad name for tourism!'

Walter looks like a scolded child and I feel terrible for him. His company is the bad guy here, but he's a lovely chap. It's not his fault and he is just trying to help, making the scolding even worse. Kudos to South Africa, though. Much as I hate the pointless paperwork shuffling, Walter is a cool guy and we have some long talks about Africa, another great source of information to my numerous questions. The importer had been charged by the airline to their account already for processing the bike, so they have to be paid something. They discuss raising an invoice, but need me to go to the office. They send a driver, and soon enough I'm in the industrial streets of Johannesburg.

The place is thriving with all manner of businesses – just like home. I've not seen big industry since Spain. You really cannot stereotype the African continent; it is just too big, too varied and too complex. The roads are beautiful;

flat, clean and pothole-free. Advertising is everywhere. Although it feels more normal for me, I hate that aspect. Confronting the two extremes is abrasive. Cars are clean, undamaged and not belching toxic smoke. My mind is not churning worry, but working properly and turning over insights.

'Stephen', a mild, easy-going fellow, drives, and asks about the trip as we go. I mention petrol and coolant (I had lost both due to the air shipment) and he says we can stop by a station on the way back. This is a key difference with the West for me. Big things here, like this shipment, are a total nightmare. Little things, with a buck here or there, are wonderfully simple. Here – 'You need me to source a petrol can, take you to the station and by somewhere you can eat – no problem friend!' Home – 'We are not covered by insurance to take you anywhere but the destination.' In the office they try it on, but have very little leverage as Glory is already imported into the country and I had done that myself. In the end it's around $50 for their time. I could argue the toss, but I would still have to pay SAA cargo $40, so it was only $10 in real terms. I pay, and leave with the final clearance papers around 3 p.m.

Back at the airport, Walter and I sip some cold cokes as we wait on more pointless yet essential paperwork. I have five different chits by the end of the day, all for various steps in the process. Eventually Glory comes out on the back of a forklift and is placed with us outside. It's a great moment. In a world of chaos she is my one true friend, and it's great to be reunited. She is key to my identity now, and I'm not truly myself here again until she is near. Freed from the cage, it takes an hour or so and Walter sticks around chatting with me. Like most African workers, he does not seem to have anything else to do and is besotted with Glory. I'm not sure what to do with the scrap wood of the crate, but once free of all my gear, the remnants of it vanish into a pick-up truck. I hate this madness at times, but I love that. The wood has value here and it will be put to good use. Back in the UK 'crate disposal' would have cost £100, and the wood thrown out.

Walter has been asking about the trip all day. Seeing the bike now he has even more questions – the same kind I have been answering for months now.

'So how did you ride from London to Ghana? There is an ocean there, no?'

How did I do it? *I got my bike and I rode it there. There is a continuous road from here to the vast majority of the world. Yes, there is an ocean in the way, but they have boats that cross it on a regular basis, which you can use to cross the ocean with a vehicle. All you have to do is move down the road. Not only is it possible, it's quite simple really.*

I did not say that, but find it hard not to be sarcastic as I answer these questions. I can't understand how people can comprehend what a vehicle can do, but not get the wider implications of its potential. They likely use a vehicle of some sort every day, but the thought of that vehicle going further than their own country seems to be impossible for them to grasp. Here, and at home. I might be giving up a traveller's secret here, but it's really bloody simple. People jest I have no belief structure, which I find deeply ironic. I believe I can do this trip and I am doing it. *You don't believe a trip like this is possible, yet you believe in a heaven after death with no proof? Where a man with a beard meets you at a gate, to assess your life's merits and if you are suitable or not to enter?*

Did people ask Amelia Earhart the same question?

'Amelia – well done! How did you manage to fly across the Atlantic solo?'

She summoned the gumption, learned the craft, properly prepared and just fucking did it. Asking *why* she did it is a much more fruitful question, but people rarely ask that.

As I leave the gated cargo area, the woman is flummoxed by how I arrived in a car, but am leaving on a motorbike. I came as a 1, but leave as a 0. Late in the day, in low chat mode, I have to comment, 'You do know what happens here, right? Things get imported via air?'

Back at the hotel, behind a huge brick wall, I let out a big sigh of relief and relax. I walk to a supermarket and stock up. Walking the neat heavily stocked isles is a revelation and I nearly cry. The world is a fucked-up place, and I will never understand it.

I hunt down a nice restaurant in another hotel for a proper feed, only six blocks away, so I walk. At the other hotel, they cannot understand how I am not in a vehicle when I arrive. That screwed-up face again. It's odd for me, too, walking up to a gate designed for cars and trying to buzz my way in. There is no door. People don't walk on the streets here. Much like Walter, the restaurant staff think it's some kind of miracle I arrive safely and have not been eaten by lions or robbed by anarchists. The 'compound life' is the way of life here, where most wealthy white people shuffle from one compound to another. Everything nice here has an eight-foot wall around it, with barbed wire on the top. There appears to be no middle class at all. Like West Africa, security itself is a booming business here. I'm sure if you had experienced hard violent crime, you would have a huge wall around you, but I don't see any of it at all.

I have lunch in a mall and continue to watch yet another new world go by. It's more like home, but still vastly different. I'm disturbed how familiar the act of shopping makes me feel. I find myself aimlessly wandering the aisles at times, in need of nothing, but subconsciously calm for the first time in ages, in an element of normality. It's calming, but also disgusting. It says a lot about me that I don't want to hear. After a few days on easy street Glory is back on form, I'm rested, stocked and well fed, so we hit the road again, leaving Johannesburg at sunrise. Still fearing someone might try to steal Glory, I reason criminals sleep in the early hours. *Not this one …*

Back on the road, I try to process this new cultural reality. The road here has no rhythm at all. You come to know roads generally and how things move, but South Africa is an entirely new pattern. I say 'pattern', but there isn't really one, it all just kind of happens. Cars move suddenly and violently, in unreadable ways. The road is good quality and there is space to move. Everyone is either driving like my grandmother or jacked up with road rage. It's a bad mix of high speed and unpredictability, and at one stage I see triple overtaking on a two-lane road, which has to be a first.

I pass through what are clearly white neighbourhoods, and clearly black neighbourhoods. It's stark. The white neighbourhoods are much like Europe. The black neighbourhoods much like West Africa but with basic services here (electricity and water). Seeing the two in close proximity is jarring. *I'm in Europe, no I'm in Africa, no I'm in Europe, no … fuck, I have no idea where I am.* From the back of the bike, it looks like the black people walk into the white neighbourhoods to work for them in the day, and then back to the black side at night. Both races occupy the same territory, yet are completely separate. It appears there is no mixing apart from work outside of the bigger cities.

I pull into a services off the motorway, the first services since Morocco. It's confusing as there are several people hanging around, mainly as I pull out. It's a pickup point for manual workers. A boss comes over in a truck, much like the US fifty years ago. They collect the ten hardest-looking workers, employing them on a cash day rate. The workers jostle about to be picked. The atmosphere is tense, shifty and sad. *Still Africa then.* I do not believe in or understand racism at all – I never have. The society here is so severe, it's nearly impossible to understand it without the stark division that severe racism causes. Like most complex issues in our world, it's something you need to see first-hand to *feel*. It's not something which makes sense on paper.

On the surface it appears black people here are apathetic, lazy and unable to understand the concept of working hard today for a better tomorrow. It's all about today and now. In reality, under the surface it's hard to determine the truth. I think black people here are more in touch with the natural world than white people, remaining closer to nature for centuries compared with Western societies. I do not believe black Africans are lazy or stupid – far from it. An African village is confusing for us, but there is an order and efficiency present. They are staying alive with very little, and have been doing so for centuries. It might be a hard life, but there is no denying its life. In the urban areas, however, the cultures blend and it seems a lose-lose. It seems they aspire to the Western style of life when it is not culturally suitable.

I think white Westerners try to push our culture on them, like the missionaries did. I see modern urban black Africa trapped between two cultures, aspiring to another way of life, yet for many reasons lacking whatever they need to proactively obtain that other way of life. Clearly part (if not all) of the problem is the psychological remnants of colonisation. Ignoring the immeasurable damage we have caused (if at all possible for a moment), we still believe black Africa should aspire to the life we lead. Who the fuck are we to do so? Black African life is too jarring for us to understand. (Just look at me in West Africa). That does not mean it's right or wrong – just different.

If we stop trying to see African life compared to our cultural framework, however, we make the first footstep in understanding life here. White Westerners need to stop trying to cram our culture down the throats of black Africans. Stop thinking 'one culture fits all'. If you add 'and it's ours' , you get the white interpretation to 'civilisation'. Black Africans need to realise that they can have their own definition and interpretation of the concept of 'civilisation'. The Western idea of it is an imperialist framework. Furthermore, should they wish to aspire to the Western way of the mass consumer lifestyle, they cannot do so without social structure, co-ordination and a long-term approach (aka work). Their philosophy of 'now' will have to change to 'tomorrow'.

It's a complex topic, discussed at length by far brighter people than myself, but I want to understand it in my own terms. The issue seems to be the concept of 'Western civilisation'. We believe we are leading the best life modernity affords not just us, but anyone on earth. Mentally we are at the top of understanding life and harnessing the best quality of life possible, for the greatest amount of people. We do this through several concepts like democracy, justice, science, equality and peace. When compared to Africa, and other parts of the world which are radically different from us (like the Middle East) we deduce they must be wrong. We are full of shit in doing so, and patently imperialistic.

Who are we to know if we have it right? Who are we to try and mould the world in our preferred shape? Our interpretation of the world rests on the idea that we are perfectly right – when we are anything but. We are trying to shape the world, when it's not our place to do so: the modern version of imperialism. A reaction to the complexity of the world, showing an inability to appreciate there is no 'right' way to do anything.

The US is not the freest country in the world, but I would argue it is the most comfortable country in the world. These are two very different things. We in the West might have the best justice system, freest elections, equal tolerant society, etc. *Yet here we destroy the world.* Not just 'our world' either – I mean all of it. Buying Chinese-made goods en masse still pollutes our world, even if we don't see it. It's we who pillage Mother Nature on a mass scale, far more than Africa or anywhere else, buying needless crap, and a few years later throwing it away so we can buy more. Often at the expense of places and people in the developing world, like West Africa. I see Africans throwing rubbish on the streets, but is this any worse than what we are doing to the world with mass consumerism?

In the West we are by far worse polluters and irrevocably damaging the earth more. Like my reaction to West Africa, where I was I not able to accept the reality I was in, the 'leading' Western world has an inability to understand the world we all live in. Why can't we truly accept that different people live different ways? Why can't we appreciate other cultures can exist, without trying to shape them into our preferred form? We may have fifty styles of tuna in the supermarket, but we also have horrific gun crime, and burgeoning diseases from eating ultra-processed foods. We poison ourselves with synthetic food. We are so far removed from nature that something 'organic' now attracts a super-premium price. Foreign powers meddle in the 'greatest political system in the world' to throw elections. It's more sophisticated than the way an election is rigged in Africa, but at the end of the day, it's the same thing. Yet we talk proudly about 'being the best' and 'leading the way'.

Why can't we let other cultures flourish, and succeed in their own unique ways? Why is it such a threat to us? Why can't we support self-determination on a global scale? Why can't we understand how damaging our lifestyle is to the earth? Why can't we appreciate, regardless of borders and races, the ecology of our one home, *Earth*, affects us all, no matter what nationality we are? It transcends all borders, nationalities, religions and all the animals on Earth. In making small bubbles of wealthy consumer comforts (like the US & UK), we create great regions of poverty, misery and conflict (the third world) which will eventually destroy us, if the earth does not give up on us beforehand. Can we see beyond the construct of our narrow version on right and wrong? Can we see beyond our doorstep? Can we ever admit we might not be right?

Can we reinterpret our world or, more to the point, see it for what it actually is?

Whether I liked it or not, that's what is happening to my mind the longer I ride out.

The landscape is stunning as I pull off the main motorway, passing the township of Moria. The green hills of the Woodbrush Forest Reserve are a nice distraction from all the mental weight. It's unlike anywhere I have been before and has a jarring effect. One minute in a shanty town, ten minutes later I am in plush cultivated green rolling hills. Turn a corner, and it's back to a shanty town. The have and the have nots could not be clearer here. I made this trip to try and clarify some of my issues about the world. I have to admit, it's actually making them worse.

Near Gravelotte I see big animal reserve fences as the land goes flat again, and hot. It's a wonder to travel 300 miles without a single pothole. I go for a lovely dinner and a beer on the edge of Kruger National Park. I've booked my first-ever safari for the next day and am looking forward to it. At the bar in the hotel, soaking up the comfort and my newfound sense of relaxation, the bartender actually makes conversation. I meet a waiter named Brenda, a very talkative young local girl with a cheeky smile. She has colourful thin braids in her hair and a pleasant slender figure. We get on very well and flirt away like teenagers – it's lovely. By the time I pay the bill she thinks we are getting married. I'm mildly alarmed as she walks me back to my room. Someone needs springing from a small town. *Someone is talking to the wrong guy.*

She wants to jump on the back of the bike and come along. Poor Glory can barely take the load as it is. As for me – who knows where to start?

Back in my room, alone, I watch television and try not to imagine the end of the world as Donald Trump wins the US presidential election. As if all this wasn't confusing enough already. For once it's calm here and turbulent at home. I did not see that coming.

The morning is full of promise once again as we pull into the park on a beautiful sunny day. I have no idea what to expect and within 200 metres we stop to see a giraffe, then in another 200 metres a herd of impala. Just like someone has turned on a wildlife switch; there are animals everywhere. I am happy to be off the bike, snapping away with the camera like mad. I found the fact Glory was not allowed into game parks annoying at first, but now I think it's far better. It costs more money, but I can really focus on the animals and not on running the bike. Not to mention the obvious. Apart from a gravel road, there is very little human interference and it's calming. It's uplifting to see a landscape devoid of litter.

We go on to see elephants, hippos, wildebeest, African fish eagles and more animals than I will ever remember. It's a wonderful day out that reminds me why I am here and what I came for. Everyone is focused on the 'Big Five', and desperate to see a lion or a cheetah. Although driving, the guide, 'Carl', has better eyes than us all, and can annoyingly see things way before anyone else. He drives along happily eating dried termites. I'm pleased to see elephants – they are my favourite – magnificent, massive and peaceful. To a point. Trees are wisdom, so anything that eats trees must be wise. Not to mention tough as nails. They do seem to destroy everything in their path, however, which is not so great.

Back at the Bushveld Terrace Brenda is nice, but also full on. I'm not sure when to mention that I have a girlfriend. When do I admit to myself I have a girlfriend? The next day it rains all day. It's wonderful to have a day of rest, when it just rains all day. I sit and smugly think, I'm not in that rain out on the bike hating it. I'm here in the dry, supremely comfortable. That's exactly what I do all day – nothing. Apart from talk to Brenda at lunch, which is now getting a bit annoying.

I unload the bike and spend a day seeing Blyde River Canyon and the nearby sights. It's a carefree day of European-style tourism, very relaxing and more what I'm used to. I also go to Mine View Point, just outside Phalaborwa, a remote industrial site on the edge of town. The road is steep gravel, challenging but tons of fun, I feel like a child off exploring. The mine itself is so deep you can't see the bottom; it's open for over one kilometre down into the earth. The view of the surrounding area is the highlight for me, though. At the top I can see for miles. The suspension on the bike makes a few creaking noises, but Glory is on top form and a totally different bike with the luggage off, far easier to control. I go through some big puddles, enjoying the off-road tyres and really giving it some, until it completely washes out on me. I pull off the track to find my first proper flat tyre. It's only 3 p.m., but the sun is still savage.

I pull out the tools and set to work, pleased I had at least packed the essentials. I hear a scuffling noise behind me and turn around. On the industrial workings of the mine there is a baboon sitting, watching my every move. I had seen him a few minutes back, but paid him no attention. I focus on the work at hand, sweating into my eyes once again. I struggle to get the tube out of the tyre. As I curse and moan, I look around to check on my friend. I'm alarmed his friends have also come to the party, and there are now over thirty baboons sitting, scratching and intently watching me closely, just a few feet away.

Not knowing their behaviour, I'm instantly spooked and wondering where my food is. Funny how we always assume the worst. It's excellent motivation to just get on with it. I don't think they gave a shit, to be honest. Back at the hotel, I'm still energised after such a long day. For the first time in ages the road is giving instead of taking. This is more what I had hoped for on the trip and positively fulfilling. Over these two days I take more pictures than the whole time I had been in West Africa.

A cockroach darts out of somewhere beneath the sink, and I kill it with one deft movement. No shock, no jumping, just fluid stealth. It's deeply satisfying. West Africa has schooled me well. Things are just easier here. Sitting at the bar I can shoot the shit with people and relax a bit. Fear held me back in West Africa, but relaxed here now I get more amongst it. People understand me when I talk. I'm confused at the state of South African social structure, but the demons are resting. They flash out now and then, but even they relent for a bit here. In my mind I've wanted this space and comfort for so long, and now it's finally here, I fully embrace it. Days like today remind me why I have come this far. For a moment I'm comfortable. When the wind does blow again it's welcomed, not feared. I gear up and roll out heading northwards, smiling. It's day seventy and I have ridden eight thousand miles since leaving Plymouth.

The road north is a beautiful ride through several fruit plantations. The scents are joyful and scenes pleasant. Its great to see land being worked. I hate to admit it, but deep down it's comforting to see order and cleanliness. The entry signs into Muscina are a warm South African-styled greeting: *'You are now in a high crime area'.* We bed down to another early night in anticipation of another early border crossing the next day.

Free from the demons, my mind turns over what it sees. It's impossible to escape racism in South Africa. I had never been before, so I wasn't sure if it was normal. Turns out it is. It was new to see it in the headlines of the Western press right now, though – talking about home. There is an alarming rise in neo-nationalism rhetoric: Trump wants a wall, LePen is making headway in French elections. Pro-Brexit voters want to halt immigration to the UK altogether. I'm somewhat used to the world being upside down here – but at home as well? Right-wing xenophobics are on the periphery of social dialogue, not in the centre. Social democracy seems like another failed political experiment when watching the news from this part of the world right now.

It appears we are moving into a new global phase, which looks a lot like the past. Universal human rights seem so 'yesterday'. Being confused looking at new things when travelling the road is normal, but you forget that from a different vantage point, even your home can appear confusing. Perhaps busy at home, I would dismiss this all as rubbish. Relaxing downline, however, watching the news and trying to hold on to some holy idea of 'home', it's all clouds on the horizon. The demons are occasionally replaced with depressing tripe like this. Guess you always need something to worry about.

The South African side of the border is somewhat organised. Another queue of five hundred tired black faces at 9 a.m. Again, I pass them all in minutes. Zimbabwe is back to more typical African standards, with no clear process and no signs at all. More 'guidance by incorrectness'.

'No, not here, you must go back to there!' or, 'This is not the right form. Why did you fill it out? Fill out this one and come back.'

Two hours later, and after countless meaningless exchanges, I am free to roam once again. The road is straight, poorly made and quiet. The villages are off at a distance to the side of the road, making progress easier and a pleasant surprise. The scenery is mostly green and cultivated, the roads are tree-lined. I have the odd sensation life happens on the other side of the trees, so you can't really tell what is happening in the villages. In Mali the road is the heart of the village. Should the smallest thing be happening (albeit rare) you would see everything as you passed. Here it's the opposite, adding a small air of mystery.

The road continues quietly until I enter the outskirts of Bulawayo, Zimbabwe's second biggest city. Off the 'high street' (yes, it's called that) there is a stone cathedral, no different from any city in the UK. It's wildly confusing to see here. The cultural confusion continues at the hotel, which is mock-Tudor style, and also utterly out of place. The suspension winces as I unload, which troubles me. I've been trying to ignore it over the last few days, but it's slowly getting louder and I feel an issue in the works.

I need some cash, but have heard reports of cash shortages in the country. As I roll out at 5 a.m. I cheekily try to use an ATM and quickly see the rumours are quite true. There is a line of people outside every bank at this hour. They have been queuing there all night to take a maximum of $50 of their own money from their accounts. A country which tanks its own currency, adopts the US dollar and now runs out of that. A compete mess. Thankfully we just don't see prolific failure like this in the West. Not so far anyways. The road continues to be secretive and quiet, delivering quick miles. Halfway through the day I come to my second police stop, but this one instantly feels different. I'm called aside, where an officer 'inspects' Glory.

'Turn on your right signal.'

'Now your left.'

'Test the brakes.'

I don't wonder why all the other vehicles are not having this little test as they rattle by, nearly falling apart. I know the answer. The cop smells blood in the air. Soon to test the flesh with a small bite, before trying to take a chunk of flesh away.

'Where are your reflector strips?'

'My what?'

'Your reflector strips, so vehicles can see you at night.'

'They are here.' I point at the headlight. 'That's how vehicles can see me.'

Non-plussed, he says, 'And if your lights are not working?'

'Then I wouldn't be driving at night. That's very dangerous.'

'You must have a reflector strip which other lights can see.'

'Oh – that's here on the numberplate. It reflects.' I surprise myself as to where the bullshit in me is coming from.

'It's yellow, and it must be red for the rear, sir.'

'Like I said, I would not drive under those conditions, and until you stop me in that situation I don't think this is relevant.'

'This is the law here, and just because you are foreign does not exclude you from it.'

I'd danced a few bars, but the wanker clearly has better bullshitting skills than me today.

'I'm sorry, sir, but this is an offence and I must issue you a ticket.'

He's salivating as his lunch is getting closer, and bigger. I prepare to dig in and fight my corner as he digs out the 'official highway code'. Nothing more than a heavily stained photocopied stack of ten dirty sheets of paper stapled together. He expertly flicks to the right infraction and points in greedy expectation as he has done many times. $5 for the front and $5 for the back. It's also forty degree centigrade in the noon sun and I'm hungry. *Dig into the wallet or dig in and fight?*

I can't be arsed to play for the crowd, so dig into the wallet. He smiles as he sees the crisp clean notes come out, my first 'moving violation' of the trip. Had to happen at some point, I guess. Nine thousand miles in is not bad going, especially in these parts. Far more worrying are the noises Glory makes as I get on and off of her. It's getting worse and I can't deny it anymore. The slight click has become very audible and has started to cloud my thoughts. I'm more concerned with getting to Victoria Falls, and giving the bike a good once-over than arguing with this arsehole.

The substantial airport for Victoria Falls is a surprise on the way into town. It's bigger than many city airports I've seen, and the largest piece of infrastructure I've seen since Johannesburg. This is the first real tourist trap I have encountered on the trip; Kruger National Park doesn't even come close. You don't notice infrastructure until it's not there. After seeing the absence of tourism over so many miles, it's sudden reintroduction is sharp. Going for a reasonable hotel is a complete rip-off. My room requires a heavy-duty bug-bombing, and I use so much my eyes hurt. Wouldn't it be ironic if the bug spray actually kills you and not the bugs? I pop into town to get some supplies and the supermarket is another cultural headfuck. I am instantly lost amongst its shelves. I wander aimlessly, wondering what it's all about. I manage to find an auto store for reflector strips, which is more like a bar in a Western movie.

I've seen reflector strips before across West Africa; now it was my turn to join in. Stickers seem to hold the cars together there. The reflector strips are a halo in their culture – the more you have the safer you will be. They believe if you cover your complete car with them, you can drive like a lunatic and be totally safe. Excellent 'logic', of course.

Eventually I'm standing over Glory like an Orthodox Jew attempting to butcher a pig. It's a machine with bolts and parts, but I'm not sure what they all do. Something has to be done, I just have no idea what. She is in pain and I can feel it. It must be related to the main shock again, as I hear a 'clink' noise whenever I sit on her. I shuffle about with my tools, trying to pretend I know what I'm doing. I unload her and have a good prod around. I think it's the wheel bearings, but they look fine. Not that I know what I'm looking for. I tighten them back up and the noise is still present. Perhaps it's the thing at the bottom of the shock, which I later learn is the suspension link.

Cue another chat to the doctor and a visit to Youtube. I look up who could help on the road ahead and send word to a Yamaha dealer in Namibia. Tomorrow I will strip down the swing arm (the bit that holds on the back wheel) and investigate further. It hangs over me all night, and oddly the thought of visiting the Falls never enters my mind. Getting stuck in an insanely expensive country with no cash is more pressing. I ponder over these developments as I get attacked by mosquitos at dinner. There are literally ten in my lap as I eat. The waiter offers to spray my table, regardless of the full spread of food laid out. I might as well bathe in the stuff at this point. I add it to the long list of things that will likely kill me, and promptly forget about it. On the plus side, the beer is very cold here.

––––––––––––

Tools in hand, I stand over Glory with purpose as the sun comes up, ready to look a bit deeper. I get one of the suspension link pins out and grease it up as it's bone dry. A good sign. I see one key bolt, which it all seems to hinge on, and instinctively loosen it. The whole bike breathes a sigh of relief and the noise magically disappears. I later learn this is the pivot pin, which the whole swing arm rests on (the bit that holds the back wheel). I consider removing it totally, but it has three sets of bearings through it, and I'm sure if I do get it out

I won't get it back in. It's one foot long and goes from one side of the bike to the other. I grease up the ends of it and put the end bolt back on, but slightly looser. I then mark the position of the bolt with a pen in case it moves and comes loose. The noise is gone as I ride around the hotel parking lot, shouting with joy. Another huge cloud lifts off me. Maybe I can keep this thing going after all? Bike fixed, I clean up and head for the Falls feeling victorious.

It's blisteringly hot, but I'm clearly not going to miss this. I walk the grounds for a few hours, starting on the east side, working my way west towards Zambia. It's hard to orientate yourself at first. The landscape is a wild river, thoroughly natural and refusing to follow any order. It's also a tourist attraction in Africa. It's the low season, and you can clearly see eighty per cent of the falls is not running. The normally wet rock now exposed to the harsh sun is fascinating. I'm sure it's not supposed to be intriguing, but it is, like a turtle fully out of its shell. Something never exposed to light, suddenly under the hard sun. Even in this punishing African sun, it keeps the colour and look of damp. The patina of cascading water on the stone is enchanting, other-worldly.

At the base of the Falls is an odd green colour body of water, not really moving. The hues remind me more of Ireland than Africa. At full pelt this would be a spectacle, but you would not see what I'm seeing now. Most people talked coming in the low season down, but I found it interesting to peek at the inner workings of this beast. To only see a curtain of water would have been fun for five minutes, but not worth the journey in my book. I do have the inevitable feeling you get once you reach a major tourist destination however, namely, 'Ah, that's it, is it?' The fancy brochures and alluring words fall away as you finally stand there making up your own mind. You can see the angles from where the best pictures were taken, and realise you have been slightly taken in. I'm still glad I came and feel very fortunate to have seen the Falls, but it's largely what I expected.

Back at the hotel I study the road once more. Consulting a map is like going to the toilet on the road. Wherever you go and whatever you do, you look at a map several times a day. I am headed to the Caprivi Strip, so must transit two borders in one day, but the distances are not huge. Although the noise has stopped on the bike, I still have one eye on her as we set off into Chobe National Park. Being a main transit route, bikes are allowed in here, and I don't see any wildlife at all. I don't see anyone or anything else moving.

Over the border into Botswana elephants are indeed everywhere and cross the road right in front of me. Just the northern tip of the Chobe flood plain looks enchanting. I have a huge row with a policeman here over a stop sign, but he just wants to hear his own voice. No one else is following the sign, but it appears I have to. It's funny how sometimes you let them win, but other days you simply have none of it and tell them to fuck off. Must be instinct. I stay in another joint on the river and shower with riverwater again, arriving as they are professionally fumigating the rooms. I can't tell if this is a good thing or not. I sit out on the river, waiting for the toxic smell to go, watching the crocodiles. Dinner is unremarkable, but hot, and it's another early night. My travelling game is rock and roll.

The Caprivi Strip is one of the those land features you look at on a map and scratch your head over. Even since I was a boy I've wondered why it exists. Named after a general who negotiated it for the Germans in the ruthless 'Scramble for Africa', its purpose was to secure access to the Zambezi River for trading. In theory, from this point you can use the river all the way to central Mozambique, where it enters the Indian Ocean and all things east. Clearly of value, but what German Chancellor Leo von Caprivi did not anticipate was a small obstacle in the way called Victoria Falls. With this substantial natural feature blocking the way, no freight could travel this route, making the whole thing pointless. The land agreement stayed and is still here today, another imperial cast-aside from a hundred years ago still impacting Africa today. Now it's used as a natural corridor for elephants moving back and forth between Zambia and Botswana and attracts a lot of tourism. It has to be one of the better colonial cast-asides and abstract borders of Africa. Not many of them do so well.

On a motorbike, it's a long stretch of dead straight tarmac. Back in the day this was a wild strip of sand, but for me it's just two quiet hot lanes. In this quiet I can hear the engine clearly and decipher by sound what 71 mph sounds like, and also 69 mph. By pitch my wrist holds 70 mph, a subconscious cruise control as the miles fall. It strikes me Africa is either too calm, like this, or too intense. There seem to be no middle gears. You are either bored or thinking you are about to die.

My accommodation is another lodge on the river, Angola just fifty metres across it. I consider the skeleton coast ahead as I plan the next few days, happy to be in Namibia. It already feels calmer than Zimbabwe, or even South Africa. The expanses are so big and empty, my mind can really open up. It's Africa's least populated country. Without as many turbulent social scenes,

I can really soak up the vast landscapes. Dinner is plentiful and delicious, but another conflicting social scene. Fat white rich people eat, skinny poor black people serve.

On the terrace outside the restaurant, I sit alone with my daily smoke. It's a silly thought, but at this moment I feel very much like I am 'in Africa now'. Earlier I imagined getting a boat and just rowing over to Angola, it's so close. Now it's pitch black, but not lifeless. I hear shouting and sense movement. I imagine sitting on the other side, looking at us here in this little castle, gorging ourselves. Muffled voices rise and fall in the breeze. I can sense magic playing in the dark across the water, running free in the wild dark, Angola radiating a dark energy.

I think I'm staring at Angola, but I later find out it's apparently the United Kingdom of Lunda Tchokwe and part of the Union of Free African states. Not something which appears on our maps back home, and nor will it anytime soon. It's a push in West Central Africa (mainly Angola), to break up the country into historic tribal clans. The European borders not relating to anything on the ground, this is a grassroots efforts to change them back. In theory it's a positive thing. This minimal effort to achieve independence is suppressed by the minimal state force in Angola. It makes me think even more about borders. If Africa was to rescind its 'imaginary' European borders, and go back to real tribal zones it would make the Balkans look like child's play. Three hundred countries could spring up over night. The choice is outright war, or to remain how it is right now. An old shitty boss of mine once said, 'We're fucked whatever we do. That's not the question – the question is, *how do you want to get fucked?*' In Africa they don't even seem to get that small consolation; people just get fucked.

The ideological rebel in me loves the idea of anarchy: the favelas of Brazil, the spontaneous order that springs up there and the undeniable sense of life in rebellion. In reality, when a state is absent or fails, things become far worse than better. I've always seen the downside of the social contract for the majority of my life, but the upside of it is crystal clear here in Africa. It's a hard adjust for me over the miles.

I hate politicians. They are all lying scumbags, no matter which party they represent. I've spent so many years hating the idea of a state, I can't swallow the idea of a positive state. It chokes my Orwellian heart like a blood clot. Rebellion has been my identity for so long I don't know if I can put it down. I don't know who would be left sitting here. So much of my life has been about rejecting everything I see. Rebellion is a sense of identity for me, an anchor. It's easier for me to reject the entire contemporary construct of human thought than wade through the shit. It's riddled with rot, and nothing positive will ever come from it. If I whittle it all down to two simple words at this precise moment, they undoubtedly would be 'fuck it'.

SEVEN

DEATH IN THE SUNRISE OF DREAMS
Namibia

'And those that were seen dancing were thought to be
insane by those who couldn't hear the music.'
Nietzsche

Into Namibia proper, it finally all falls into place. The landscape goes on
forever and there are marvellous vast spaces to roam free in. If I had a clear
mission when setting off on this journey, which I most certainly did not have,
it would have been to get here. Physically and mentally, to cross huge great
stretches of land, and vast distances of the mind. Here in Namibia you can do
both. There is so much of the world, and so much of our minds to which we
have never access. Anyone who thinks they have seen and thought it all is lying.
Movement in one promotes movement in the other; they are symbiotic. We
see them as two activities, when they are one. Conscious progression through
physical movement.

Pushing the boundaries of my geography, I'm pushing the boundaries
of my thought. If there is land, I want to see it. If there are thoughts, I want
to think them. If there is life, I want to live it. Our lives exist between destiny
and will. Sometimes destiny takes the upper hand and sometimes if we push
hard enough we can make our will take the upper hand. In the middle is the
dance of life. The best defence against dying is living. At this moment, right
here, I am living with all my being. A mix of destiny and will have put me on
the C42 this morning. I had plotted, schemed and spent to get to this precise
moment. I can sense it in all my being, the feeling of accomplishment as vast
as the landscape. The further I can see, the more I feel I have accomplished.
Charting your own course is pure empowerment.

My journey was not about *what* I was doing – it was the fact I was doing
it. I am alive. It's life itself, a living breathing thing. By doing this trip I am
breathing life into my life, making it take shape. A shape I want, not one I
was given. Great things are not always enjoyed, but having done them brings
a sense of enjoyment or, better yet, *peace*. In the vast dusty plains of Namibia
I feel a deep sense of accomplishment. The further I go, the more peaceful I

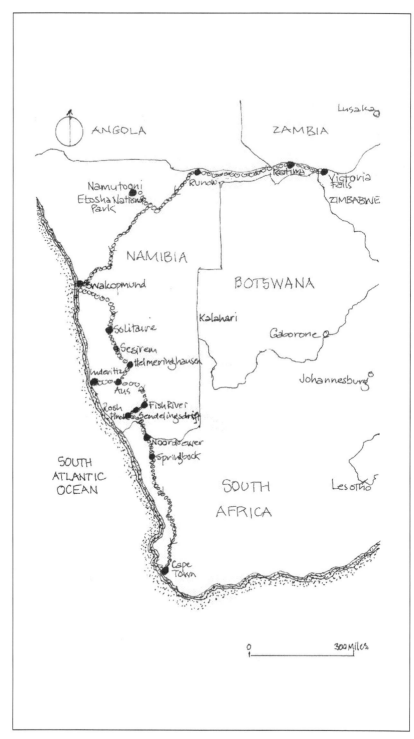

become. I see some of this colossal world we live in, and drink it in with relish! People rarely ask why someone makes a trip. This is why: to be here – *now*.

Namibia inspires from sunrise to sunset, the entire planet in just one country. Endless desolate coastline. Vast empty deserts. Gentle rolling hills. Jagged mountains. Windy surface of the moon plains as far as you can see. The colours of the rainbow dancing across the land all day long. Most of all, it has space. Vast, enormous, glorious, infinite space! I feel like I have not breathed out since Spain, and I exhale here for what feels like days. Glory and I roll on through the huge landscape towards Etosha National Park. Yamaha in Swakopmund, only a day's ride south, have responded to my call for help back in Victoria Falls with a wonderfully welcoming message: 'Any Yamaha rider in need is welcome here.'

Worried about my machine, words like these are magic. They give me peace to focus on Etosha, and sort Glory later. I am still worried about the crucial pivot pin and want a professional opinion. As I roll into Etosha, I wonder how any animals can live in this hot and desolate environment. I find a very nice hotel outside the park called Mokuti Lodge. Passing so much poverty on the way here gives me more conflicting thoughts, but I am normalising some of them. I join another game drive in the morning, and get out on the 'pan'. The Etosha pan is home to hundreds of species of mammals, birds and reptiles. A giant salt lake which swells and shrinks in the seasons, the name *Etosha* means 'great white space'. I could see it on a map, but as usual, it's nothing like looking directly at it.

I want to get out into it, amongst it, inspired by the big clean miles I have been getting in. Standing here now I can see that would take days. It's half the size of Switzerland and, like everything here, impossibly vast. We do manage to see a lioness, slowly walking across the plains at her own speed. I'm struck by how calm and unconcerned she is. Queen of the jungle, right in front of me. We sit for nearly an hour, watching intently. I can't help think the animals feel we are invading their privacy somehow in these parks. If one animal is spotted, the call goes out on the radio and suddenly ten cars are sitting watching it. The animals are clearly free, but it seems like some kind of a false freedom to me. Maybe after being stared at for two months straight I could relate. Sometimes you just need to be left alone.

Back in the hotel, it's a German holiday camp. The food is obscenely plentiful and the manicured grass lawn sticks out for miles in the bone-dry desert. How anyone sees this as in keeping with the surrounding area is beyond me. Whenever I stop like this, I can't move for a couple of days. Happy to be motionless. I have a full day off and it flies by as usual. It takes over two hours to get the room straight and repack again. By now a cycle has developed on the road: arrive, find comfort, unpack, relax, breathe out, sleep, rest … then prepare to depart, fret, get stressed, have a little fit, put your life back into impossibly small containers, breathe in and depart. The more comfortable the hotel, the sweeter the arrival, and the harder the departure.

The ride south to 'Swakop' gets better and better as I go. I stop for pictures often, the landscape simply breathtaking. There are no checkpoints at all. The flat low-lying shrub has a mixed green and brown colour. It goes on all the way to the horizon, where low brown mountains meet the sky. Like a bigger version of California, stretched – jumbo size. The sky blue and vast, the roads immaculate. There are even rest stops every five miles or so, where you can sit at a picnic bench in the shade and have lunch. With bins! Wonderfully comfortable, even familiar. Rubbish is disposed of properly in Namibia, another welcome change that dramatically enhances the landscapes. With no people around, there is no staring, so I naturally relax, and open up to what I see.

The B2 through the Namib-Naukluft National Park on the way to Swakopmund is a high point. The landscape previously had low-lying scrub; here it opens up to rocky desert, only the occasional hearty tree or shrub off in the distance. The mountains in the distance grow bigger and more jagged, becoming even wilder. It's big country – as big as it gets. Even better, it's relatively untouched by humans. There are no power lines or rubbish anywhere. No shacks or buildings at all, just vast open spaces. It feels bigger than the Sahara. I've never seen somewhere so big and raw. It's deeply satisfying to take it in.

The wind picks up as I near the coast, first sight of the ocean since Ghana, two and a half thousand miles ago. Rolling down the high street I'm completely bemused. It's a lovely street, well-maintained and looked after. Shops have paint and are well cared-for. The windows have attractive, full displays of wares. *People care.* It's not like anything I have seen in Africa thus far. It's like a small town in Germany or the US, and I'm completely taken by surprise. I call directly into Duneworx, wasting no time to get Glory looked over.

I'm met warmly by Mario at the garage. Glory is shoved to the front of the queue, cleaned and then stripped down as I walk around the shop. On the wall there are several photos of famous overlanders who had done similar journeys. It's refreshing to be around people who understand the trip and support it. The whole suspension link comes off; all three bearings in it had gone dry and sticky. The shock itself had no grease at the top or bottom, hence is not moving freely as it should. *Thanks again, Yamaha Corsica, you useless French bastards.* This crew are no standard dealership. They know Glory well and roll up their sleeves to do whatever it takes.

It's soon quitting time, so Glory will spend the night there. Marco introduces me to Yahn, who owns the shop, and also an active overlander. At this stage it's great to have company. They kindly take me out for a couple of beers down by the beach at sunset. Fancy that – after all these miles, Yamaha actually bought me a drink! They are really sound guys and we have a great chat about everything. Later I go for a walk and find a bunch of restaurants. I try a German place called Butcher & Brewer and have a lovely schnitzel dinner with a huge stein of beer. It's superb. Best of all there is 'customer service' and the waiter actually gives a fuck!

The next day the sun is out as I walk down the high street to the garage in high spirits. I dub Swakop 'little big Germany'. It's clean, calm and relaxing. The food, architecture and way of life seem more European than African. It's a little town, on the edge of a vast space. The towns here have an edge which doesn't look out on fields, but vast stretches of nothingness. The edge of town looks more like the edge of the universe.

The cars are in great shape, food is easy, clean and plentiful. Another bizarre cultural offshoot, I would have never anticipated. Africa keeps confusing. The people are portly here, very German. The food is plentiful – hearty, stewy and rich. Coming from bits of bread and crisps on the bike, it's hard but pleasant work on the digestive system. Most guide books say Swakop gets a love/hate reaction in most people. After the sewage-strewn streets of Senegal, I find myself on the love side.

I hang out with Mario and Yahn in the garage, chatting away. We remove the pivot pin and roll it on the floor. Thankfully, it's straight as an arrow. No new parts required, just grease. I learn a lot more about how Glory works, and she is very happy and clean when we finish. It does us both a world of good.

Yahn kindly gives me lots of advice about the route ahead, and advises a scenic flight to see the desert as it's hard to do on the bike. I go for it, and book one the next day. He also advises heading to Sesriem as the jump-off to Sossusvlei, the giant red sand dune. He and Mario both have stacks of advice, so I take as much as I can get. I talk to Mario about the road surface, as he has done a lot of sand riding. He teaches me a simple phrase: 'Get up, look up, open up', a phrase I go on to repeat a thousand times in the future.

The scenic flight is like a recurring dream I've had. In the dream I'm on a commercial plane flying somewhere, looking out the window. We descend over the ocean to just a few hundred feet, hurtling along at full speed, then we rise again. We descend once again to land, just like the ocean, and can see everything up close, but passing by very quickly. Then we rise again. Up and down. In the dream the flight never takes off or lands. It just keeps going on and on like that. The only variation is what's on the surface. I struggle to take it all in as we move past it so fast. This flight also goes up, then down, then back up and then down checking out different stuff on the surface. It's very cool.

The plane is bloody loud, however, and far worse than riding Glory. No one is able to make small talk, which is a bonus. We head south-east to Sossusvlei. Its spectacular to see the land change below, from dusty plains to red-hot desert. There is a singular faultline where the land drastically changes. One seam of green life separates two different worlds of arid desolation. Only from the air can you see it clearly. There is a winding dry riverbed with some trees in it. Arid brown clay soil on one side and rolling red sand on the other. At a distance the sand dunes look more like waves on the ocean, moving in sets, with absolutely no human interference as far as you can see. Another view I will never forget.

Further out, the dunes get bigger and bigger. They are beautiful and wonderfully dangerous, utterly inhospitable. We pass over Sossusvlei, but it does not have a big impact on me. It's the overall setting that blows me away. It's not one dune alone, no matter how big it is; it's all of them together as far as the eye can see. The scale and colour of the land is totally unique. Yahn was right: air was definitely the way to go. We head west to the coast. The dunes mellow the closer we reach the sea, turning a softer colour. Near the coast we dip down to 300 feet to see a giant boat wreck in the middle of the desert. Pure Indiana Jones territory. We go over the water and come back over a huge seawater flamingo colony. We dip again to see a seal colony on the beach, then rise. Up and down for another shipwreck, half into the water this time. It's hypnotising. Soon we are over Wallis Bay, and descend into Swakop. The flight path to land goes right over the shanty town and I see the other side of

Swakop, a stark reminder of all things African.

The shacks are more substantial here, some even with power. Differently from most shanty towns, there is a lot of space here. It is spread out, loosely on a grid system. There is a skip on every block, so rubbish is properly collected. Of all of Africa, Namibia seems to have the best refuse collection system in place. Several roads are a surface I have never seen before – salt. Back in town I stop at the garage for my overlanding gallery picture, which I hope is still up there. Later I meet up with Mario for a night on the town.

Mario knows the owner of a nice restaurant, and we get well looked after there. It's a boozy affair. We have a huge meal, and then settle into an odd dice game with the bar staff. Its good fun, but despite playing for two hours I never really learn the rules. Each time you lose you have to do a shot, and I lose count after eight shots. It all goes a bit blurry, but somewhere in there is a nice waitress called Tina. Perhaps we kissed, or perhaps I declared my undying love to her, I can't be sure. My notes are wonderfully short on the matter, but I know there were a lot of laughs. It's a huge night, which sets me up horribly for the road on the next day.

Breakfast is poor – more birds on the buffet, and the roads are twitchy in the heavy mist. I roll on through Walvis Bay and out the other side on to the C14. I am completely shocked and mystified when it turns into gravel. How did I miss that? It's a main road on the map. I am on the right road, it just isn't sealed, and I still have 200 miles to roll on a massive hangover. Silly boy, someone relaxed. It's eerie entering such a vast plain of nothingness. The road surface changes constantly, and it's hard work to pay attention. There is little vegetation and not many hills in the distance. In the flat light it's hard to keep my bearings. I can't really see where the road ends and the sky starts, a giant beige pea soup, like being out at sea. Eventually the sun comes out, but the land does not reveal much more. Just a single track of gravel into the horizon, heading to where I can't see any further. When I get there, I go on to where I can't see any further, and so on. I've never seen a landscape so big in my whole life. Vast is an understatement – it's Brobdingnagian.

I see some people for the first time in hours as I pass the Tropic of Capricorn. Around lunchtime I feel I'm losing the fight. The dust is intense and the handlebars are about to vibrate off. I'm standing the entire time and the bike is all over the place. I try to take it slow, but it will take for ever, so I slowly speed up – until I nearly lose it in the gravel and have to slow down again. In Solitaire, I pull off for a much-needed break. The sun breaks through and the temperature instantly rises. A few of the cars I passed on the way all wave and come to see the bike. I sit, deeply hungover and exhausted, near a nice German couple called Dieter and Anita. Dieter is also a biker and understands how hard the road is for a bike. They are struggling in a truck. It's like someone just flicked the hardcore switch on out here. My hangover is no help whatsoever. It's amazing scenery, however, just really raw.

Back on the road again, the GPS mount snaps. Glory is taking a proper beating with all the vibrations and so am I. Tomorrow we have 200 more miles to run, and once again I wonder what I have got myself into. I stay in another lodge again just outside Sesirem. At the bar there I bump into Dieter and Anita once more, who kindly offer to lift me to the only restaurant down the road later in the evening and we end up dining together. They are lovely people, just on a 4X4 holiday for two weeks, and it's nice to have some company.

The food is delicious – the biggest BBQ I'd ever seen, with every type of game imaginable. Just what my hangover needs. The sunset is stunning. Another hue is added to my mind's palette as the sun meets the red dusty hills surrounding the camp. The night sky is clear and you can still see the hills through the darkness, casting a subtle afterglow. It was a difficult day, but I have a deep sense of peace and accomplishment. Finally – a sense of adventure. Terrain like this used to be off limits for me, but now I'm just taking it in my stride. Namibia is feeding what I've been seeking. Freedom, space, adventure and, at last, a break from all the attention.

I'm up again before light and head out in the dark. It just feels right. It promises to be a hard day, so I grab every minute of daylight I can. It's breathtaking in the morning desert sun heading out south on the C27. The road continues to be tricky, but rewarding. There are no cars or anything else for that matter. I'm on my own. The morning mist slowly rises from the ground, the hills silent and stationary in the distance. The landscape is by far the most beautiful of the whole trip. I feel warm inside as the landscape massages my brain.

Despite bouncing around and having the crap beaten out of me by the road, I enter another realm. This is the sunrise of dreams. 83 days since leaving home, I feel I am finally traversing the hurdle of my mind. I feel no fear today. In this other realm there is no noise, no movement. I am the wind, earth, fire and water all at once. Elementally connected to the mystic cadence. Breathing freedom. A rhythm you don't hear, but can feel in your blood, electricity fed through your eyes, powering the active subconscious. Beauty radiates from the silent vociferous landscape. Desolation feeds the diorama. I am staring at infinity. I am lost in it, but also free in it.

Deep in the subconscious mind, a movement on the road snaps me back to the singular present realm. A herd of impala is on the road ahead and they have just seen me for the first time. They stare, necks turned, ears up and then hear Glory charging for them. They break and run. For a moment it's fun to slowly follow them and see them leap up the road en masse. There are nearly two hundred of them, and they are a wonderful sight. Eventually they tire and break to the sides, over the game fence and on out into the vast expanse. One straggler remains and continues to try and outrun me. I slow further and change my position on the road to help it understand my direction of movement. It works it out from this and bolts left, increasing speed as it goes to jump the fence. It misses it by a big margin, however, and its neck viciously jerks as the fence throws the animal back in the direction it came, its whole body contorted in a violent unnatural movement.

It's immediately apparent the animal will not survive as it continues to twitch, but cannot get up. The implication for me is also immediately apparent. I dipped into the amphoral realm for a moment, but was jerked back instantly. I park the bike, grab a knife and wander over. The impala feebly tries to get up, but cannot. It's one upward eye on me, at first in panic, then peace, it gives me a peripatetic look. One nomadic heart sensing another. It knows its fate, and it accepts I will be the one to change it. It does not speak, but I can clearly feel its thoughts, their meaning clear. It senses to me, *'I have lived, now it is your turn. Embrace the lifeblood of vitality through me.'* I may be charting this road by will, but destiny brought me to this moment. Destiny always has the final say. It places this knife in my hand. Being alone reinforces the madness, or the clarity – it's hard to tell the difference.

I eat meat, but have never slaughtered an animal before. I grab a horn, apologise and lamely try to jab the knife in its throat. It barely goes in. The knife feebly falls out of my hand and to the ground. I think I'm going to be sick. The animal is surprisingly smelly up close. I look out for any assistance, but there is nothing in all directions. It's just us. The animal is in enormous pain.

I have to put it out of its torment quickly. Somewhere deep within me comes what I need. I grab the horn properly this time and move the knife from right to left across its throat, just like in a movie. It's amazing how easy and deep the cut goes – nearly two inches. Blood flows profusely, soaking the sand a bright red. The pain leaves its eyes as its spirit leaves this earth. At home this might be routine, but out here alone today, everything is mysterious.

I have never been so completely in a moment. This is why I was here; it's fantastic and complete. The blood gives me fresh energy, which I take forward. It's macabre, but beautiful, distressing, but cathartic. In killing it I evolve, connected to the earth once again. The blood in the sand makes me calm yet determined. Seeing the fragility of life propels me to live with all my being once again.

The ethereal realm is heavy. One minute here is like a year in the human realm. It takes a moment to collect myself and fully re-enter normality. *Did that just happen? What does the death mean? Does it have to have a meaning? Maybe it simply was. Maybe it was the death of my fear, which I had to physically kill to finally get over?*

I continue further on the surface of the moon. The moon of Namibia is the moon of my mind. Sand appears and quickly grabs at the front wheel. I am up and down on the pegs all day. The road constantly changing keeps me focused, and helps put the impala out of mind for now. If possible, the landscape becomes even bigger than before. The road seems to stretch on forever. I reach the horizon several times. Like a Spaghetti Western landscape on acid. I think I am tripping, until the road calls me back again as I come to a nasty stretch of sand for around ten miles and lose Glory twice. The sun is relentless. Getting her upright again is met with profuse sweat.

There are no conscious thoughts. I am purely in the moment – doing it. I feel like I have crossed the universe when the blacktop of the B4 magically appears like a mirage. Back on sealed road, the miles fall easy as I head West to Luderitz. The road drops into another plain, once again of yet another new world. Namibia refuses to stop stretching the mind. There is only a single stretch of road, with absolutely nothing on either side of it for over fifty miles, and no touch of the human hand. At the end of the horizon a wild jagged mountain range. I've never seen this far into the distance before. I stop to take it all in several times. I cannot get the smell of impala out of my nose, and it adds even more to the crazy vibe. So much of this trip has been a battle, but I am away now. Transported, transfixed, in the moment.

I am looking at the enchanting 'Sperrgebiet' – the 'forbidden zone'. Just the name intrigues me, but seeing it is phenomenal. Near the diamond mines you need a permit to stray from the main road. What Saint-Louis in Senegal took out of me, the Sperrgebiet is restoring. Like Iceland on steroids, I am riding to the end of the world. It's hugely disappointing to end up in the bizarre town of Luderitz. A Wild-West-style outpost, complete with a ghetto, and a twist of something unidentifiable but negative. I'm too tired to try and work out what the vibe is. It's all a bit odd. I feel like I have been in a fist fight after the day on the bike. My body and mind are wrecked, and I have reached both maximum thought-processing power and maximum physical output for the day. I have nothing. I can't process anything more. I sit dumbfounded, smoking and oiling the chain in the car park, both of us utterly rinsed. People stop and stare, but I can't really see them. I still feel transposed. I am high on simply being alive in such a place. It's like magic, but there is no illusion – this is real. I made the whole trip to Africa for this one day.

The next day Glory and I are warmed by the sun, and more stunning moonscape once again. Normally I hate a dead end, when you have to go back on yourself, but this is a treat. I'm heading to Fish River Canyon, where petrol will be an issue. I call into the station at Aus to top up and try to get some kind of reserve. I stupidly ask if they sell jerrycans, when the pump attendant wryly smiles, and pulls a couple of used bottles of coke out of the bin. In a glorious disregard for health and safety, I bungee-tie them to the spare tyres on the back and set off down the road for more adventure. Soon I'm making the turning off the B4 and again into the unknown.

On a day like this, with off-roading involved, I always hold my breath until now. Now I will see what kind of a day it's going to be. The tarmac before doesn't really count, even if you run over a hundred miles on it. The day is decided solely by the off-road element. It makes or breaks you every time. I stop at the gate to fill up from my 'jerrycans' and take a leak. Staring down a long empty road to nothing, wondering what's to come, there is only a simple lonesome gate to nothingness. Joyously, I pass through it.

The landscape constantly changes further into the canyon. There are some small foothills, which are like rollers on the bike, and great fun. Occasionally there are gates and I have to stop and open/close them. I don't see anyone. Around fifty miles in there is a turning for Fish River Lodge, with a further twenty miles to roll. The road gets hairy, an off-road roller coaster, with steep banked turns and blind rollers. I have to lean forward to stop her pulling massive wheelies and throwing me off the back the terrain is so steep in places. It's exhaustingly good fun. Although shattered, I can't help but to charge it. Glory and I both received another royal thrashing, but we are operating as one now, in full unison. I pray we don't get a puncture. She is having trouble getting into gear for some reason, but if I can just rest for few days I will have a look. It's a relief to finally come to the lodge, perched right on the canyon edge, the most remote place to bed down on the trip yet. Dust in my eyes, nose, ears and even my mind at this point, it's time for another deep rest.

The lodge has one main building in the middle and ten self-standing units fanned out either side along the canyon edge. It's all style and low substance. They shut the water off in the night and to wash a pair of socks in the laundry is over $3. The food is delicious, however, and the hospitality second to none. It's mainly trading on the view. The rooms look cool, but are really unpractical. I give the bike a once-over. The GPS mount is truly shot. The clutch cable is seventy per cent frayed, which explains why it was hard to get her into gear. Thankfully we had fitted another right next to it ready to go, so it's only a five minute switch out. I give the chain a proper clean with petrol and oil it up again. We will be needing every bit of help possible to get out of here.

I hang out in the main building by the bar to use the Wi-Fi and plan next steps. I meet another interesting girl who works at the hotel called Tanya. She is very similar to Brenda, except even more keen, and even more attractive. A dangerous mix. I am not sure what was happening. I certainly never received this type of attention back home, sadly. Tanya is very pretty, but not very bright. Clearly. While charming, her endless giggling while getting me drinks or food is not productive. As a service industry worker I know that if you only have one skill serve the drinks and food efficiently. Banter is a plus, not the other way around. I did consider acting on her advances many times, but reason it's more hassle than it was worth. I have some 'companionship' coming in Cape Town by an even more attractive girl very soon, so should just chill.

Southern Africa has the worst HIV rates in the world with over 50% of HIV/AIDS sufferers here. Botswana has the sad title of the worst HIV-impacted country in the world, with over 26% of the population having HIV/AIDS. Charming as she is, she is definitely not that charming. Our chats are good fun, however, and amusingly pass the hours away. Dining solo in a crowded room you welcome any chat – let alone with an attractive young lady.

I spend a day doing a 4X4 trip to the canyon floor, which is truly beautiful. It is the second largest canyon in the world and a nice break from the bike. On my last night another biker, Nick, arrives from the US and we naturally strike up a chat. Nick is a California 'dude', with long blond hair and a cool breezy manner. He carries the California surfer look, but is a bright guy. He's about ten years younger than I, but has a similar spirit and we get on well instantly. He is on a two-week trip from Victoria Falls to Cape Town, on a rented BMW bike. We have a beer and decide to ride out tomorrow morning together southwards to Rosh Pinah. It's a lot of off-road, and having a partner would be sensible out here. We have a drink with an English couple at the bar who had done a similar trip years ago, and after dinner it's high spirits for the next day.

I have high hopes for the Orange River. I feel Namibia can do no wrong in my book. Literally. For all its faults, the lodge is in an amazing place and staffed by lovely people. Everyone I meet here is like-minded. It helps me contextualise where I am and what I am doing. Over extended periods solo you can easily lose that and get lost in your mind's pitfalls. I enjoy being on my own, but hanging out with cool people like this is also fun sometimes.

We are up before sunrise and eat big before setting off. In the parking lot it's long goodbyes with the English, who are excited for us, and also nostalgic for their trip. I could see myself here in 25 years, wishing some young morons good fortune and reminiscing. This is the first companion on the whole trip, so naturally has a different vibe. The last person I rode next to was Nick, back in Hampshire when I was leaving. We push each other to go a bit faster than normal, but I don't think there is too much showing-off stupidity thankfully.

We run the twenty mile 'driveway' and then tear off into seventy miles of off-road. After that it's the main road for a forty-mile blast, down past the town of Rosh Pinah, then once again off-road down the Orange River itself. Beyond that we have another eighty miles of off-road through the Ais-Richtersveld Transfrontier Park, on a surface we know little about, before crossing the border and back into South Africa. From there its a simple eighty miles on a sealed road south to Springbok for the night. All in all, it's going to be a very mixed bag of riding.

It all starts on the D463 – a long windy stretch of gravel road with huge views. The trail is in good condition, and with the macho factor we are pushing over seventy miles an hour. At one stage I have to check my speed as I am doing eighty-five on gravel. How things have changed. Nick has a GoPro on, and is filming some of this. I am leading on one section, when I spot deep gravel. I wave to Nick to slowdown as I lock up fully on the rear brake, desperately trying to slow down myself. We are going entirely too fast. My front wheel washes about a bit and I can't hold it. Eventually I go over for the biggest drop yet, even rolling off the side of the bike like a stuntman. At least, that's what I told myself.

The tank bag rips off, and the panniers take another big hit. It's not too bad and I have the bike up again before Nick can get to me. He's filming all of this, of course, and runs up to me with the camera rolling, shouting, 'How was that!' *Wanker*. When I try to move Glory, her back wheel just digs a hole in the gravel. We cannot push or power her out. I take off the panniers and Nick lifts the back end, hoping we can get some traction, but the wheel just spins further and the hole gets deeper. She is now down to the rear axle in hard gravel. I don't need the side stand as she just holds frozen in position, bolt upright. Jackets and gloves off, we dig for some time. I finally wedge a huge flat rock under the back wheel, and we power her free again. Less than an hour in to the day's ride, we are already sweating and shattered – but having a great adventure.

We haul down the gravel road further, having a blast as we go. Reaching the tarmac of the C13 is a nice break for the muscles. The off-roading sections here require constant standing and excessively wear the wrists and ankle joints. We grab some simple provisions in Rosh Pinah and head off-road again for round two. Rosh Pinah is a weird vibe, just an odd town in the middle of nowhere with connections to the mines. I wonder if I'm in a Western movie again, or on the surface of another planet. It's weird, but the feeling is becoming normal. We are near Oranjemund, or 'Mouth of the Orange', another odd town, which is really not a 'town'. It's one of the bases of the De Beers diamond-mining empire. Access is severely restricted and you have to have a special permit to enter. The streets and infrastructure are supposed to be every bit as good as the US. It's not built with public funds, but private diamond money.

Rumours fly across southern Namibia about draconian security and elaborate heists gone wrong. Apparently you can't even take a car into the town, they fear diamonds being smuggled out so much. I imagine a simple wedding ring that some chap spends a month's salary on for his future partner. Around two grand for a one carat stone. This mine spits out two million carats a year, and has done so since 1936. That's four billion pounds a year, or roughly £324 billion since it opened. Where did all that money go? It certainly did not land in this town, or anywhere else in Africa from what I can see.

If there is only one story to summarise the white exploitation of African resources this is it. De Beers was establish by Cecil Rhodes in 1888, and supported by the Rothschild bank. They capitalised on the resources here and profited billions. There is more information on the controversies they caused through price-fixing and conflict diamonds than there is on the company itself. Little is known about either entity, apart from the fact they are uncomprehendingly rich. Here on the ground, it's a small dusty town in the middle of a beautiful nothingness. Shrouded in tall tales and mystery. Fascinating and sad, the African story framed in one view. Ask yourself why Africa is so fucked-up and if you think we have a part in it. Think about this when you covet that diamond ring on your finger.

The road is a mixed surface and washy in places, but we keep pushing. We stop for a few pictures and have a laugh here and there. The river is on one side and a mountain range on the other. The sun is out and its great riding. The river is running low, but snakes a wide colourful path. The only life here hangs on the river's edge. Apart from that it's desolate desert mountains with little vegetation. The rocks are savagely formed, dusty and dry. You can see the centuries of formations in them. The river looks like it could change levels substantially, but the only thing that has come from the sky recently is dust. Occasionally there is a small rocky pass to tackle with a few twisty gravel corners, but nothing too crazy.

We ride close by, then separate, then come together again, stopping for pictures in different spots. It's a great pace to appreciate it all. The water gives all the colour here, in the same blue colour range as sky, but deeper. It's not named 'Orange River' for its colours, but in honour of William V of Orange. It is the longest river in South Africa at 1400 miles, starting in Lesotho and flowing out to the Atlantic. Away from the river it's big country and very rough. I smile, thinking how I savoured every mile of Namibia from the top to the bottom.

We stop for lunch at the park gate, pleasantly chatting in some shade. We naturally drift into politics, having a long discussion about the ills of Africa.

Nick is convinced it all comes down to education. He makes a good argument that education can solve most of the world's issues, especially here in Africa. I disagree a bit, as from what I could see Africans lack drive. They fundamentally don't care, making education pointless. We go back and forth. I can't help but feel that it's all fresh for him. He has a fresh energy for it, but has only been here for a few weeks. I am apathetic about it all at this stage, having been in it for months; it's rubbed off on me. I urge him to see West Africa and then have the same chat with me. What I saw in those villages was apathy on a massive scale. I had no idea what the answer for that was, or more to the point, was not sure it needed to be changed. You can either view poor Africa as exploited and forgotten, or perhaps consider they actively choose to live this way, maybe both. I exaggerated the idea in the discussion to prove a point, but I could not escape the apathy I saw. A small touch of it is toxic to a country, especially a small impoverished one.

All of the elements involved in Africa will never be amassed into one catch-all of understanding. It's simply too vast a topic to summarise. As such, Africa retains elements of extreme mystery and madness. It can be enchanting, intimidating, mystical, difficult, inspiring, depressing and at times appear like hell on earth. It always drives me back to the fundamental question, however – *is there anything wrong with living like this?* Yes, they suffer, but is that the price of living free? Do we have to impose our sense of comfort and affluence? If we stop thinking we are right, however, our way of life appears meaningless, hence we struggle to take that viewpoint.

Are we at the leading edge of civilisation? For me, we simply are not. We are at the leading edge of comfort, that much I can admit. No one has cracked 'this life' perfectly, so why should we lecture the culture here on what is 'perfection', when it's a culture we can't even understand. We can't even fully understand our own culture. No one has grasped a universal meaning of life. Thus no one can assert their way is the best. We could all use a little humility, and a lot of acceptance.

The question still remains – is it right or wrong to live like this? The second question – if the answer to the first is that it is wrong – is how can it be made it better? The third would be, whose responsibility is it to make it better? The first question leads to the next. However, I feel everyone in the West just jumps to the second one and sets about doing charity work. They don't even ask the third question. I don't feel like helping if living like this is not wrong. Questions here just lead to more questions and nothing ever really gets answered. People just talk a lot. Riding across Africa is never a simple ride on a quiet road.

We cross over the border with a small lecture on the South African Customs Union, 'our version of the EU, don't you know?' Yeah, that's going well, isn't it, mate? Immediately things are green and prosperous again. The road is in beautiful condition, and after the

exploits of the day, we are happy to smoothly ride to a few cold beers and a big feed. It's great to have company of a like-minded person and our chats continue over dinner. Further south the road passes through some huge farming country; the fields are possibly the biggest I have ever seen. The road goes flat and then rises again over Piekenierskloof Mountain near Citrusdal. The views coming down are stunning and I think I could be in France. From there we continue our path hard south. With Nick's GoPro camera he is able to capture a picture of me on the motorway as we catch sight of Table Mountain for the first time. A picture I will cherish for life.

We part at a petrol station outside of Cape Town and I ride on to the suburb of Millerton. I am pleased to have met Nick. He is sound, and opened my eyes to riding with other people, something I previously imagined I would not enjoy. We make a plan to meet for dinner in a few days before he leaves. It's day 89 since leaving Cornwall, and I have ridden 11,122 miles. In standard style I celebrate with a six-pack and a pizza in my hotel room, alone. Jo arrives tomorrow and we will celebrate properly with a few cocktails in town. For now it's business as usual tending to Glory.

With a few twists and turns aside, I am happy to have reached a lifelong goal. I feel a new kind of tired – deep in my bones. I'm very happy Namibia delivered the 'African experience' I was questing for. Despite all the preparation, expense and fear in getting here, this portion of the trip alone was worth it. What I sought in the Sahara, I found in Namibia. *That feeling*. The childlike buzz of excitement and wonder. That richly fulfilling experience of striking out and seeing this huge wonderful world we are all lucky enough to live in and appreciating how stunningly beautiful it is. That energising feeling of seeing a place unlike any you have ever seen. It was a delicious tangible mystery which I ate up.

A cigarette has never tasted as good as this one. Looking out at the setting sun on Table Mountain, I try to hold back the tears, but fail. Looking across at Glory and once again thinking, *No one is laughing at you now, girl – no one. Well done, girl, well done.*

Cape Town is a wonderful break for a few weeks. Food is easy. Having a washing machine wonderful. Glory is securely parked at the airport, locked and covered, having a well-deserved rest. Jo arrives and we spend a few days getting to know the city, before getting a rental car and driving east on the 'Garden Route'. We have a big night out with Nick before he leaves, and it's another amusing boozy evening. It's easy travel, small distances, good roads, nice hotels with lots of downtime. We talk and learn more about each other. We do a full loop of Cape Town and find it surprisingly big. Table Mountain frames every view and is the best landmark I've ever seen. Leaving, we head immediately for Stellenbosch and get wonderfully drunk in the vibrant street bars there.

Date four is a long one at three weeks, but we have lots of fun. We see Cape Agulhas and the southernmost tip of Africa. Then Mossel bay, George, Wilderness and Knysna. We rent a canoe for a day in Wilderness, and bikes for the day in Stormsrivier, spending some time in Tsitsikamma National Park. Eventually we reach Port Elizabeth. The land is beautiful, but fairly boring and supersafe compared to where we have been. Although chilled, my mind is still processing so much conflicting information. We stay in some fabulous hotels and spend a lot of money, but you only live once. Our favourite is Views Hotel on Wilderness Beach – a lovely room with a balcony overlooking the sea and wonderful food. For all purposes we are back in the Western world, and the hospitality is delightful. The days fly by.

Instead of turning around, we head north to loop back to Cape Town, passing through the Karoo Mountain range. Yet another landscape in the vastness of South Africa opens up, unforgiving and rugged, but alluring nonetheless. On the way we pass through Groot Swartberg Nature Reserve, where I miss Glory. The views are fabulous. We have one last hurrah in wine country, staying at a super expensive hotel in Franschhoek and sampling some wineries. It's lovely. We call Franschhoek 'Fanny check' which is a source of many jokes.

Back in Cape Town again it's time for some serious downtime and to tend to Glory properly. We check into an Airbnb I had booked for three weeks and I put down roots for a bit. Glory safely in the garage, I start to take her apart and clean everything. She has several layers of dust and dirt. My mother arrives from the US and she meets Jo for the first time. We have a nice dinner and a day exploring Robben Island, before Jo leaves for the UK right before Christmas. I spend a lot of time sleeping and eating well. I start running again and get a bit of fitness back. Mostly I sit online and plan the next stages of the trip, while visiting with my mum. It's Christmas, and it's lovely to be with family.

We celebrate with a simple dinner, a drink and some television – perfect. Glory goes to Yamaha for some more TLC and a good once-over. She is sparkling once again and in sound shape rolling out. All the gear is thoroughly cleaned. Including my boots. Somewhere offroad in Namibia I had ridden through a puddle on a farm and got mud inside the boot. It had a strong smell of African Farm, which kept giving for months. Having a washing machine is so pleasant sometimes I change clothes in the middle of the day for the hell of it. Of all the home comforts, it's my favourite.

For New Year's Eve we go to a safari park a couple hours out of town. It's a glorified zoo compared to Kruger, but I didn't have the heart to tell Mum that. She has a wonderful time and felt she had been on a real safari, so I didn't want to spoil that. Eventually the time comes to say goodbye and she leaves for the US. It was a great visit and I am grateful she made the long trip over. Riding out, I'm sad to say bye to Table Mountain, but feel I will see it again one day. The bike is solid, and I am better equipped mentally than ever before for the road ahead.

I know it will not be easy, but nothing substantial ever is.

EIGHT

MOANING IN MAUN
South Africa – Mozambique – Botswana - Zambia

'For my part, I travel not to go anywhere, but to go. I
travel for travel's sake. The great affair is to move.'
Robert Louis Stevenson

I set off north-east heading for Beaufort West, and on to Bloemfontein. After
such an enjoyable break it was going to take some time to get back into the road,
so I throw myself headlong at the task, eating up 1200 miles in three days. In no
time I'm back to uncomfortable hotel rooms, shit Wi-Fi, poor food and feeling
exhausted. That said, it's wonderful to be back on the actual road. I forget my
happiest moments are simply rolling down the road – riding, exploring, with a
clear purpose in the simple act of A to B. In the early mornings the Karoo have
a moving mist on top of the their jaggedness. In the mist the landscape keeps
changing, reinventing the scene constantly. The clouds take away the colour
and give it back again, like going back and forth between black and white and
colour television.

Out of Bloemfontein the sunrise is really special, driving a rising mist
up off the fields. The mist completely envelops me at one worrying stage, but
coming out of it again is fantastic. Just shy of the border I pull in for fuel and
a coffee. Sitting here I watch a minibus driver fill up with petrol. I have seen
people shake their vehicles to get more fuel in, I do this myself. However, this
chap takes it to the next level. He gets back in and circles the pump once in the
bus, then fills it up a tiny bit more. Then drives a loop around the pump again,
then squeezes a few more drops in. He does it five times as I watch. I've come
to dismiss things like this now simply as 'African'. There is no point trying to
understand it: you can't.

Over the border in Lesotho, its back to 'Africa proper' again. I climb into
what I can only describe as 'Africa does *The Sound of Music*'. The conditions
take me by surprise once again, with full-blown mountains and freezing
temperatures. People have blankets around their shoulders as they sit on the
side of the road watching you. People still do a lot of that. I guess that throws
out the 'heat causes laziness' theory. The hills are green and fertile, and for

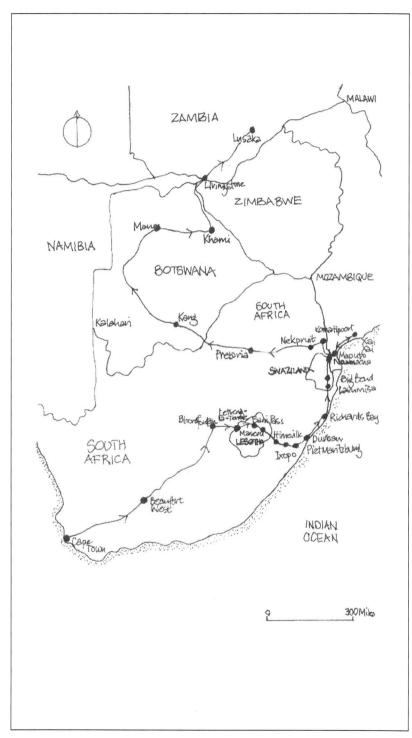

once the rivers are running full, nearly raging and a pleasant change. Still just huts, but not much litter.

The passes get higher and higher – 2,500 metres, 3,000 metres, 3,300 metres as the temperature plummets. The road surface is mostly fresh pristine tarmac. I keep expecting it to go to shit at any moment, but it doesn't. I continue up through small villages and waterfalls, stopping for pictures often, and trying to keep my hands warm. It's all so unAfrican, at least the Africa I had seen so far. When you think you know this continent, it becomes something else. I could be in the Pyrenees right now. Just as I arrive on the border above Sani pass the mist fully descends and I can't see further than ten metres. At the border there is a girl with beautiful blue eyes. She gives me one look with those eyes, which won't be one I'll forget. Strange to find such a beauty here, but everything is strange here.

After the border post, the beautiful tarmac finally stops, in a big way. It's just rocks and gravel in no man's land. This would be stunning in the sun, but also probably pretty hairy if you could see it. The pass is very steep, technical and wet. It reminds me of Dumbarton Street in San Francisco, but with a loose rocky surface and waterfalls on the corners. The whole thing looks like it could slide out at any moment in this damp, and it's super-slippery. You can only see the corner ahead, and next stretch below you – no further. I have no idea how many switchbacks there are going down. With no traffic I am alone, which helps me remain calm.

I travel slowly so I can remember every metre of it, and there is a lovely mystic quality to the descent. Riding so technically in these conditions alone is a mix of trepidation and buzz. I feel like I am in Scotland or Wales in the damp mist. If Lord of the Rings *did motorbikes* … Thankfully I have no issues on the steep hard section. As the road flattens, however, visibility improves and reveals ten miles of wet clay. I regret my last tyre choice in Cape Town as they are road tyres, so take it as slow as possible, hoping for the best. Several times I have to put both feet down to try and stabilise, like some kind of adult training wheels. Just four days since leaving Cape Town perfectly clean, Glory and I both are immediately covered in clay. My beautiful clean boots are soon clogged with so much mud I cannot work the foot controls.

A few miles in we have our first drop, slipping off the side of the road. Once you touch the side, you have no hope, as the clay is over six inches deep. We creep a bit further for another drop. Glory does not want to start after this one, and I'm fed up as well, so we stop for lunch right there on the road. A few cars pass and honk. After ten minutes break she fires up again fine. A mile takes over twenty minutes. Another mile down the road we have a big tumble. I roll off into the hedge, cursing like a madman. The newly repaired tank bag is ripped off again. Glory passes that point of ninety degrees where she becomes impossible to pick up alone.

I give in at that stage, having a sulk on the side of the road and waiting for destiny to intervene. Within minutes a man appears, and then another. Thankfully they help me get her back up, but it takes all three of us. They motion I am through the worst and will be OK from here. There are few words spoken, but they can read how grateful I am. We boxed again, except this time we went down. My whole body is wracked, Glory has fresh scars, and we're both covered in mud. I find a waterfall flowing over the road and try to clean us up a bit, but it's futile; the clay just spreads on everything and sticks. Soon the rain stops and the sun comes out, so the mud bakes in. Back on the road again then.

The Drakensberg mountains surrounding us are stunning. Lush dense rolling green hills with waterfalls and rivers. Super vivid greens from the constantly damp conditions. Above the rolling hills the mountains have odd stone step formations near the top. The rock is different colours in places, but mostly shows damp. Another wildly different landscape. The waterfalls are small, but stack up like pillows; one falls into another, slowly gaining strength. Rolling into Himeville we look a right state, feeling like a rock band after a three-day bender. It's a lovely quaint rural town, with big farms and horses, and the dramatic mountains in the background. I find the digs, some hot food and promptly pass out.

The next day the sun is out and I'm in excellent spirits after tackling the pass the day before, some kind of afterglow in effect. I'm a mess and not entirely focused on the road, but really happy deep down. I have a renewed sense of identity in it all. I am a motorbike rider. I get up every day and eat miles. That's what I do. Keep moving, keep riding, keep passing through the lands of Earth, drinking them all in. Don't stay too long anywhere, don't let the chat get that deep anywhere. Then when in the helmet again, let the thoughts wash over you, let the miles cleanse you. All thoughts − past, future, present, all of it. It is not becoming my identity anymore. It is my identity now. I am bruised, battered and not ready for another 250 miles, but I'm exorbitantly happy. I feel triumph and jubilation at the simple feat of taking on the Sani

Pass. It wasn't the pass itself, but the drama and trials I found at the bottom of it. We wear our scars proudly.

Taking a perfect bike, spotlessly clean, in a spotlessly clean set of bike clothes (first wash in 120 days) and throwing them both down in the mud was a release. We are realising our full potential. Sweating, cursing, shouting and all. It's not a hard pass to tackle, but looking at miles of wet clay, on slick tyres, was finally a battle that I was not going to easily win. It was the stuff of motorbike stories, and pictures I had become hooked on over the years. Except these memories and pictures are mine. The power of it gives me goose bumps. I had slogged my guts out on that hill, slipping and falling in the mud. I gave it a fair whack and came out still fighting. I lived that day. Today I'm in the after moment, relishing it. I woke this morning like I was hungover. Like I had a huge blowout on the tiles, including a one night stand with a super model. I feel a huge sense of release, coupled with a 'fuck it' attitude. My monkey has been fed.

The roads south-east to Durban are far more twisty than anticipated, but Glory and I just roll with it. We head south to Ixopo, and then out on to Highway 3 near Pietermaritzburg as the road just gets better and better. There is a lot of logging around the area, and some farming. I see the white/black divide again, but the road takes most of my attention, or maybe it's becoming more familiar. A white box truck slows and indicates to turn right at one point. Either he signals late, or I don't see it as I'm not really with it, still drunk on yesterday. I go to pass on the right as he is about to turn right, but thankfully he hears me at the last moment. Classic accident scenario. It all happens very slowly, thankfully. If we were going to connect it would have be at a slow speed, but it doesn't happen because he was paying attention. We look at each other as I pass him going too fast, and he is nonplussed. I wave an apology, but he is rightly not amused. Thankfully he completes his turn after I've passed.

My head is clearly somewhere else, and I curse myself suitably. Pay attention, moron. We do not build roads like this in Europe; they are far too tight. The road is a badly built tarmac rollercoaster and, like most roads in Africa, it's dangerous, but good fun. Heading into Durban I think my mind travels a lot further than the bike.

As you roll through the lands, the countries, the people of the world, you would think you become more connected to it all. I find the opposite is happening: the further I go, the further back I pull back from humanity. Pulling back from my home, from the religion I was brought up in, from the school of thought I was taught, from the economic system I lived in – back further. Back as far as you can go. Dumping your complete identity. Causing you to further question nationality, religion, and a reason for being. Question everything. When what can only be described as a sense of 'outernationalism' descends.

In different lands, they build things differently. They run things differently. They have different customs, fears, cultural norms. Ideologically we actually have very little in common. When you start to question it all, suddenly you can't stop. Nothing seems reasonable or part of you. None of what you see reflects who you are, or how you think. It's both beautiful and sad to roam the world wholly unbelonging. Why is it so difficult to all get along? Why are we so different, when we are really not that different at all? How can we hate so much? Why do we fight so hard for our stupid little ideas? Why is it all such a big fucking deal? How do we make it all matter so much that we can kill?

Humanity is a paradox. On the one hand individual people are kind, loving and beautiful. As a whole we are a disgusting, Earth-destroying, hateful people. I always see paradoxes and want to destroy the maddening idea. The more time on the road I spent, the further back I viewed things. I feel as if I have pulled back so far I am in space, looking at the Earth as a whole. Not from above – travelling does not make you some kind of god amongst humans. More seeing it head-on, right in front of you. How can something matter so much? How can one place be so special? Why do people feel an intense connection with just one space – home? How can you take a religion so seriously when there are so many different ones? You are either saying I am weak to believe only this construct, or worse, my construct is the only right one, and you would be wrong either way.

They are all constructs for weak minds, fixed only on what happens after death. Can you not just live your one life as much as you can? Can familiarity with a place be a negative thing? Is the idea of 'home' detrimental? A space which is no different from all the other spaces on the planet? This sense of 'mine' and 'not yours' driving division. Can familiarity with an idea also be a negative thing? With over six billion people, how can anyone actually be important? With so many towns, cities and countries, how can any one individual place be better than another? How do you claim one amongst hundreds as your home?

Rolling through, I enjoy seeing and learning, but I feel no connection to one piece of land or one group of people. At times not even my home. Simply a confused drifter, the only thing clear is that I need to keep moving. The mind is so infinitely powerful, yet unable to fully reason the world we are in. Logic is ultimately a broken set of principles that can never truly explain the world we live in.

I have no destination in life, and none in Durban either. I'm heading to Richards Bay, but do not take the turning, instead naturally wandering into downtown Durban to have a look about. Southern Africa has me back to my normal habits, following my nose. A state West Africa never seemed to induce. Durban is South Africa's third largest city, after all, and home to the largest Indian population outside of India. The road is very hilly as I approach, with great mansions on either side in expensive affluent communities. Likely gated and alarmed.

Downtown it's a similar urban vibe to Cape Town. Durban is a thriving place of industry and the busiest port in South Africa. It doesn't say much to me, just a lot of noise. Near Richards Bay there is a dirty great big power station that goes on for miles. The hotel is suitable and I pull in for some downtime and laundry. Hanging out with the staff as usual, chatting shit and drinking beer. I'm tempted to head north into St Lucia and on to Mozambique, but after research find the road involves one hundred miles of deep sand I rule it out and plan to head through Swaziland. After the elation of Sani Pass, it all seems a bit static.

Swaziland is calm and organised enough, also part of the South African Customs Union. There is a slight moment when the officer asks for ownership documents on the bike. He immediately reads the top part of the UK logbook, which clearly says 'this document is not proof of ownership'. Somehow I manage to talk him around it and he lets me go. Twenty crossings after leaving the UK, he is the first person to notice this absurd wording. Swaziland smells sweet, highly productive with sugar cane, and, surprisingly, distilling. USA Distillers at Big Bend has a large processing plant, with a lovely scent that goes on for miles. A very welcome change to some of the other scents on the roads of Africa.

The road is simple but quiet, with a red strip of clay either side of the potholed tarmac, and lush green beyond that. It makes for a strange sightline. A big strip of red along the roadside with green fields beyond, eventually meeting clear blue sky. A surprisingly colourful effect, with flashes of the Caribbean.

It's one of the smallest countries in Africa, but has the lowest life expectancy in the world, at just forty-nine years old (just beating Lesotho). It's a lovely climb through green hills up to the border at Namaacha. The ride is a strange sensation, with Mozambique literally over the hill to the east the entire way. Borders lines are fascinating everywhere, especially here in Africa. You've seen the map many times before, but you learn it all over again when you see the land first-hand; the feeling never gets old.

Once inside Mozambique – for the first time crossing a border in Africa – things noticeably change very quickly. There is an explosion of language. I can't understand it all, but I can get the intonation much better – a highly expressive and rapid Portuguese. The poverty is staggering. Buildings are collapsing – but there are buildings! Giant great collapsing shells of clearly European-style colonial buildings. They are falling apart now, but once would have been impressive. African life is in full swing around these former carcasses – the usual street sellers, turbulent roads, horn honking, and constant staring. It feels different here, though. Interestingly, they don't go in the buildings or use them at all, just occupy around the bases of them. The Caribbean and Brazilian vibe continues. There is the same poverty as most of Africa, but a different kind of happiness. The people seem more vibrant, and far less apathetic. With a wild element once again, I can feel a sense of fear rising inside my subconscious. 'Africa proper' pushes my guard up again.

I can still function in this state, but it's a more of a refined state of mind. The focus is on critical systems and logic, with no long walks into my subconscious, no daydreaming. Everything is a potential threat and has to be analysed. My mind strictly focuses on only what is in front of me. What that thing is doing, how it's moving, what signs it's telling me. Be it a person, a vehicle, an animal, a road. It shuts down the cerebral conversation where revelations and unexpected travelling surprises happen. A focused sense of survival, where there is no space for rolling the dice. The idea of 'random' closed down. I have no doubt fear is the base cause. Something I did not feel in South Africa, and definitely not in Namibia. Being this focused for long periods like this is exhausting. When your every move is constantly studied by hundreds of people I find it tiring and intimidating. If I am a computer, in Africa proper I go into 'safe mode'. Unlike West Africa, however, I am now able to understand what is happening.

In Maputo I have a look around, but find it uninspiring. Maybe I'm just back in that zone and it's hard to cut through to me. I walk the streets to the main train station, and have a mooch about. It's a lovely European building, which has been freshly repainted recently. The grounds are well kept, and back home it would have been suitable. Here, surrounded by filthy, dirty and noisy African street chaos, it is entirely out of place. Everything around it crumbles, yet this one thing designed and built under the imperialists stands out proudly. It seems backward that they celebrate and maintain such an entity. Like a bizarre manifestation of the Stockholm syndrome, on a national level. They are simply incapable of the organisation, planning and commitment it takes to build something like this. That does not mean Africans are lazy or stupid – it means a building like this has no place in their culture. Hence it's even stranger the way it's being revered.

I find a nice-looking hotel called Nascer do Sol Lodge (Sunrise Lodge) online, just past Xai Xai. It looks perfect, but has a six-mile sand driveway to the beach. I call and speak to the owner, Peter, who says, 'Yeah, we've had bikes here before', which is enough to commit. The roads are thick, slow-moving NAV the whole way. With police everywhere it's tedious progress, but I pull off the main road just before lunch. The trail is sand, but firmer in the tyre paths from the trucks. Around halfway in I have my first drop, quickly followed by second and third. The fourth drop is the worst, as Glory passes the fatal 90-degree angle again and I cannot lift her. I resign myself to sitting under a tree and have some water, momentarily defeated.

Sometimes you have the fight in you, and sometimes you don't. I don't even get to sit before a family comes up from the beach in a 4X4. The father gets out and tries to help me lift her, but we can't manage it. She just slides across the sand, blocking the single track even more. The whole family of six jumps out then and even the kids help to finally get her upright again. Say what you will about the world, but I find ten times out of ten, regardless of where you are, people will pitch in and help. We expect it from family and friends, but the kindness of strangers always touches us unexpectedly, and always seems more profound.

I sit under a tree panting, and eventually summoning the gumption to carry on. The heat is oppressive. There is a strong correlation with bad shit happening just before lunch for me. It's always a terrible coincidence, which is likely my fault, but I will never admit it to myself. I remember Mario's advice and open her up once again. As we approach the beach the sand gets deeper still. With one final hill up to reception, we go down heavy in a gully at the bottom of it. I roll off, cursing very loudly in a blind rage like a child. The sand must be over a foot deep. I sit for a bit once more to try and regain some strength. It's around 40C in the shade. The hotel entrance is only fifty metres away and in clear sight, but we are both overheating uncontrollably. I get her up again, and we eventually reach the top of the hill, where a man comes out to greet me.

'You must be Will!'

'Yes, you must be Peter.'

'Yes – nice to meet you.'

'If I had more energy right now I would punch you!'

He apologises as I try to see the lighter side of it all. He is a nice guy actually, and it wasn't his fault; I'm just in child mode. He kindly offers to help me get back out again when the times comes, which I will take him up on. He also buys me a beer to say sorry, which is welcomed. Most things are forgiven with cold beer. At reception I try to check in. They give me a form to fill out, but the sweat is running so profusely off me and mixing with the dirt on my arms it stains the form. You can't read a thing on it; it's a disgusting mess. The receptionist kindly advises that I go get cleaned up and come back later. Outside reception I go to move Glory and she just topples over like a sack of shit. I just have nothing in me. Six drops in six miles is officially a new record. It's also Friday the 13th. The 'room' is a small beach house in an amazing setting. Just up from the water, and next to the restaurant. Like a child, I have a feed, and then a nap.

I wake as an adult once more, and set off exploring along the beautiful white sandy beach. Every view is simply a postcard. It's mesmerising to just watch the water lap the beach. There is a cooler breeze on the water's edge, and it's supremely peaceful after the manic road. There is no one staring at me, as there is no one here. The beach has a harsh drop-off, which is slightly intimidating. The water seems to go for five feet on a steady sandy incline, and then just drops off a sheer edge to darkness. The water moves in an odd way, as it looks like the waves are too big, but the ledge just cuts them off at the shoulders as they come in. The great power of the wave is neutralised. I've never seen a beach like it – it looks dangerous as hell.

It takes me a while to realise how different this is from most beaches I have ever seen. There is nothing on the water or around the beach. No signs, adverts, boats, noisy engines, docks, litter, people, animals, tracks – nothing. Just the calm lapping of the waves and white sand meeting blue azure water to the horizon. We do not have unchanged expanses like this at home any more; it's a small slice of wild heaven here.

Dinner is out of this world, and one of the best meals I have in Africa. Simple spiced fish with rice and vegetables. Beautiful. I have a look over Glory and once again she is in a state. I wonder if cumulatively the trip has also had such an impact on me. Living this hard takes it out of you. We both are in need a day of chilling, so we take one and stay another day. I sit by the beach and read. I parked Glory under a tree full of birds, so wake up to crap all over her. I do treat the women in my life badly. I give her a clean and move her. I had cleaned her in Richards Bay as well. After pulling in here we look like we just crossed Africa, but it was only six fucking miles! As usual a 'day off' lasts about an hour. I walk up to Peter's house and have a nice coffee with him and his wife. They have led quite the international life, and are lovely people, very hospitable with some great stories. I don't think you can live here in Africa without amassing several fascinating stories. We make a plan to link at 6 a.m. the next day with his pickup truck, so he can take the luggage and I can ride behind him. That way he will be on hand if I get stuck.

A huge thunderstorm passes through in the night and the next day everything is wet and miserable. Peter is perfectly on time – bless him, on a Sunday and all. We load up the truck and off we go. Glory flies with the weight off and is substantially easier to control. All of the dips coming in are now unexpectedly very deep puddles. The sand is compacted by the rain, making it easier, but the puddles are a worry. I speed up and head right for the middle, the water black with who knows what in it. I try not to get any in my mouth and clamp it shut every time I charge another one. Several times the water is so deep it goes clear over my head when I go through them. I'm wet down to my toes within five minutes and still have eight hours of riding to do today. But – I have a huge smile as I smash out this trail Indiana Jones style.

At this speed it's over quickly, and we are soon back at the roadside, without a single drop. I show a small smile outwardly, but inside it's one of my greatest triumphs yet on the bike. Glory and I are both dripping wet as I load her back up again. Peter nods as he inspects her, agreeing she is an amazing piece of engineering. At the last minute, while saying goodbye, Peter hands me a bible. He explains he used to be a Gideon and hopes this will help me on my journey. The religion is totally lost on me, but the sentiment is not. Although

I had wanted to punch him forty-eight hours ago, I now give him a hug. He is a human at our highest form in that moment, inspiring nothing but love and respect with a simple act of kindness. When you are alone, far from home, small gestures like this go a very long way and are never forgotten. It was just what I need at a moment like this, some perspective and consideration. I gently turn to face the pouring rain and more endless NAV, happy I made it here.

It's a Sunday, and in the rain the road is empty. The only movement is churchgoers, continuing the religious vibe. It's fascinating to see everyone out in their Sunday best. It must be a nightmare to keep clean in all the mud, but they all manage it well. That seems a miracle in itself to me. It's interesting they care about looking good for church, but seemingly nothing else. I can take another road back to the border, skipping the capital. However, Peter warns me off it with the rain. So it's five hours of backtracking to the capital, Maputo. On the outskirts I see a truck hit an old boy clean off his moped. He walks it off, more pissed off that his Sunday best has been ruined.

The city is beyond filthy in the rain, the dirt sticking to everything like glue. Everything looks like a mudslide has just passed through; it's on every surface you see. I get lost again in the city, and lost in myself for a bit, cold and confused. I slither back into South Africa and find a grill place for a hot sandwich and chips, thinking about Mozambique. After hot food it's a new day once again. I can think clearly and feel my toes again.

After the stark segregation of South Africa, thankfully skin colour does not seem a 'thing' in Mozambique. I had not seen one mixed race couple in South Africa, but there it was more common. Much like Brazil where colour is seen as a sign of beauty and health, as it should be. People love the simple act of life, which is infectious. There is an energy for life, not of hard work and a career, but for essential things like family, friends and enjoying life. In so many countries people *try* to be characters, here they naturally are characters. It's cripplingly poor, like the rest of Africa, but it has some class and soul, charming really. It's the first time I have been able to perceive a noticeably different culture here in Africa. If only they had all been like that. Perhaps it's me, and I'm finally starting to notice the small differences.

I roll into Nelspruit and the highly recommended 'La Roca' guesthouse. The hosts Marlea and her husband had been adventure bike riders back in the day and I am very well received. Much like La Villa 126, it's one of my top stays of the trip. I am so comfortable I stay another day and have an outrageously expensive and delicious dinner. The setting of the hotel is lovely and it's another delightful place to pass a day researching and catching up on things. I meet countless people while travelling, but will only remember a few. It's always those who enjoy hospitality I like most, and Marlea is definitely one of them. I recommend this place throughly.

Sometimes I wonder what I'm doing out here on these hot dirty roads. Trying to find something, not on land, but in my mind. If I ride far enough, perhaps I will find it. Every time I approach 'it', however, it seems to morph into something else. A beautiful game ensues, where a myriad of shapes, colours and emotions are unlocked by distance. It takes so much bitter to unlock just one moment of sweet, when it all just clicks and thoughts flow effortlessly, making it totally worthwhile, some kind of 'travelgasm'.

If only on one day a week, or even only one day a year the weather is clear and the temperature is perfect, enabling your mind to open – this is that day. A map can never show where our minds have travelled. Maybe these words are my mind's map. The trail I tear across unknown lands. Or is it the unknown lands that tear a trail across my mind? The unknown lands becoming known.

I suddenly find myself staring at a gleaming prosperous city. I stock up at a supermarket in a posh mall on the side of the motorway. Local guys are smoking and intently look on as I pull up to the bike with a full shopping trolley and manage to get it all on. No struggles with this kind of thing anymore; there is plenty of space on the girl. As usual I get pissed off with the attention and blurt, 'You getting all of this?'

They smile, thinking I have nodded hello, but one lady smoking hears me and laughs. We smile; at least one person can understand me. Here in Pretoria my loop of Southern Africa crosses for the first time – over 6,000 miles later. I'm headed to some friends of my sister who are in the army and live here. Lizzy, Freddie and their friend Dickie are all thoroughly English and very welcoming. They are also people who put a 'y' or 'ie' after every name. Typically people I would probably avoid. But they are lovely hosts: kind, warm and very humorous people. We sit up chatting into the night about the world at large and it's a refreshing slice of home.

Before departing South Africa, I spend my last rand in a petrol station on random items just to get rid of them. I have entered and exited South Africa four times now, but this will be the last time, for now anyway. I say my goodbyes to it in the remote border post of Skilpadshek. Both sides are very straightforward. On the Botswana side the usual onlookers sit there watching my every move. They even have folding chairs set up outside the customs booth. They do not work here. I often wonder what the fuck these people do here all day. They are at every border, just watching. I'm not going to stick around to find out.

The landscape is hilly bushland, with no one around apart from the odd cow or goat. With no police about I hit 85 mph, and finally bank some serious milage. There is no confusion on which road to take out here; there is only one. Eventually I reach my hotel in Kang. Another spot with nothing more than a bed, food and fuel. The only noteworthy thing is watching bugs eating other dead bugs. In the restaurant seven members of staff watch a football match, and me, the only guest. They take turns between watching the match and watching me, like a game of tennis. *A pass in the game, he takes another bite of food, a pass, another bite of food, a pass, a swipe at a mosquito, a pass.* They are all still probably there now, watching whatever comes into view.

I roll out the next morning in the dark and watch the sun rise over the Kalahari. Standing here alone watching the sun come up is another massive moment. It's not another sunrise of dreams, there can only be one of those, more a sunrise of reality. Here I am in the fucking Kalahari Desert! The road is busy with wildlife, but Glory is the only vehicle all morning and we have a beautiful run. I see wild dogs, oryx, impala, African fish eagles and a lot of vultures. Domestically, I see horses, goats, donkeys and mainly cows. They use the free grazing on the edge of the road, so are often in the road. There are giant flocks of butterflies. At times they nearly block the sun out there are so many. Glory is intent on catching as many as possible. There are wings and guts all over her in the oddest of places. Swallows dive through the air and I nearly hit one or two, ducking like a lunatic in the process.

With all the roadkills there are decomposed corpses around in various stages of rot. At one point I interrupt over fifty vultures having a feed. They are big savage-looking things, but I smile as Glory scares them away. Everything runs from the bike except the donkeys. People say the biggest killer in Africa is hippos, but it's actually donkeys as they cause so many bloody car accidents. I get within inches of them, and they don't even flinch.

The only thing suspiciously absent is the desert. The road is green and verdant. I cannot see far enough into the desert, which is slightly sad. It's not possible to take Glory in there. You need a 4x4 and to stay in the expensive lodges or camps. I reason it's for another day. I set a personal best and get in

175 miles before 9 a.m', which is a great feeling. There is something deeply satisfying about simply covering massive distances. Soon enough I'm in Maun, sitting at a police checkpoint, the copper just wanting to chat as usual.

In town I get lost, and pissed off with the obsessive attention. Kids shout and wave, dogs run out and try to bite my legs, everyone stopping and just bastard staring. Going from being alone in the wilds to the endless attention of the cities is abrasive. I'm looking for a scenic flight for the delta, and eventually I find the airport, but have no joy on a flight. Smoking the daily, I'm full of doubt once again, and unsure I have the next leg in me. The hotel room is the only place I don't get attention and can feel calm. The only place of normality for me. I keep finding it bloody exhausting. Everyone wants to watch you, everyone wants to talk, everything is difficult and falling apart. It's all really taxing, and I come to think I hate Africa. The phone rings and there is a scenic flight tomorrow if I want, so I jump at it.

After dinner I go for an unusual second cigarette and sit by the pool contemplating. It's full of a toxic-looking green water. I don't think anyone has been in it for years. For some reason the life-saving ring is in the pool and is doing circles on an unseen current. It loops over twenty times as I sit mesmerised by it.

At the airport I meet my fellow passenger. He's a middle-aged Korean, head to toe in trousers, a hat and has a healthy dose of sunscreen which looks like it has not been properly rubbed in. He looks utterly lost, like he's on his first day of school. As we hand over our passports, the crown on mine has worn off, it's bent in the shape of my arse, and dog-eared from sitting in my sweaty pocket for months. It's a piece of art to me. His comes out of a protective case, which is kept in another protective case around his neck, and looks brand new. He also sizes me up, of course, as I slouch in shorts and a Zeppelin T-shirt. I can see him trying to work out how I can afford to take this flight. I just smile. He doesn't talk.

The pilot is a young South African, who has already spied the bike outside and is a fellow rider, so we chat bikes. The plane is much smaller than the one in Namibia, and thankfully quieter. After my funk yesterday I am ready for a change of scene. We've been putting in a lot of miles recently; to be off the bike and also off the road is a refreshing change. I expect to be instantly on the Okavango Delta, but we have to fly for over ten minutes just to reach the edge. I'm not sure what to expect, but in typical form it's not what I'm seeing.

There are trees and lakes everywhere, the land incredibly damp and fertile. Wild game paths snake in all directions. They refuse to follow any direct form like a road, and simply meander freely. I am surprised how many tracks there are, like some kind of natural anarchy. Small copses dot the huge green expanses and the animals wander free. The green shades match those of England, perhaps a touch lighter, but with the same vibrant variation and depth. It's wonderful to see big game roaming so freely. We see giraffe, elephant, wildebeest, hippos and several other species. Not just one or two, but in groups of over fifty. How anyone maintains a sense of direction on the ground is beyond me. It's teeming with life down there, natural and wonderful. It's no fake freedom either – definitely the real deal. On the loop back I spot a lion. We circle back to see a pride of them, which is a real highlight. As we come in to land, I reflect on how Africa does that to you. You get worn down dealing with all the hot chaotic bullshit, and then you get a big bolt of 'worth-it-ness' that energises. These two hours make the whole 800 mile journey getting here totally worth it. It's joyful, natural and uncomplicated – quite simply one hell of a sight.

I come violently back down to earth at the hotel watching Donald Trump get sworn in as president. My brain overloads as depression completely envelops me. I had hoped this trip would make life make more sense, but it's been anything but the case. I have been knocking on the door of meaninglessness for years, but here in Africa I finally burst though it to discover without any doubt: life is utterly meaningless.

As I sit in the same bar again for a second night, I can feel the depression on my skin. This place is a dump and likely to give me food poisoning. It strikes me after all these miles that I might have just reached the destination. So much of our lives is given to the constant need to give a fuck about everything. For the first time in ages, I finally feel like I don't. I've reached a point where what will be, simply is. That is Africa. Africa does not make sense – it merely is. For those who can cope, at least. I know I'm not one of them. It's a land where it is what it is, and there is nothing you can do about it. Throw all your assumptions on life out, or perish here.

After dinner I smoke by the pool again. The life-ring is still doing the rounds in the green filthy water with the bugs. Perhaps it's still there now.

Round and round. I think it symbolises life here in Africa and everywhere. Useless circles. Why does it have to mean anything? What does anything actually mean anyways? It's a whisky moment. Drinking life itself, I stare on in that murky water trying to find some meaning to this illogical human life. The most severe depression of this trip bites down on me here in Maun. Elation has turned to depression and I'm tired of battling with my mind all day. Being uncomfortable and unsure over long periods is too taxing. At least at home I can be unsure, but comfortable. Each dip in my mood on this trip feels like it goes one step lower each time. The highs also seem to get one step lower as well, my mind on a downward trajectory. Africa is no place to question life, but it's all your mind is driven to do here. Whatever the right balance of travel is on the road, I hate admitting that I'm not finding it.

In the morning I'm collected for a Mokoro trip down the Delta. One man hands me off to another, and yet another, each taking a small cut of my cash as we drive deeper into the Delta. Typically I would be mildly worried about driving off solo into the bush with a stranger and wondering if I will ever come back. But after yesterday I don't give a fuck. What will be, will be. The truck thrashes around in the sand as we head through a town called Boma and out to the water's edge. There are several mokoros by the water – traditional canoes made by hollowing out a tree. It's disappointing to find these are made of fibreglass and fake. Apparently the government does not want locals cutting down trees, so had these made and gave them away. I assume the people took them with both hands and did not look back. Until they destroyed them all, and then they asked for more. Whatever the story is, I'm pleased to push off and float down the river for a bit. My guide is called Shadrack and thankfully he's a really cool guy. He was born in Boma, and has lived here his whole life. He also does a lot of guiding in the lodges, so speaks perfect English and can understand everything I say.

My blues drift away as we float down tiny corridors of water. Reeds blow in the breeze either side, and there are iris flowers on the surface of the water everywhere. I feel like I'm in an impressionist painting. The land is vast and quiet. We stop at a bank of land and walk inland for a bit, Shadrack explaining the land as we go. Back on the boat for a while, and then walk again, a slow pattern of exploration in this quiet and calm beautiful place. It's just what I need to lift my spirits, Shadrack is cool and peaceful.

It's crazy to think in the summer these water channels are bone dry; the seasonal variance is so extreme. On the way back we cross another boating party of Koreans heading out. I'm a paranoid traveller, but this lot take the prize. Twelve of them are covered head to toe in clothing: hats, gloves, face masks, as if scared of the air and worried the sun will melt them. They look more like a biohazard crew at a chemical spill than tourists. I'd love to see the local reaction to them on the street. Even I catch myself staring.

Back in town the funk is still passing through me. It's in my blood here. I can distract myself, but I can't escape it. I've been in Maun for three days and it feels like three years. I question the road ahead once again. All I do is question things. The enormity of the trip is suddenly hitting me here and now for some reason. Maybe it's as I turn north; it's hard to see clearly so deep in it. My brain has been melting here in Africa for over one hundred days, most of which have been alone. I slowly reach the conclusion that I have reached 'Max Africa'. I have my first thoughts about leaving the continent altogether, and they clear the funk immediately.

The thought of getting on the bike and simply riding for my life is appealing. Just tear across the land in one bolt of movement. Fly on the ground. Point the bike north and relentlessly smash it out. See how long and hard we can run, leave Africa and get some perspective. With that the storm blows through me. I feel rejuvenated, with a renewed sense of purpose. After days of confusion I find clarity. I pack in earnest, and after a sleep I am ready at 4 a.m. to hit the road – *hard*. I do not need another day here in limbo, moaning beside the toxic green pool. I commit to Lusaka come what may tomorrow. In my mind I left Africa right at that moment.

––––––––––

In the morning I break the record – 181 miles before 9 a.m. The road is fantastic and full of game. I come upon some ostriches in the middle of the road. I'm not sure how to proceed, so slow down. Thankfully they run from the bike like everything else has done, but are hemmed in by the game fence, so end up running alongside the road with me. They run at full pelt, around 50 mph, alongside me. Amusingly, they do not take their eyes off me. Their bodies run ahead at that speed, but their heads are turned 90 degrees to the left looking directly at me. Despite the terrain changing height, they keep the same eye level with me by moving their necks up and down in some kind of high-speed death stare, which has me in fits of laughter. It's another fulfilling day of adventure on the bike. Apart from wildlife, the road itself is quiet and the sun is out, enabling solid progress.

On the A33 north to Kasane there are elephants everywhere again. Somewhere near Pandamatenga I get collared for a speeding ticket. For once there was a sign, and I ignored it. 89 kph in a 60. The cop sprang out of the bushes and sent me grovelling to his boss, cleverly tucked behind a thick set of trees. He asks for 500 pula, but I only have 300 ($30). I apologise, and he says no worries. Nice cop. Unlike Zimbabwe (now over 5,000 miles ago). I am clearly guilty, so don't sweat it or get wound up. It was fair play: I call into Kasane and get some more money for the border tomorrow.

The hotel is another one on the river, close to the ferry terminal with a really nice manager. She is half Sri Lankan and half Botswanan and speaks excellent English. We chat and drank beer into the night, enjoying a lovely lamb curry together. I try to play it cool as hundreds of small monkeys live in the roofs and scurry around like mad in the night. Not to mention another flotilla of bugs. The Indian influence in Africa continues to confuse me, another cultural mix I had no idea existed. After a long ride today, it's great to just drink cold beer and chat. I start drawing a link with being solo for extended periods and depression. I know this is obvious to most people, but a big part of being human is finding these things out for yourself. Maun was an episode and this lovely lady is the first person I speak with in recovery mode. It's like learning to communicate all over again.

I'm in pole position before the gates on the border open. There are busloads of people asleep, slowly rising. They emerge from the bushes as people relieve themselves, the noises leaving no confusion as to proceedings. They drift out of the trees, half awake as the place slowly comes to life. It's a pot of madness and the gas has just been lit as the sun comes up. Slowly it comes to simmer; at 6 a.m. the gate opens and it boils over. Everyone runs for the correct door. Slow-moving, placid and apathetic Africans suddenly running at full speed to beat the queue. The immigration staff sit and finish their cup of tea, having a good debate on exactly when to start work as hundreds of people watch on. Eventually they decide they might as well. Botswana is pretty ordered in the African scale of things, but Zambia is another story.

Down by the water the first boat is coming over from Zambia. It comes in too fast and drifts in an odd direction, something clearly wrong as there is shouting and panic. The boat loses power, drifts and smashes into the pier. It's wedged and can't move as the water works against it, pinning it down. With a big leap one brave passenger bounds off the front and on to the shore line. The others follow like lemmings and soon surround us. I thought they were passengers, but they are all fixers from the other side, and like a pack of wolves they seek prey. Someone sucks oil out of a pump on the boat and spits it into the water while we wait and watch. He swings a hammer at the generator on the boat and it grumbles back to life again. Happens all the time, apparently.

In the shuffle I find a fixer clinging on to me, who just won't fuck off. 'Bishop' thinks he is in the Bronx, complete with a thousand-yard stare and Western style hip-hop clothing. I think he is bipolar. It's the same old story for me. I think, no, I'll do it myself, it's no big deal, I've done it a thousand times now, then I get here. In reality I always have a dollar or two in local currency that is worthless when I cross the border, so decide to give it to a fixer at the last minute. All they really do is point you in the right direction. They will try to extort from you, but you learn the routines – the tactics and the hard sells. They also get the vibe when you know what time it is and ease up the pressure. It's another dance.

This border promises to be the hardest one yet, so I figure for a buck it won't hurt to have some help. I tell Bishop I will be holding my own documents the whole time, and double-checking every price with the officials directly. He nods, staring off into the distance. I also make a deal that I will pay him one dollar if he gets me through in under an hour. He accepts the challenge. The boat barely sticks above the waterline as we chug over the Zambezi. I look into the water, and wonder what's been thrown in there over the years. The locals 'go free' as usual, and that leaves pretty much me to pay the bill. The ticket man walks over and Bishop comes to life.

'It's 120 pula, get it ready.'

The man gets closer and I ask him directly, 'How much is the ticket?'

'50 pula.'

I pay and turn to Bishop, raging.

'Really, that's how it's going to be, motherfucker? I told you, don't fuck me about!' I have zero patience at this stage in the trip and fly off the handle often now. It's the only way to stay sane.

'Um, uh, I didn't know it was less for bikes.'

'Don't fuck me around – I don't have to give you shit, remember?'

'OK, pull up to the green roof ahead on the right.'

Down the rabbit hole we go. People swarm the bike, but when they see Bishop they step back and calm down a bit. Once they know you have someone, they actually back off, which is another reason to go with a fixer. I won't even attempt to describe the steps here. It's fucking bonkers. There are several different buildings laid out in the oddest formations, with open sewers running through them. No signs anywhere, people everywhere, rubbish everywhere, people in your face. Scenes that make you scratch your head and question life. Epic inefficiency. Doing the rounds takes us across it all. Immigration and Customs are easy. Beyond that there is carbon tax, council tax and road tax. All for a few bucks here and there. None of it is expensive, just overly officious. Through the process I amass six different bits of paper. When I return to Glory, a crackhead is cleaning her with a dirty rag, making her even dirtier. He puts his hand out for money. I normally tell people where to go, but I discover a 20 rand note from South Africa left in my pocket so just give it to him. He looks at it and then me.

'What am I supposed to do with this?'

It takes nearly two hours in total. Alone it would have been four hours minimum, I expect. All of this has to be inspected before I can even leave the compound. Then we have to sort insurance, the final piece. Chit number seven. I follow Bishop to a sea container off the 'road'. Inside there are several youths watching a James Bond movie on an old computer powered by a generator. It's an odd scene. They all start making excited noises when an Aston Martin dives into the scene on the film. I can't help myself.

'How come you lot watch that and can understand them speak fine, but you can't understand a fucking word I say?'

They all bust up laughing and shaking their heads, but do not move their eyes from the screen. More dirty sweaty handshakes ensue. I tell Bishop it's been over two hours so he won't be paid. He looks off into the distance again. Caught a winner here. At least I'm through. It's not even nine yet and I have 350 miles to roll today, so best get on with it. A stack of fully complete paperwork is neatly stapled together. Back at the bike the crackhead is back once again. I thank Bishop and slide him the dollar. I have some pula left, and ask if he can exchange it. He offers me some obscene rate, of course, and I naturally tell him to fuck off immediately. I don't even know how much it's worth; it's simply my role in the dance. He would be disappointed if I didn't. I'm sure it's a criminal rate, whatever it is. With months of practice I have not fallen in love with the dance – just the opposite in fact. At the top of the road

I hit my first road block, still in sight of the border. A policeman asks for my documents, and as I pull out the stack he just smiles.

'Oh no, sir, not a problem. Carry on, have a good trip.'

Maybe Bishop wasn't that bad after all. The nice tidy stack stapled together certainly looks the part. I press on to Livingstone as once again my southern African loop nearly crosses itself. Seventy days ago I was on the other side of the Falls here, learning about pivot pins. I pull in for a coffee in a nice spot where I can see the bike, and tuck into a massive apple fritter and a coffee. These are the moments I love. Suited. Glory fully loaded and fuelled. No more border hassles, full stomach, nothing to do but ride all day. Clarity.

I hear several warnings about speeding here, so keep it slow. There are cops everywhere, but I only see one proper speed camera. The downside is that it takes a long time, the upside that it's the best fuel economy I've seen the whole trip. The skies darken and I get a quick ten-minute blast of it and then it quits. I pull in north of Mazabuka for quick bite, but there is still a giant wall of purple on the horizon. I've never seen a cloud this big. It's not really a cloud, it's everything. The sky just seems to stop and become something else, dark and sinister.

I set off again, but it's only minutes before I hit a hard wall of rain. Within three minutes I have to pull in and seek shelter, completely soaked through. I can't see a thing; it's biblical. Even the lorries pull in and everything stops moving. I try to get shelter under a tree (there are no buildings), but I'm soaking wet. I stand in a way so the drops don't go down my neck. Fortunately after thirty minutes of heavy downpour it slows down. The world slowly comes back to life again. Thank fuck I never saw this in West Africa. With no infrastructure here, there is no drainage and nowhere for the water to go, so it just sits. The road is extremely dangerous after heavy rain. I slowly roll on, mesmerised by the big skies and turbulent clouds above. Things are just on a different scale here. Into Lusaka I can't help but think that if urban Africa is dirty normally, it's truly disgusting in the rain.

It all goes blurry again as I pull into the hotel. Another surprisingly expensive dump. I get the usual attention in the car park and even the manager comes out for a chat. At this stage I don't really feel like I'm me, a touch delirious. There is a guy chatting away down in the car park next to a bike – but it's not me. This guy is way more talkative than me. I'm not consciously there, just going through the motions. The trouble with these big days is that when you stop it's a really hard stop.

The next day I head into town to have a mooch about. The heavens open again and just walking around town is supremely miserable. I'm met with a billion stares, as usual, as no one white seems to walk around here. At the hotel I do some tinkering on Glory, and a keen hotel worker joins me for every step of the way, with a thousand questions. Why people can't see you're busy and just leave you alone is beyond me. I give him quick clipped answers, trying to get him to piss off, sweating as I tend to things. He only asks me to speak up, pushing for more, not at all sensing the mood.

'Do you have a gun?'

'Yes', by now I lie about this daily.

'How can you afford this if you have no money?'

'Ah – you can't'

'Well, how did you do it?'

'I worked really bloody hard and saved up.'

'How long did you work for?'

'Ten years.'

'Wow, what do you do?'

On and on and on it goes. Finally, he asks a decent question.

'Was it worth it?'

I wasn't really talking to him, more thinking out loud, but had to be honest with myself.

'*I don't know.*

NINE

CHASING DEMONS IN THE LAND OF DEL MONTE
Zambia – Malawi – Tanzania – Kenya

'Don't stop for nothing – it's full speed or nothing, I'm
taking down, you know, whatever's in my way,
Getting your kicks as you're shooting the line, Sending
the shivers up and down my spine.'
Motorbreath – Metallica

The Great East Road heading out of Zambia is *great* fun. I'm simply charging it at this stage, no holds barred. If negative thoughts on Africa cloud my mood, making the bike go as fast as possible clears them. The road climbs into plush green wild hills, with no police and few animals. The pace is brisk, my determination clear. It's overcast and cool, with only a lot of freight and buses to contend with. With no signs, it's slightly confusing; there are no 'confirmations' along the way, just a very long stretch of road. I am not sure which town I am in several times, so simply keep heading east as there is only one road. Around halfway, it returns to NAV and naturally I have to slow. It's odd to follow along the border with Mozambique so closely, for so long.

It makes you wonder how all of these border lines were drawn up. While I don't know the particulars, I do know its part of the sad 'Scramble for Africa'. A rich Englishman and a wealthy Portuguese man, likely sat by a fire somewhere having a drink and simply made an agreement. To this day the poor locals have to deal with a border that has no relation to centuries of their tribal history at all. A border that makes no sense to either of the newly independent countries, but now defines them. As I ponder it, the road abruptly stops for a ten-mile construction diversion. Dust clouds everything as vehicles make their own scramble for bits of land to drive on.

The border with Malawi is calm in the morning, but there is no one open to buy insurance from. I wait an hour sitting in the morning sun, parked up outside the office, where a local farmer strikes up a chat. Unlike the vast majority of 'characters' you meet on the borders, George is calm and interesting. A long comfortable chat ensues as he speaks passable English and is fascinated with the bike. He also wants one, and wants to take my phone number so I can try

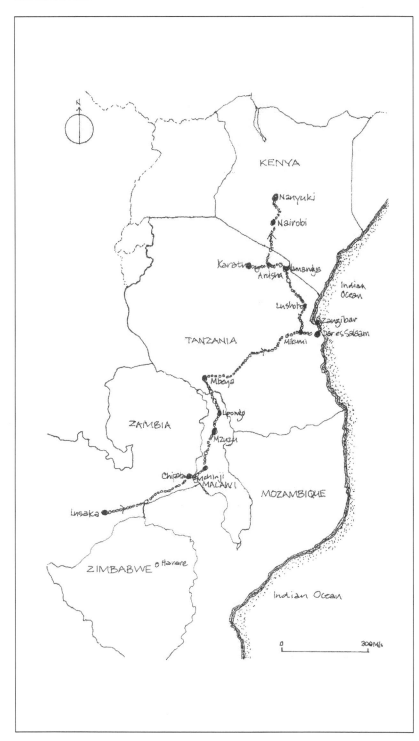

to import him one from the UK. The smallest of conversations here result in a request for contact details. People think you can be of great use to them at some point in the future. I never hear again from any of them.

Equipped with insurance, I ride on into Mchinji. The roads are like a festival here. People are everywhere, walking in groups of hundreds, laughing and joking. Vehicles come second on the road; it's more of a giant path for pedestrians. People come alive at the sight of Glory and start hollering more than usual. It's intimidating. At a checkpoint another cop tries it on again;

'Do you have some relish?'

'Relish?'

'Yeah, when you cook food you put some relish on top, my friend' he says, with his hands sprinkling something in the air.

'You mean like mustard? Why would I have that on a motorbike?' Smiling, knowing exactly what he wants.

'No, "relish" makes things better, right, my man?'

I shake my head, looking confused, and his shoulders sag.

'I have no idea what you mean, I'm afraid.'

'OK, have a good journey, my friend.'

You get used to the routines. It's not a proper bribe, just a little nudge – discretionary like. Charity, perhaps. If you are going to give, however, there are a lot more needy people here than these crooked cops. When they are half-arsed requests, or really weak, I sometimes just belt out, 'Oh, you're asking me for a bribe? Is that it?' Upon which they cower a bit and shake their heads.

'Oh no, of course not, sir, I wouldn't do that.' *That's what I thought.*

Despite extreme poverty here, there is large-scale cultivation of the land, mainly tobacco. The huts are far from the road, there is not much litter, the sun is out and it's a good side of Africa, just beautiful. Further north the road rises, with heavy logging industry around. The views are stunning in the afternoon light. On a high plateau I see a totally burnt-out bus, and stop to have a look. It's like a ghost town. The entire guts of the bus are gone and there is nothing left but rusting metal. The road is actually really good fun and I continue to charge it with a smile.

I find the hotel after taking a few token wrong turns, and it's another wonderfully expensive dump. A soviet-looking relic, untouched for years, and another fascinating example of African hospitality. Later in the car park I find two other massive adventure bikes, with Brazilian plates. After all this time, it's only my second encounter with other overlanders. One of the owners comes out, we start chatting, and end up having dinner together. They are state prosecutors in Brazil, which is really odd to me for some unknown reason. They are on their own bikes, but have only five weeks to get from Cape Town to Egypt. I thought I was a mad, culturally insensitive rider. We have a few laughs over some beers, and as we are headed in a similar direction north, we decide to ride out together the next day.

It's overcast as we flow north-east towards Lake Malawi. The road slowly gets worse the further north we go, but the scenery improves dramatically. Watching the morning mist rise through the hills of Northern Malawi is spellbinding, a sight and an emotion which I will never forget. Supernatural. We pass through new levels of poverty, where kids run up to us as we pass with their hands out, shouting, 'We're hungry!' I start to feel like an Eskimo describing snow on this trip when it comes to describing levels of poverty, there are so many stages to it. I don't yet have terms for a scale, but I can see different levels clearer now.

We catch our first look at the lake before Chiweta. It's hard to get a feel for it in the overcast skies. The sky and water colours look so similar, like a dull blue watercolour painting. You can't see a line of the horizon, which gives no depth to the lake. Naturally you think you can see the other side, but it's over thirty miles away. The vegetation is still lush and green as we slowly make our way down to the waterfront on some steep twisty roads.

At the border the sun comes out, and we immediately roast. Thankfully it's a quick crossing, although the Brazilians have a huge row with a money changer. It's normally me losing my temper, so it's fun to watch someone else do it for once, the Latin temper making it far worse. They are surprised when someone tries to mess them around. That's simply the way it is here. Agree a price and they will change it mid-transaction, trying their luck, and every sob story or technical hitch seemingly possible gets trotted out. On the Tanzanian side it's high bureaucracy, taking up valuable hours. It's nice to be in a team, however, as while one of the Brazilians watches the bikes his friend and I can tend to the paperwork. We separate for a bit, and I end up in a 'restaurant' just outside the border gate solo, waiting for our insurance to be completed as a huge downpour blows though. Another random place full of border types, but they are a cheery lot.

I chat with some of them, enjoying sitting back a bit, and watch things for once. No one openly hassles me, so I can really observe it all. White people are far more common in these parts, although I don't see any apart from us right now. There are a few food outlets and shops, all converging under one makeshift roof, with damaged plastic chairs about, all in various states of disrepair, but still in full use. Everyone sits in a funny way to stop their chair from collapsing, making the setting all the more bizarre. The roof is partially plywood and partially cardboard from used drinks crates. Water drips through several gaps and you have work to find a dry spot. Then the wind changes and you catch a few dirty drops. The cardboard is slowly rotting away, the gaps for water getting bigger and, as usual, no one cares. It's easier to avoid the drops than actually do something about them. It's typically filthy.

It doesn't feel like total chaos anymore. It's just what it is − basic, disorganised, and full of dubious characters, doing dubious things in broad daylight. A different setting with the same scene, this feels normal now. People don't need to speak the same language as me. Over the months I now have the look perfected. They can read my looks and mannerisms, as I can read theirs. They can sense I don't want to know, radiating an energy of my own which simply says, steer clear. I am watching now, instead of being watched, and it's sadly empowering. This pseudo-reality of border towns, now familiar, is tamed as a result. It has shaped me over so many miles.

You need to learn fast to normalise this mini world of border towns. Someone shouting in the middle of the road: instant snap judgement − it's a town crazy, don't make eye contact and look away. A concerning size-up by a shifty guy in a doorway − stop in your tracks, and just stare at him. Let him know you can see him, know his game, then watch him get uncomfortable. Someone offering you their services on the border, tell them where you have come from and that you know more about this than them. They all back down. You can never tell the infinite variety of approaches people will make on you, but you can control your reaction. People can see how quickly you reason and know they are not going to get far with you. Instinct rules here. It's the first look − the size-up. They are looking for weak prey and if you do not show weakness, they won't advance. If you head into the scene paying no attention, they will take you then and there.

After another mountain of pointless paperwork, we finally set off on the wet road. It's great riding in a three; there is a strength to it. Even the cops are not sure how to handle three of us.

The scenery in Tanzania gets better and better. We slowly gain height entering Tanzania and reach five thousand feet, with stunning lush green views either side, continuing on the spine of a low mountain range, meandering up and down steep rolling hills.

With the Brazilians, I find a new humour to it all. They love the attention and with three of us, it takes the intensity out of it, a totally different experience in a group. It rains on and off as we continue, the scenery is beautiful, and the most 'African' I have seen the whole trip. Every view is an 'African postcard', something out of a coffee advert. Tight rolling green hills, heavily cultivated and productive. The sun breaks through the clouds occasionally, casting a beam of light on this hypergreen landscape. Coffee and fruit are everywhere, lorries being overloaded with bananas.

With all this, the roads are lively, agricultural debris everywhere on them. We continue on the spine, overlooking a huge flat, highly fertile and colourful expanse below, eventually dropping back down around Mbeya. The Brazilians want to keep going and keep pushing out the miles. When we lose each other on the streets of Mbeya, I am not surprised. I never learn their names, or got any contact details, so they will simply be know as 'the Brazilians'. That's how it goes on the road sometimes. I hope they made Egypt. I have a reservation in a coffee lodge, set a few miles off-road on a hill, another fabulous place with a great view. Once again I collapse in the car park, unable to unpack as I smoke and stare off into the distance.

Back in the solo zone again, I push hard up the A104 eastwards in the direction of Dar es Salaam. Mbeya was still on a hill plateau, and at the end of the main street there is a huge hill straight down, like a rollercoaster track. Right next to the largest rubbish tip I have ever seen, half on fire. The freight inches along very slowly, making overtaking constantly required. The road has the worst 'ripple' yet and it's very catchy when overtaking. Every time I overtake something, it feels like I might lose the bike under me, the vibrations are so strong on the handlebars.

Tanzania is the size of France, but only 9% of its roads are paved. The ones which are sealed suffer unbearable wear, especially on the hills. The tarmac is heated to over 35C every day, and then overloaded freight slowly creeps up it, at less than five miles an hour. Deep grooves soon form, which I call 'ripples', a bit like corduroy. It's another hazard to navigate, but at this stage I eat it up. I'm on a mission now and battle-charging the whole way. I have a huge distance to cover to Mikumi – over 300 miles on heavily policed roads. The roads feel even more chaotic than the rest of Africa, on steroids, things moving quicker, in even more unpredictable ways than West Africa. The trucks have thundering horns, which make you jump out of your skin. Driven by people with little experience and no concept of safety. The stakes on the road are quickly ratcheting up.

A new phase creeps through in my riding in these conditions. They are the worst I've seen in Africa so far. The same danger is everywhere, but it's at a higher speed here. I soon have my first proper close call of the trip as I go to overtake a lorry, thinking I have enough time to get around it. However, the oncoming lorry is going way too fast. It also kindly speeds up, trying to cause an accident for fun. I have to bail out onto the tiny hard shoulder on the opposite side of the oncoming lane, which is just big enough for the bike. The truck thunders by just inches from me, with a chorus of horn tooting and light flashing. Perversely, it gives me more confidence I can survive the road. Glory and I are a true unit now; we move as one. The road becomes a mix of battleground and playground. With a full day, I push hard, finding a calm clarity in the furiousness. This emotion quickly builds momentum and the rush starts to feed on itself, getting stronger by the minute, and becomes very difficult to switch off.

There is no wallowing about, or worrying about dangers. I'm all in, going for it, and having a fantastic ride. The road changes constantly, keeping me focused the whole way, a furious high-speed meditation. There is no time for other thoughts. I'm not thinking, I'm automatically responding to what is happening around me. Processing thousands of pieces of information like a supercomputer, with no reaction time, it's all real time. My entire brain is in the present and thoughts happen at the same time as the reactions. It has to work like that to stay alive here. My wrists and feet are moving faster than any conscious thoughts. In the moment – clear and beautiful. Danger here, opportunity there, along a backdrop of *push, push, push.* Making haste, and enjoying every minute of it.

Most people would call me a cultural heathen, given the sheer amount of things I am passing at ninety miles an hour, but I don't care, this feels right. I am having a bloody good time, shouting the whole way with the music pumping, just thrashing it out. This is my culture. I'm easily doing double the speed limit all day, as a bumbling moron of a cop jumps out of his car near Iringa and, against my better judgement, I stop. I guess it had to catch up with me at some point.

'How are you, my friend? Why were you in such a rush?'

'Um, I wasn't.'

'How fast do you think you were going?'

'55 kph?' I say, wondering myself. My speedometer was still in mph. I had no idea, nor did I care.

'You were going 61 kph, my friend and this is a 50 kph zone.' He was equally just making this up and had no real idea. It's a simple shakedown. He goes on trying his luck.

'Why were you in such a rush?'

'I'm trying to catch up with my friends,' I say, lying through my teeth as usual.

'Ah, the two Brazilians on the BMWs?'

My eyes flash up, naturally. 'Yes, that's them.'

'I gave them a ticket just twenty minutes ago.' *Wanker.* 'Do you want a receipt?' he asks.

'What are my options?' I say, hoping I can skip the paperwork and halve the price in the process.

'There is a 30,000 kes fine, no matter what. If you want me to write you a receipt then you will have to wait.'

I can see his game a mile away. It's textbook and without flair. Even when it's working against me, I respect some originality. It angers me further.

'Well, you fill that out, and I'll go for a piss in the bushes while you do so,' I retort.

'OK, but you must give me the money now.'

Always the money now. Whenever you check into a hotel in Africa, they want payment immediately, before you have even seen the room. There is no trust at all. Money now, money now. They won't lift a finger until you show the money.

Over a bridge in the dusty desolate town of Mbuyuni, the road climbs into the surreal Valley of Baobabs. The sun passes the midpoint, casting these magnificent trees in a stunning light. It's such an original shape for a tree, totally distinguishable. I have seen several of them in Africa, but never this many in such close proximity. Set twenty metres apart and going on for miles, it's electric. In the background are dense lush green hills and blue sky, forming a perfect setting. Their trunks are unbelievably thick. In Australia, they used hollowed-out baobab trees for jailing people as there is so much room in there. It's amazing anything so strong can grow in these conditions. It's an intriguing place by daylight, but I sense in the dark it's another story. Onion is the biggest crop in this part of Tanzania and you can smell them for miles on the air. Naturally, along the side of the road there are several onion vendors. All are selling the exact same thing, and all are without any customers.

I call into my hotel victorious, and come down hard from the frenzy. I'm exhausted and wired at the same time. I have a crazy look in my eye, my mind completely shot but still wide awake. 330 African miles in eight hours, through all terrain and weather. I'm running a race against myself and getting stronger by the day. On nothing but crisp sandwiches and a bottles of water. Great fucking stuff! I can't wait to wake up and attack it all over again.

Out there on the road, I feel like I am chasing the demons now. I'm doing it with raw spirit, harassing them back, and it feels righteous. It's vengeance time. I know it can't go on forever, but it's fresh and exciting. A new drug high, of which I just want more and more. The bullied becomes the bully. It's not about the countries and the cultures. Rightly or wrongly, there is not a lot of culture here, to me anyways. There is equally not a lot of culture in me either. The joy is what it always has been – the simple act of just riding the bike hard. Childish, simple and pure. There is nothing better than belting out huge great distances. What is it today? Road, gravel, sand, mud, desert, mountains, hills, rain, sun, fog – all of these? *Let's fucking have it! Throw it at me!* Set yourself an impossible goal for the day. Tell people your plans, and watch their faces screw up in disbelief as they shout, 'That's impossible!' *Then go and do it.*

Deep satisfaction at the end of the day is your prize. Momentum is your best friend. It's backwards, but the frantic motion leads to a quiet mind. That's what this trip is all about, going for it. Covering ground, surviving, and seeing the world from the back of a motorbike. Bonding with Glory and charging the road it all comes to life. This is the world? This is my reaction. Somewhere in the middle of the filthy dusty chaotic streets, blaring horns and heat, I realise I'm having the ride of my life. You sure as shit can't do this at home!

The morning mist on the ground is heavy as I ride through Mikumi National Park, still foggy myself after the giddiness of yesterday. Wildlife is everywhere – giraffe, buffalo, impala, elephants, and none of them like the sound of the bike at all. They all run. Misty morning African wildlife and early Metallica thrash metal make for an interesting combination. The mist blows quickly through the landscape, and with a muted rising sun the herds of wildlife are a surreal sight, broody and intense. The morning hills steam some kind of quiet magic.

I'm better at spotting the cops by now. It's more about being able to anticipate where they position themselves. I slow at these spots and am mostly right, then speed everywhere else. I laugh when I see a pole with a yellow box on top of it in the distance. In the UK we know this is a speed camera and instinctively slow down. Closer to the pole here in Africa I always find a tall skinny African, with a yellow bucket on his head, waiting to cross the road as I burst into laughter. Eventually I find myself fifty miles outside of Dar es Salaam. I stop for a breather, as I'm sure it will be a taxing ride in.

It's hard NAV from that point on. Like Dakar, the city seems to start thirty miles out of the centre and you have a foreboding 'belly of the beast' vibe the further you go in. Thirty miles of slums and chaos. The tooting and shouting do not slowly escalate, but are just suddenly happening. Like the TV was at level two all day, and then suddenly the same show is at full blast. Tuk-tuks in full swerve, lorries on ripple roads trucking about like trains, mopeds zipping around them all. Buses stopping, then racing, then stopping short again. Add in pedestrians, livestock and pedal bikes with no discernible patterns. No signals, black smoke and dust, it's a symphony of madness.

I dig in, fighting quick and dirty myself, right back into the crazed racing zone from yesterday. I fight every battle bloodily, pass by pass. I am amazed how quickly it comes over me, an electric superpower. Whatever it is on the road, no matter how big, how fast, how wildly manoeuvring, how much toxic smoke it's belching – I'll take them all, one by one, gaining strength, speed and confidence as I go. I don't care what else is happening on the road. If it's in, or about to be in my way, it's a factor. If not, it's just noise and unimportant. Pure ruthless focus. Fire up, brake hard and tuck in. Small gap – have it – fire up, brake hard. I gain a steady rhythm, and other road users know I'm not taking any shit. The attention reduces as I am not about for that long to be stared at.

Overtaking or undertaking, whatever is available – just taking. Smash them all out of the way! There is about two feet of tarmac on the hard shoulder and it gives me more room to operate. Take one outside, one in, one out, one in, a high-speed drunken zig-zag line. Cut and burn; if there is a gap I'm through it. I don't wait for people to give me space, I simply take it, coming in hard. They admire the ballsiness and hold back. I'm blind to it all, fully committed.

It's hugely reckless, but it seems the only way to get through it. I don't care, and it's totally liberating. There is more risk in this thirty-minute ride than perhaps the whole trip, but I've never felt so alive. *I can do it, Glory can do it.* Don't trust one of these fuckers, just get round them all. Honest, unapologetic and fierce. I'm not holding handlebars, they are steel swords, and I'm hacking a path like a possessed lunatic through a jungle of pandemonium. I laugh at the day back when I almost dropped Glory pulling out of the driveway in Cornwall. Now she's like a ballerina, in a demolition derby. Running up the dotted line full speed, like an oil tanker on ice skates. It's not the sport attack riding of yesterday – this is a step even further. I'm out to kill; it's a nasty, bloody business. You can't do this often, it will quickly catch you out. But when you need to it's absolutely liberating to be able to ride a motorcycle like a fucking lunatic.

It's an outright attack on Dar, and surprisingly good fun, the best ride of the whole trip. Certainly the best riding I've ever done. Focus and push, focus and push, kill 'em all! I land in Dar hot, heavy, ragged and ruined, but victorious. We both collapse in the hotel car park. The room is spinning as I put my head down. *Where am I? What just happened? Who gives a fuck … I'm alive!*

———————————

In Dar I run some errands. The street is another complete overload on the senses. The pavement is a calamity with building materials and generators everywhere. The power cuts out every two hours and the street chugs to life as the generators kick in. You can barely hear a thing over them. The air is thick with exhaust fumes and dust. Everyone wants your attention: 'Yes boss', 'Hello, my friend'. Dar es Salaam translates as 'home of peace', but that's not at all what I find on her streets. My room is on the twelfth floor, and I'm slightly hesitant to be in a skyscraper in Africa. Sure enough, when alone in the express lift the power drops to the whole building. Small panic, and thankfully the generator kicks in, and I continue.

I research the route to Zanzibar. Everyone has grave warnings (as usual) about taking the bike there. The police are supposed to be on the next level of corruption and you need a special permit just for the island. Glory is as tired as I am. Her chain is now grating and causing me a lot of concern, so I investigate my options on that front also. I decide to leave the bike at the hotel for the Zanzibar excursion, and give us both a break. I spend more time on the streets, trying to sort silly small things. Top of my list is the bike. There is a Yamaha dealer in town, so I naturally head their way, trying my luck. I chat with the sole importer of Yamaha bikes into Tanzania.

'What type of bike do you have?'

'A Tenere.'

'A what?'

He's clueless, but checks out the bike, gives the typical praise and says he can get parts brought in. I send him an e-mail, and he never answers. It's Africa all over, and at this stage I'm just sick of it. I hear of another backstreet joint in town which might be able to help called 'Tuk-Tuk'. It's not where it's supposed to be, and I spend hours circling a chaotic block downtown near a huge mosque and melting in the stifling heat. Eventually a man runs out and asks if I'm looking for Tuk-Tuk. He says they left four years ago and are across town now in Kariakoo. *The one place I was told to avoid.*

The street reaction to the bike is intense, more so than anywhere else. At street lights vendors selling coat hangers or lighters start talking to the windscreen of the bike, crazed. Making noises and smirking a lot, like she's a horse that can only hear them or something. Anything goes on the streets of Dar, and in my new zone of madness, I thrash around like I own the place. I've totally lost respect for proceedings at this point, *there are no proceedings.* It's the only way to make sense of it.

I'm coming undone. Once you start to not care, it's very hard to care again. I park Glory up and cover her for a few days, showering her with positive comments. The pier to the ferry is more steaming hot hysteria. I feel incomplete without Glory as we've had such a good run of late; without her I feel I'm just a tourist for the taking. She gets attention and people stare, but she is a hell of weapon – big, scary and noisy. She's a snake, which can snap out and bite at any moment. People come close when you stop, but when you fire up the engine, they jump away and it protects my sense of personal space.

As we pull out on the ferry, we pass by the main port for Dar (we are on a posh tourist boat), and it's another scene like Saint-Louis in Senegal. Too much for the eyes and brain to process, a completely soiled disorder. I arrive in Zanzibar, and it continues. The streets carry a heavy Arabic look and feel. This place has a serious international reputation, but it does nothing for me. I walk the spice market and old town for hours, but find little to grab my attention. There is crap everywhere and no one really gives a fuck – it's certainly still Africa. I have to conclude most people fly here, get whisked to the nice side of the island and then fly out, which would be another experience entirely. To arrive here overland, having seen all this in various guises the whole way, is the experience I'm having. There is little romance for me as it's more hot dusty chaos, and poor food in Stone Town. My hotel is dry as well, so I find a bar on the waterfront and get drunk. It helps.

I head over to see the beaches on the other side of the island, and it's a package holiday 'resortville'. Another compound, with its own private beach. The food is good, and the bar well stocked. I sit on a balcony for two days contemplating the world and slip into another all-consuming European depression. Given the wider state of the world, it's unsurprising. Things seem upside down at home and they are certainly upside down here. My mind is unable to find north. You can't run this ragged alone for so long and stay on solid ground.

Things go from crystal clear to opaque as my mind chokes on mental pollution. Comfortable, uncomfortable, comfortable, uncomfortable. Moments of everything, but nothing lasting, just streaming by on the television. Thoughts spilling all over the place in turmoil. I know where I am heading, yet I have no idea where I am heading. I skirt the incomplete circuit of logic, chipping away with metaphors, and weak half truths. Paradox and paradoxes, forming a pyramid of paradoxes, the same ecstatic dead ends. The human condition is usually the quiet stranger in the corner, watching. Here it's a thief with a knife, attacking my mind.

Back on the hill, in your mountain of dreams. Sometimes the candle just blows out, sometimes it starts an inferno. The fire eventually dies and the residual stain is a broken system of logic, the ideological tower of Babel. It's not just our language that the idea of God muddled – it's also our logic. We took our confusion, and through copulation, and the weak concept of nationality, multiplied it infinitely. Here we are today, a fractured humanity at war, rife with inequality, division, fear, and oppression. Buying useless shit to make our lives better, just to throw it out shortly thereafter when the next new essential thing comes along. Ephemeral. A fragmented, confused and stable, yet also unstable world. *As long as our bit's stable, it's OK.* Thousands of shattered ideas guide our lives, none of them unlocking the greatest question of all. It's not the elephant in the room, it's the whole room. I see it like the Hollywood sign up on every hill I pass, in big white letters – *Why are we here?*

Ready to collapse this great big lie of a world we live in and all the lovely realities we've created. We demystify it one day, only to sleep and wake up mystified again the next day, a maddening cycle of total futility. No one has answered Nietzsche; he broke me, he broke us. I'm staring at the gauntlet he laid down, wondering if anyone will dare run it. I've tried to run it across Africa, but it's gone nowhere. It's clear, and yet impossible to decipher. There is no one to consult with, as usual. I'm lost in a dream of ideas; there is no map here.

Nietzsche hacked a giant wound into our collective understanding, opening the real Pandora's box. In doing so, he frees us, but we don't know how to live free in anarchy. The open wound stays open – we've simply learned to deal with it. We treat it, but we cannot cure it. Buy a new iPhone or escape to the beach in Thailand for a week. Go to church on Sunday, have a child – it's not going back in the bag, try as you must.

Why can't this set our minds free, instead of imprisoning them in fake constructs like religion and nationality? Logic will not unlock your life: abandon it, cast it off immediately! Venture forth into new lands of the mind. That's where I want to go – the unmapped lands of the mind! Everyone is talking about a paradigm shift and ignoring the construct of the paradigm – it's a trap. *Destroy the whole fucking concept!* If there are numerous questions about humanity we can't answer, is it too much to admit our system of thought and language cannot explain our world?

We must venture further, like the journey to the centre of the earth. It's the journey to the centre of the mind. Running further than any road we have ever know, further than the distance to the sun. We must roam farther than any other human mind ever has to find 'truth', whatever the fuck that is. This is where I am trying to go. It's not Africa at all.

Only I can sit on a beach in the sunshine and see a turquoise sea of disillusionment.

The days blur as it all goes sideways. In the end I'm stood at reception about to check out, waiting for my bill as reality starts to set back in. The extras soon outweigh the cost of the accommodation itself. What have I been doing here? Trying to anticipate the subtle ways in which every hotel is going to shaft you is tiresome. Yet another thing I am over. On leaving, I'm reminded once again of where I am. A *have*, surrounded by a big wall to keep out the *have nots*. We play in the pool, they play in the river full of sewage and pollution. We relax with all modern amenities, they don't even have windows on their dwellings, let alone running water. We feast while they starve. It's another hour of poverty the whole way to the ferry and off the bike I can observe more than ever.

The sea is rough as we head back to Dar. Outside the terminal there is a huge line of taxis, but the hotel is close so I walk. The drivers do not like this at all and all try to grab my bags. I make it past them and cross the road where another lone taxi driver is sitting away from the rest. His face lights up when he makes eye contact.

'Taxi, sir? Let me help you with your bags.'

I blurt back, 'Yeah, that's right – I walked two hundred metres past all those other drivers, sweating like mad, just cause I liked the look of you and your taxi above all of theirs' as I push past him.

He stands there watching, bemused. I step on, disappointed that I'm such a child. I need to get back on it somehow, back into it. Africa just keeps driving me down. I'm suffocating. This would be a blast for two weeks in a group of people, but here solo for months I'm delirious now, tired of it all. Not the time on the bike. That part is pure, perfect. It's all the other shit that goes with it, the constant spending, the constant attention and the lack of inspiration. My spirits instantly raise when I see Glory again, happy she is still here and untouched. Now that makes sense – *let's fucking blow this town, girl.*

Unfortunately I still have the chain issue to fix, so I find Tuk-Tuk in Kariakoo. Hussain is the man here and a real character. A big guy with a big heart, who is passionate about Tanzania, and wants the world to know it's a great place. There are people dossing around the shop, sitting on stools, and watching the street in typical African fashion. Much like the bar in *Cheers*, but with no alcohol or women. Shit really, but they are warm people and there are a few good jokes amongst the dusty moped parts. He agrees I need a 'wet' lubricant for the chain, and not the 'dry' stuff I was using. He has a cheap Chinese chain for thirty bucks, so I take it as an emergency spare. We decide to take off the chain, clean it properly and put it back on. First job is getting some wet lubricant, so he calls over his mechanic, Dili, and we jump on his moped to get around town on the hunt.

If I thought Glory was fun, this is brilliant. We bob and weave around the mental streets of Kariakoo on a little adventure. It's a totally unique place, once again, the likes of which I have never seen before. The streets are bewildering. We visit twenty shops, but nobody has what we are looking for. Story of my life. It's annoying considering how many auto shops there are here. Hundreds of shops are selling the same thing, none of it what you actually need.

Back at the garage, I sit with Hussain on the steps, talking it all over, sweating in the sun. Venting my thoughts on Africa as he gently laughs at it all. He's a good soul, an honest man. He understands the journey and what still lies ahead. He vows if the chain oil is in Dar, he will find it. It's a case of sort it out here, or wait until Nairobi, some 600 miles north. We jest about Africa, and he sticks up for it. He believes he can change my view of Africa, and in a way he does. A bit, anyways. Later he calls, and he has the right oil. I head to the shop, pay and thank him heartily, another character I'm glad to have met.

He directs me to the workshop, and with a tyre over my shoulder, I head to the 'garage' to meet Dili again. The garage is really just a roof over a dirt lot, a bike graveyard, with carcasses all over the ground. It even makes Nick's shop back home look clean. I pull in and get out my tools and I have five times more tools than them. The wheel goes off down the road again like in Dakar, and returns a bit later fixed. Magic, that. Dili tries to break the chain, but it's not happening. I panic we may be doing more damage, so we stop. We cut the new spare chain to the right length, and wrap it up again. Hussain kindly gave me a chain breaking tool which I can use in the field should the DID actually fail, which is highly unlikely. I was just being paranoid as usual.

Maintaining the bike here for me is like aircraft maintenance. There are no garages at 30k feet. Be proactive all the way. Most people would say it's probably over the top, but after 15k miles through a lot of madness Glory has not let me down once. We've had issues, but she's never left me in the lurch. It's not luck, it's the approach. I properly clean the chain in petrol while the wheel is off and use the new wet grease liberally on it. We switch out the back tyre and change the brake pads while we are at it. By now we have an audience of thirty people, but Glory is getting the attention she needs, and I'm getting the confidence I need to proceed.

I tell Dili my story as we work, and can hear him telling it to the others, who in turn tell it to the others. I can't hear the words in Swahili, but know the string of destinations as my trip. As always, they can't quite believe it and just stare at us. I'm there for a few hours and bond with the whole crew – a great bunch of lads. Bike mechanics the world over really are a decent lot. The dealers are another question. We sit and watch as the pretty girls of Dar walk by, of which there are surprisingly a good few. Dili's good fun and I can't resist making his day, so offer him the test ride on Glory. His face lights up as he grabs the keys. I think I've made a fatal error as he nearly hits a bus head-on as he pulls out too fast. After a few awkward minutes later, I thankfully hear that familiar roar as Glory comes back, untouched. Such a machine! He quotes me $5 for all his work. Two mechanics for half a day, in Dar es Salaam, for $5! I give them $15 and they are ecstatic. She's not 100% fixed, but is a lot better than she was, and we have what we need to see it out.

Leaving Dar is very different to arriving. Early in the morning the roads are calmer and I can actually take a look around, calmer myself after the last few days. There are rolling dusty hills, but it's steady city for well over twenty miles. It comes to the boil every mile or so, but never really dies out in between. The hills are covered with everything you can possibly imagine, in motion. Dar is in explosive growth, one of the fastest-growing cities in the world, and building projects are everywhere.

In every direction buildings are in various stages of development, yet never fully complete; even the occupied buildings are unfinished. Most likely tax is due on finished only buildings, so nothing gets fully finished. Several buildings are being demolished as well, as unofficial reclamation outfits circle like vultures. They take every block, clean it up, and pass it down a chain gang out to the road, where it is stacked in beautiful neat piles for sale again. Nothing is wasted, but this is not sustainability in action, far from it. There is a lot happening, but no real end results. People are just moving stuff around, and there never seems to be a 'building' at the other end of it.

In amongst this are vendors selling everything you can imagine: beds, car parts, motorbikes, fruit, food, shoes. All of these wares are out on display for all to see, and perpetually covered in dust. In between all of this, people are going about their daily commutes. Not just on the sides of the road. It stretches on like this as far as I can see into the hills. People weaving in and out of everything. A vacant field a teeming explosion of chaotic life. There are no clear pathways, just desire paths through everything. A group of school kids wanders directly through a building site, inches from danger. Four people sit at a box playing cards. A moped weaves in amongst it all. You could stare at it for hours and never make sense of it, unable to take it all in. Occasionally you see a beautiful women caked in make-up, done up and walking through the mud in heels. Every vendor is all about the hard sell, believing the more aggressive they are, the more successful they will be. Most people on the street don't need the goods they offer, or have the money to buy them.

It's all so tightly interwoven that it's hard to pick out small things, one big picture of constant movement. The history here is complex and it's not just black Africans here; there are several Indians and other races and cultures. Another bewildering part of Africa, where some of the culture blends, but not all of it. What does blend, forms hybrid cultures which are even harder to try and understand. It's a meeting point of traditional Arabic orthodox views and cutting edge modern Africa. Everything steals your glance, until you are dizzy. Then someone steps to you and goes for the hard sell – 'Hello, my friend, you need some eggs? I have the best ones here – good price, my friend! Come on, boss!' A constant blur of energy and movement. There are layers of pandemonium across these endless dusty rolling hills, a rich tapestry of chaos.

There is a choice of roads up into Lushuto and I opt for the quicker off-road option, soon to be defeated. The dirt track starts innocuously enough, but soon rises steeply as the clouds darken. I get a clear feeling this is a bad idea. The ground continues to get uneven and at one stage I hit the brakes, only to start a sickening slip backwards on the gravel. Trying to put down a foot, I meet only air and we go over hard. Glory passes the point of no return, so I sit back, shaken. Seconds later, as if by magic, a man appears, and kindly helps me raise her. Embarrassingly, he is on a small 125cc, heading down and managing fine, although he is not carrying 100kg of luggage. He advises I don't go any further and I follow my instinct back to town and up the longer road side.

I stop in town to collect myself as the children mob me with aggressive begging, their hands held out and shouting, 'Money, money, money!' The kids of West Africa just stared at me with jaws dropped in wonder; here, they just see money. You are not greeted with smiling waves, but with forceful shouts for cash. The paved way is thirty miles longer in the rain and an unwelcome extension to an already long day. On the way up I hit another roadblock. Fed up with the endless questioning, my new tactic is to just shove paperwork at the cops. Insurance? Here you go, and here is my driving licence, passport, registration, import documents and birth certificate. Just keep putting stuff in front of them, until it's too much. Choke on that, you bastards.

'OK, sir, thank you, carry on.'

The hotel is a basic but honest dwelling around 1500 metres above sea level. The owner, a charming lady called Krisha, is true to the complex make-up of Tanzania. She is half Cypriot, half Tanzanian, with an Italian husband. The hotel has been in the family for years, but a reckless uncle drove it into the ground. She is now repairing the property and doing a fine job driving tourism in the area. She has a long difficult road ahead of her, but fresh enthusiasm in her outlook. We chat as I wait for the woodburner to heat the hot water for a shower.

After dinner she invites me to join a group of her friends in the bar, a very international lot. I can't keep up with the cultural blends; it makes my mind hurt. Someone with a Christian Egyptian mother, an Indian Hindu father, who was born in Mumbai, but raised in Dar. Educated in England, with summers in Switzerland, and the like. Not super-rich, but very well off, they radiate internationalism. It's fascinating and they are a lively bunch, but it's hard to grasp where they are coming from. Where they are going seems to be a US-orientated standard of life and easy enough to decipher. They logic like those in the West. The great melting pot always tastes like vanilla in the end.

Krisha tells me many challenging stories about doing business in Tanzania. She needs to import stuff for the hotel and cannot get past the bribery, which is heartbreaking to hear. Here is an honest citizen, trying to build the local economy with tourism, being held back by a repressive and corrupt government. It's a common story, which just holds back Africans from developing Africa, and is naturally sad.

Going back down the hill is a lot easier in the dry. Soon I'm back on flat land, approaching the south side of Kilimanjaro, excited to catch a look at such an iconic mountain. I had considered going into the park and having a look and perhaps a climb, but then saw the prices. To hike Kilimanjaro is a seven-day trip, and costs well over $1,000. Too steep for my tastes. I can hike a mountain at home for free. As I approach it's the greatest anti-climax: despite blue skies all round, the mountain itself is shrouded in cloud. Just that mountain. I spend an hour passing it and the clouds do not break once to reveal a peak. I nearly crash several times trying to keep one eye on it, sure the clouds will part at some point.

The roads continue to deteriorate as the hysteria factor slowly turns up approaching Kenya. I pull in off the road to watch the mountain for fifteen minutes to see if it clears, even for a second, to take a quick photo. Despite being down a side road, a car pulls in and stops next to me as I try to pee. I cannot find peace outside of a hotel room. A woman does not even lean out of her car and just starts talking at me from inside it.

'How many countries do you go through when you ride here?'

No hello, no introduction, just straight into it, like we have know each other for years, or I work for her. Typically African.

We have an awkward chat and she doesn't listen to my answers. It's all very weird and in the end I drift off to take a picture without saying anything. If it was actually a conversation, it never seemed to start, so I don't feel it needed an end. She sits there for a few moments and drives off. This type of encounter is becoming more common. I find the constant attention more stifling by the day. The more people look at us, the more I get angry, becoming a deranged madman running around East Africa. Like Dennis Hopper in *Blue Velvet* – *'Don't you fucking look at me!'* It must be an introvert thing. This was not on the to do list in my preparation, as there were worse things to worry about. I don't know how you can prepare for this to be fair. It's something I wish I could stop, but seem powerless to do so. I can't seem to reframe it all. It surprising how much it brings me down and makes me glum. The longer I'm here, the worse it's getting. Now that I am fully aware of it, it's a weight around my neck, getting heavier by the day.

On arrival in Arusha, there is a new road under construction – they are always under construction, never complete . Built to make things better, ironically it brings a new level of disarray. It's intended as a two-lane road on both sides, with a divider in the middle, so the heavy traffic can move quickly in and out. What's happening is both sides are going both ways. You can follow it 'in motion', however, at junctions commotion quickly ensues. There is no order.

With a lot of developmental aid in town, the UN has an office here. Onwards, past town, the road gets hotter, and quieter. There are concrete dips in the road which are large enough to carry water, some kind of overflow in rainy season, I guessed. With no water in them now you can go full tilt though them. It's the opposite of a humpback bridge, and quite amusing on the bike. I put on some music so I can't hear the chain noises and hope for the best.

I'm heading to Ngorongoro crater, as Krisha advised checking out the world's largest inactive unfilled volcanic caldera. It's on the way to Serengeti

National Park, which to access you have to pass through the crater. Both are $250 a day to visit, but as you can only access Serengeti through the crater, it's $500 to see the Serengeti. I find this hard to stomach, given none of the money seems to reach the crater itself, or the locals. Krisha advises if I could only see one to see the crater as it's such an unusual land formation and a cool place to see the game.

On the way I get lost, and meet a tour operator (likely preying on lost tourists like myself). Leonce is naturally operating a crater tour the very next day with some Germans. He kindly helps me reach the hotel,and invites me on the tour. I finally pull into Crater View Hotel after another hard ride. I'm deeply shocked there is no view of the crater from the hotel. In the morning we run errands in support of the tour. As ever, cash is the first order of business, and I need to get more. Always the money first. I sit on the back of his 125cc 'Bob Marley' edition bike and we bob off down the dirt streets into town. He waves and shouts to everyone as we go and we chat away African style. He's pretty shifty, but also kind of likeable. I have a fresh set of questions, so start firing away as he laughs.

'Leonce, I'm dying to know, why is it every town here has a group of moped riders who just sit round all fucking day, doing nothing but watching the road? They all shout and holler when I roll by on the bike. Like that lot there,' I say, pointing to a small gathering. He laughs.

'No one ever asks me that question! They are taxi drivers, and they are waiting for fares.'

Why did I not work that out myself?

Eventually we meet the Germans, who are furious it's thirty minutes past the agreed time to depart. They had been cycling across Tanzania, so were hardly new to 'African time' – just German, I guess. We have the usual argument about money before anything happens, the mid-transaction change of terms an everyday thing now. We thought there were three of us, but there are actually seven. This time the price goes down, making a nice change. For once, I feel in power haggling, as I'm sure that I'm their profit margin and threaten to simply walk away.

Soon we are bumping down the road in a truck that does not feel like it will make it. Again, Leonce hands us over to another fellow, but we stay in the same vehicle. In turn he gives us to a third driver, further down the road. You never do a deal with one person in Africa. The road in the park is in terrible condition, extremely dusty, bumpy and very steep, and a very uncomfortable ride in this piece of shit. At the top, however, the view is truly stunning, making it all worthwhile. The crater edge is around 2000 feet high and a mighty sight. We descend into the crater itself, which is around 100 square miles. Every view has the crater in the background and it's a fascinating place to see in its own right, let alone with the game. There is an ethereal quality to it.

We see Grant's zebra, Cape buffalo, hippos, wildebeest, eland, Thomson's gazelles, elephants, waterbucks, lions, and impala. At a giant natural pool there are forty hippos bathing in it, which is fascinating to see, although it smells like a sewer. Watching the elephants wander with the crater in the background is superb, all of Africa in one single view. Like a natural zoo, the crater rim keeps everything hemmed in, but should they really want to roam out of it they can. It's a fantastic day in a really magical place and I'm very happy I made it here.

Much as I would like to brag 'I've been to the Serengeti', after the world-class parks of Kruger and Etosha, I think it would have been great, but much of the same. Ngorongoro was special for me and a great recommendation. I return to the hotel buzzing, and to a dinner which is the most awkward meal of the whole trip. I'm alone, and there are three members of staff serving a buffet. Other guests are coming later, but I am first, and stupidly sit facing them all. They watch every move I make through the whole meal, especially the first bite of anything, trying to judge my reaction to their work. It's hugely awkward and draining, I find it painful. Thankfully the food is decent, which helps.

I wake in the night, sweating, too hot to sleep. At 3 a.m. the music outside is banging, similar to a music festival. Three competing sound systems are battling it out, with driving bass lines and the occasional melody blasting out, a tinny muffled wall of noise. This is common in most urban settings across Africa at night. I imagine it's only a bar or a small business advertising the fact its open. Occasionally a motorcycle engine blasts off as someone tears up the high street. There are other noises I cannot place, coming from all directions, drifting on the night air. Just as I nod off someone screams. It hangs in the air for a moment and then is overtaken by another crashing bang. It feeds the dark side of the imagination as you try to imagine the scene. People could be dying. Locals live like this every night and I think of the kids having to endure this daily. Occasionally shouting grows to what sounds like violence. It's impossible to know if there are just two people at it, or several.

It's the literal heart of darkness as engines come to life and die. With no street lights, no one knows who anyone is in the dark. Shadows move through the dirt streets. There is no safety net here at all. It's not 'like' anarchy – it is anarchy. This paper thin wall my only defence. Sitting in bed listening to all of this, vivid images grow and fade. It's hard to know when I'm dreaming and when I'm awake. The shouting comes and goes. In my mind a group of angry bandits surround Glory and start to remove her parts, then set her on fire. I rush to the window and she is there, covered and locked as I left her. No one is even in the parking lot.

I stand at the window and stare into the darkness. Goose bumps rise on my arms. I have no doubt I am staring at the unseen wall of this cruel universe. They are out there in this night, and in my mind right now. Our imaginations are limitless, our minds infinite, but in them are unseen walls we can't get past. Their foundations set in fear. Some ignore them, some try to deny their existence, some try to study them, and some run headlong at them. I've been trying to knock down mine my whole life, exceptionally hard this past six months, but have failed. It makes me weary, yet I cannot find sleep.

On the border with Kenya there are the most Westerners I've seen the whole trip. For once someone instead of the locals stare at Glory and me. I go through the familiar inhuman process of amassing all the essential bits of pointless paper. I lunch on the steps outside, with a lovely ham sandwich I picked up back in Arusha. This could well be the last border I cross in Africa. It's bittersweet – but more sweet. I might make Uganda or Rwanda, but it depends on how Glory holds up. For now I'm heading to my sister's house and some bloody normality. Just as I go to take a bite of the sandwich, the afternoon call to prayer blasts out. I can't escape the irony that here in this dusty dirty African world I am the filthy one eating pork. Have some of this, you bastards.

Kenya is more affluent than any of the other East African nations, I see advertising immediately, with large-scale industry and infrastructure. Nairobi is another massive hellhole of chaos. It's all familiar now, back in attack mode, and thrashing around everything. The median gap between lanes on a motorway becomes a green belt speedway. If I can find a path, I gun it to avoid three lanes of gridlock. Instead of getting upset, people seem to cheer me on. I don't really hang around to see their reactions. It's hot and nasty riding that can't continue forever, but is needed today. In town I run errands again, and all the other general stupidity that goes with a trip like this.

The next day I'm on the final straight heading to my sister's house, three hours north in Nanyuki, at the base of Mt Kenya. My brother-in-law is in the army and presently stationed there. As Africa goes, I won't find a safer haven and I try to hold back the emotion as I ride there on the truly insane roads of rural Kenya. I suddenly feel very vulnerable so close to the end. It's the end of one road and the start of another. For now it's just about collapsing into safety. My sister and I are in tears as I come up the drive. 18,000 miles across Africa, through nineteen countries, totally unscathed. I am a complete mess as I step off the bike. Elated, and wondering what the fuck just happened. It's amazingly beautiful to find family here and in no time I am in the garden playing football with my niece and nephew. For the rest of my life I will remember this moment.

That evening there is a fancy dress party, with all the expats in town. I'm still in Africa, but I might as well be in a pub in the UK. The beers are never-ending, and the party chat wonderful. It's soothing to hear English, to speak and be understood. The theme of the party is 'Best of the British', and continues the surreal theme of the trip. I'm home, yet a long way away from it. This is normal, but it's madness. I have no idea what's happening, but finally, for once, I'm truly not worried.

A month passes in a day. The days are long and restful. I play tennis with my nephew daily. Unlike at home, with this much time I get to spend quality time with the whole family and get to know them better. The children are developing characters and its great to interact with them. My sister takes me to Samburu Park and Ol Pejeta Conservancy, which is brilliant fun. I'm happy to just stay put, rest and gather my thoughts on the last six months.

It takes a while to build myself back up again and stabilise. Some days I barely leave my room. It's wonderful. It's also a great chance to balance out my African thoughts as I see a large thriving community of expats, happily living in Africa and making the most of it. There is an extensive support network that makes this possible and it's lovely to be welcomed into it. They are some happy carefree days in Nanyuki. Nick sends down a new chain from the UK and I order some other parts to get Glory fighting fit again. I also plan ahead for the next adventure. Always more planning to do.

I stay with some more army friends in Nairobi, Alice and Will, who were really supportive. I also spend some time at the famous Jungle Junction, talking with Chris there. He has more bad jokes than me and we shoot the shit as we work on Glory. He talks about when Ted Simon stayed and many other stories of famous overlanders who have passed through. It's just great to unplug from the daily hassle of the road. I finally have some time to process it all, while not being stared at. It's deeply restorative.

TEN

KENYAN DAYS ON AFRICA
Kenya

'If you're only tool is a hammer, you will see every problem as a nail.'
Gambian proverb

I wanted to see Africa with my own eyes. I travelled 18,000 miles, across nineteen African countries – a lot to some, just a glimpse to others. Africa is the second largest continent on earth, containing fifty-four countries and approximately one billion people. I sampled life in the west, south and east, but did not see the centre or the north. I travelled as a tourist, with a comfort blanket around me, staying in nicer places and eating Western-style and expensive food. By no means whatsoever did I live as a local. I doubt I could, unless I had no choice. My thoughts are based on common observation, as I tried to make my own impressions of Africa and reconcile the radically different way of life to ours that I saw there.

Africa is easily the most confusing continent on earth. The origin of life itself, and the zenith of human exploitation. The size of it is staggering, the range of culture bewildering, its growth distressing. The way of life is paradoxically unchanged for years, yet simultaneously blasting ahead into the 21st century, causing complex anarchic social situations (not structures). Africa's sociological history is massive and sad, but its future bright and challenging. Africa will break any model that tries to contain it.

The vision of Africa we in the West are presented with is of a wild and savage place. In the West Africa is positioned as a forgotten land, full of beauty, but ultimately suffering. We exploited Africa and benefitted as a result. Our society has gained a higher quality of living through exploiting black slaves and stealing the natural resources of the continent. The famous line from the US revolution says it best: *'The cradle of liberty rocks on the bones of the middle passage.'* The US revolution and ultimate separation from the English Empire was heavily funded by the slave trade. The foundation of the 'new world' and its 'order' is in exploitation and genocide, the ugly truth always removed from the victor's school books. Despite these atrocities being committed by their forefathers' generations, white people naturally feel a sense of guilt. We live in stability, provided by wealth, the very wealth created through exploiting the developing world. We naturally have a complex emotional mindset before even setting foot on the continent, as we should.

What follows are my thoughts on my experience first-hand, and I begin these thoughts with several important caveats:

Firstly, I am not racist, nor have I ever been. I believe all people *are not* born equally in the social sense, but *are* born equally in the mental and physical sense. You can be born poor and be smart, you can be born rich and be stupid. I do not believe in a super-race, or any other fascist ideologies. If one human life is valuable, then they all are, no matter who you are or where you are from.

Secondly, I am clearly not a historian or a sociologist. I am a philosopher on a motorbike, at best. I try here to make sense of what I saw personally and in doing so move forward after experiencing it. As generalisations, they are by no means perfect or absolute, and only employed to help challenge ideas. Despite repeatedly saying we cannot understand such hypercomplexity, I'm very aware it's ironic I try to do so. I don't do it to create governmental policy,but merely for my own sanity and education.

Thirdly, self-determination is vital in everything, regardless of cultural belief or outlook. Yes, we can accelerate knowledge through education, but at a base level the real university is in life. It is for me anyway. It's the people we know and the world we live in; there is far more to be learned here than any classroom. The school of empirical observation is available for all and free of charge, provided you can physically see. While I believe you cannot alter your ultimate fate, you can influence your life. All it takes is effort. Some can learn faster than others, and some can learn more, *but all can learn.*

My mind formed a framework in an effort to understand what I was seeing in Africa. I would move a piece here, leave it, absorb more, and move it again. Each of these pieces evolved as a singular thought, then were slowly stitched together. Piece by piece, mile by mile, a framework which could hold everything I saw evolved. It became a formula, written on the back of scraps of paper.

1. **The culture has such an ingrained apathy towards the bigger picture, they are not motivated to change it. It's viewed by them as beyond their control.** Unfortunately, they are not entirely wrong. Every structured government, black or white, national or foreign, has exploited them for hundreds of years. The apathy extends even into small-scale cottage industry, where it's a culture of subsistence. There is no promise of tomorrow, so working hard today in the service of a better tomorrow seems futile. It's a culture of 'now' only. The immediate goal is survival today, rather than long-term stability.

2. **There is very little industry in Africa.** Hence there is little employment and wages for spending. Apathy does not drive business, it represses economic activity. People have no money to spend or drive industry. The culture also does not trust big corporations or businesses, thus does not get the benefits from it (products & infrastructure).

3. **In turn the state system cannot raise any central tax funds.** The government has to squeeze hard on what few streams of income it can gather, such as import tax. In doing so it drives most small-scale business underground, where the majority of business is done in cash and they can't touch it. It also stops organic medium-level business development.

4. **Hence the countries cannot build infrastructure, invest in social services, or provide stability and security.** Long-term projects are impossible, basic social services are not in place. Common crime is rarely policed and institutional fraud is even harder to harness, blocking basic economic growth. Large-scale government business development initiatives are impossible. Imagine London without any airports, trains, only 20% of its roads paved and no police, social housing, clean water or regular power and where 80% of business is done in cash, without any trading standards. You start to get the idea.

5. **This leads to an unstable political regime, which to stand must have the bare minimum of funding – opening the door to corruption.** This in turn influences the first point, creating a turbulent scenario in which business will neither invest nor grow. Leaders are a case of 'it's better the devil you know'. Ironically, Somalia has done better under anarchy than under a formal government, the pirates believing they are 'collecting taxes' as the government cannot do it.

6. **This leads to other nations being able to take advantage of Africa.** Both historically and presently. If there is any large scale industry, it is only agreed to by corrupt governments, to benefit the few elite and not the many. The vast wealth which is raised by this industry goes abroad and does not benefit locals. The West and the East have a meddling hand in African politics and all developed countries are guilty. Historically, it was Europe and the West, but China has joined in and no one's hands are clean.

This loop repeats, and is how I understand Africa. It's not poverty I see, it's this loop, as the overriding framework of why life is 'the way it is' in Africa. You can argue which was the first domino to fall, but this is how it looks to me now. It is of course a Western interpretation of why Western societal structures cannot stand in Africa. It does not address the fundamental question of if our interpretation, *our idea of civilisation*, is right or wrong for Africa. As a result, wherever I go from here is skewed. This is more about how Africa *looks* to me, in the common comparing and contrasting practice of definition. Why it operates like this is a much bigger topic, talked about at length by far smarter and more eloquent people than I.

The Culture

The culture of Africa feeds into every stage of the 'loop'. It is both shaped by, and shapes the loop. Does African apathy cause the loop, or does the loop cause a sense of apathy in Africa? That is an excellent question. The more ingredients in any scenario, the harder it is to decipher cause and effect. It's never one thing, it's a whole host of them coming together under certain unique conditions. Of all the things I encountered in Africa, it was the apathy that struck me the most. I have never seen such disregard for life, and so many people not caring about things. West Africa filled me with a deep sense of hopelessness and I was only there for a few months. Nothing I read or saw beforehand prepared me for this tidal wave of apathy. I had to see it to believe it. This is the most significant factor in the loop for me.

Most of my thoughts are focused on West Africa, as it was the most shocking part to me. It challenged everything I think about the modern world and my place in it. It still does every day. It shocked me to experience a life so radically different. My first thoughts of Senegal, Mali and Burkina Faso stuck with me for miles, slowing turning over in my mind. The abject poverty and apathy, a complete lack of hygiene, cleanliness and order. The word 'poor' redefined many times over. People here are able to get by with so little, it's unbelievable how basically they can live. It's inspiring they can be so happy in these conditions, but with so many differences from our culture it's bewildering for us, the biggest sight to reconcile I've ever seen. I remain disappointed in my inability to fully process or understand it. That said, I also struggle to ultimately understand life in the West.

In the fight for survival in Africa, a culture of 'now' emerges. If there is no tomorrow, what does today matter? With the life most Africans are offered, it's not a surprising way to think. Litter is not an issue when there is no tomorrow – it's completely trivial. Social institutions are a supreme waste of time if there is no tomorrow. Anything beyond food for the day and immediate shelter (shade) is a pointless hassle with no tomorrow. If there is a tomorrow, it's met with apathy as little can be done about it, evolving a culture of passive anarchy. Not with violent intent or organised rebellion, just an unwillingness to do anything that requires more effort than the absolute bare minimum.

To say there is a fundamental different viewpoint on life here is a colossal understatement. Our systems simply do not work here. In the West we have a culture of order and structure – we do something today, we reap the benefit tomorrow – and beyond. In Africa it's the opposite: it's all about today. There is no point in doing anything for tomorrow, or following rules which further the idea of tomorrow.

Take a motorway, for instance. For us it's about high-speed travel between major cities. It's convenient and enables growth. We did not invent the road, per se, but we did invent the motorway. A motorway in Africa is still seen as a country lane (not an upgraded express version of a road) and as such it becomes more than just a motorway. It's a place to graze animals, to display and sell goods, a path for walking, a meeting place – they make it their own. In doing so, they make it more dangerous than it already is. Without rules and respect, it appears like chaos to us. Of course people will have accidents if they wander close to fast-moving traffic; they either don't sense that danger, or don't care. They cannot follow our system, yet use our invention. Ideally they would make something more suitable for them, but in the loop this is impossible.

Africans approach everything with a wonderful sense of anarchy. That impulse is fantastic and it could be the key ingredient in the future of Africa, but it's nearly impossible to channel anarchy by definition, so things fall apart before they even start. It's impossible to build anything which will stand for time. Most things are immediately reinterpreted and repurposed in a way the locals prefer. If you want to experience anarchy and study it in real life (instead of a textbook), Africa is the best example you can find.

Many would say Africa is over-populated and birth control would help. What many in the West fail to understand is the African psychology regarding children. They are your insurance and the system in place to help you when you are older and cannot farm the field. There is no social system to look after you in old age. Sadly, the children are also likely to die. A typical family in West Africa will have around seven children, expecting two of them to die before the age of five. By having more children you are raising your chances of survival, by having more people to gain an income for the family. What they don't realise, of course, is that they are creating more mouths to feed. On the wider implications they are also making it harder for anyone to get a job, as there are more people than the stagnant economy can handle. The result is young, unhappy, bored populations, ripe for radicalisation by either the state or religious fundamentalists.

I saw people sat around in the heat, doing nothing but staring. They have nothing to do; there are no jobs or industry. Even in jobs people don't do much. The model is to pay people as little as possible and throw as many people at the problem as you can. Thus a job in the West that would take one person gets over five in Africa. There is not enough to do when 'at work' to keep one person engaged, thus people become apathetic in the working environment. This culture spreads though the workplace – rapidly. People lean and stand around chatting, more talk happens than work, and no one is motivated to do anything. Things are built with the bare minimum of materials and skill, so they don't last. It's cheaper to pay fifty people with scythes to cut grass than it is to buy a lawnmower. Let alone maintain an industrial lawnmower, or secure it. It directly challenges our notion of development, making it appear that time has stood still here for hundreds of years, with no progress.

Relics of colonisation appear across the continent; the ways they were intended to be used are radically reinterpreted. Railways lines and sealed roads are more used by pedestrians than by vehicles. Without central stability and organisation, African countries are simply unable to build infrastructure. Much press has covered the opening of Kenya's new railway line connecting Mombasa to Nairobi, the largest infrastructure built in Kenya since it achieved independence from the British in 1964. It cost approximately four times the equivalent being built in other countries. Why? *Corruption, we assume.* That aside, it's 80% funded by the Chinese. East Africa's most prosperous country cannot even build basic infrastructure. Once complete, vandals attempt to destroy it. Why? Apathetic anarchy? Taxation without representation? Lack of education? Anger? Africa is so complex, it repeatedly tears itself apart.

Education is the common drum to beat. Without education, Africans cannot learn what hard work can deliver to them. If they can learn this, but still have no security to build for tomorrow, why bother? It's a vicious cycle of repetition, where every outcome seems to end in suffering. I'm merely trying to put what I saw into words, and how my mind processed it all as a traveller, not an expert. One would imagine, however, if there was an 'African Expert', they might have solved Africa's problems by now?

Road Safety & Respect

Driving standards are poor and testing is limited. Let's assume there is no training or testing and it's all conducted in the school of life. All Africans know someone who has been hurt or killed in a road accident. Therefore they should conclude driving and roads are dangerous. Naturally they should respect the danger or it could hurt them. Simple logic, a=b. Yet they don't respect it. It kills them or their family and they still don't respect it. I fundamentally believe any human mind can draw that conclusion without any formal education, yet either they don't draw that conclusion, or do not act on it.

Take an everyday scenario of a group travelling in a car.

(1) ten people are in a car designed for five,

(2) no one wears a seat belt and children are not secured properly,

(3) the driver might have little experience or no licence,

(4) the vehicle is in disrepair and not working properly,

(5) the vehicle is overloaded with goods, causing it to be unstable and not handle properly,

(6) the road is busy, and has a lot more activity on it than driving,

(7) the driver does not use common sense and drives faster than their ability or the conditions allow. (I saw this every day in Africa, and I don't think anyone would deny it's a daily reality in Africa.)

1. Is education at fault here? Or is it common sense that one seat is for one person? The African anarchic interpretation says the more people in it, the more efficient it is. Which could be positive. Education by the

State should cover this.

2. Education is at fault here. The government should push this educational aspect, and implement laws to enforce it over time. The Western world also had to be taught how to use a seatbelt when they were first introduced. This is the State's responsibility.

3. Government is responsible for making sure anyone driving has the ability, and need to police this. If people respect the road properly, they should also know being on the road without the right skills is dangerous. Both parties are responsible for this.

4. The government is responsible for sufficient vehicle testing, to a degree. Beyond that a person must use their common sense to know if their vehicle is roadworthy or not. If they believe there is a risk, then they shouldn't take the risk to the road, endangering others, and not wait for the government to stop them. Both parties are responsible for this.

5. Education should teach what happens to a vehicle when it overloads. However, people can also learn this in the school of life. There is a spilled load on every main road in Africa. Both parties are responsible for this.

6. Both the government and African citizens should have a basic respect for roads – they are clearly dangerous. The government should not allow dwelling or activity near the road. The people should know from everyday life that roads are very dangerous. They should keep away from the roadside and fast-moving vehicles, and make sure their children and livestock also do so. Both parties are responsible for this.

7. This is on the driver entirely. The people are responsible for this.

With no government in play, we can't rely on them doing anything as they don't exist. The loop stops them from having any proper existence. The people themselves are still not acting on their side of points 3, 4, 5, 6 & 7.

3 – If there is a licence, they should have one.

4 – They need to make sure their vehicle is up to the task.

5 – Arguably education helps here, but there is also a common sense in all people.

6 – Africans do not respect the road, but the school of life teaches this lesson well.

7 – The more near misses a driver has, the more it should slow them down, yet this does not happen.

Point 7 is the only one solely on the driver, but it's arguably the most significant factor in a crash. The lack of a system is letting the people down, creating apathy, causing them to not bother with their obligations in the scenario. They are also not learning from the school of life, which is harder for us to understand. This is of course me trying to deploy Western style logic on Africa, which will never work, illustrating how our minds struggle to comprehend Africa.

What is my point? If thirty people die in a motorway pile-up in Tanzania it's a tragedy and a waste of human life – doubtless. Should I feel guilty based on what I have seen? No. They didn't value life or respect it. To be totally clear, I don't wish anyone to die, anywhere. The institutions of government are letting people down, but they are also letting themselves down, as both groups blame each other. If they even care. All we hear is 'life is cheap' in Africa, and feel guilty about it, but when you don't respect life, *it is cheap*.

Recently several petrol tankers have blown up in Africa.

(1) A truck carrying petrol crashes and people loot the petrol off the truck,

(2) syphoning it into unsuitable containers,

(3) someone smokes a cigarette nearby,

(4) it causes an explosion, and several people die.

Here you could argue the people are not properly educated on the dangers. Maybe they don't know how petrol works. You would assume some common sense, yes, but if someone has never had any formal eduction, they could miss this. There is no school of life, apart from the story itself, and filling up in petrol stations, which a lot of people do not do (petrol is often sold in old water bottles, by unofficial vendors).

If one year later this same scenario occurred near the same crash site and the same thing happened again then it's on the people for simply not learning the dangers, or not caring about them. A culture of now does not care; there is nothing to lose. These stories are told far and wide when they do happen. One blew up in Kenya in 2009, killing 111 people, another in the Congo killing 230 in 2010, yet it still continues to happen. People do not gauge the potential danger, and as a result, die.

African people do not respect the road, and thus have a hand in their untimely demise. Conversely, I travelled far on my trip and didn't have one accident. You could of course argue I was lucky. I would argue back that I have a fundamental respect for the road, and I am very aware of the danger involved in using it, thus I treat it with respect. (By and large, there were obviously a few instances of 'red mist' like Dar es Salaam). I make sure I and my vehicle are up to the task, but I have the ability (money) to do so. In my mind it's 90% respect and awareness, and 10% luck. The African version seems the opposite – 10% respect & awareness and 90% luck.

Hygiene & Disease

I was appalled by the hygiene in Africa, where there is a strong culture of touching. Just about every type of disease is active in Africa, and several have their roots in this. Disease does not just cause humans to suffer and kill them, it also removes them from jobs and being productive. There is no food safety at all. Animals are slaughtered by people who are taught by their older generation. There is no empirical understanding of the risks involved, or practical measures to limit risks, similar to the UK in the 1600's. In the West we understand the notion that cleanliness promotes healthiness, the backbone to having the highest mortality rates on earth.

If you don't have a clean environment to prepare/cook in, it's a moot point. If you don't have electricity, you won't have a fridge. If you have nothing to cook with, you don't care about eating something raw. Everyone learned about Ebola from West Africa. Has this stopped the act of touching in neighbouring countries? I doubt it, and if it does it's short term. There have already been flare-ups in surrounding areas, so the message did not fully get through. People did not fully learn the dangers of this deadly disease. HIV/AIDs is another point often discussed. African countries are educating people en masse on the dangers of HIV, trying to stem the spread, yet it's not getting through. Some Africans believe they can cure HIV through sex with a virgin. They have been educated otherwise, and still ignore it. Why is this?

I had to see subsistence living on this scale first-hand to understand it. You cannot chastise people for not washing their hands when they have no running water or soap, it's simply not possible. In the world of today, it's a tomorrow idea. Food and hygiene will remain a difficult point for the discerning traveller to Africa. Their construct is fundamentally different to ours. I doubt this will change and it really doesn't need to. If they can exist eating the food prepared this way, if it works for them and keeps them alive, who are we to intervene?

However, their life expectancy will remain low

Disease is another matter. No one disagrees there is needless death in Africa through treatable diseases. Education plays a part, but the state also has a responsibility to its citizens. Sitting in a hotel with all the windows shut, under a mosquito net and on antimalarials, you will always think of the people outside. A whole family in a hut the size of my bed, with no door, mattress or windows. Bugs everywhere, biting them through the night. Who's at fault here? Every stage of the loop is, causing it to keep repeating. There is no 'social structure' to be failing. Why does it always have to be the developing world which makes the sacrifices, having shorter, miserable lives and not the prosperous Western world?

Attitude & Work ethic

I really struggled with the attitude in Africa. The apathy is endemic. As a tourist you deal with hospitality-based businesses. Apathy and hospitality are a horrible mix. I was seen as a hassle and not a source of income. There is a binary way of doing things in Africa – yes or no. There is not much scope to vary the way things are done. People can't break the binary pattern, yet they are some of the most resourceful, anarchic and ingenious people I have ever met. It's conflicting.

Africans are larger than life in a group, full of personality and humour. They are mostly extroverts, who talk and shout with everyone on the street. Yet singled out they get uncomfortable and self-conscious, which also conflicts. I never got a straight answer from anyone and it was infuriating. There is no confidence to answer a question and approval is apathetically sought from a more senior person. There is a common extrovert comfort, and an individual lack of confidence in people.

Simple tasks take five times longer because there is a string of people relying on a chain of events, all of which are inconsistent. They become used to interruptions of everything, be it milk, petrol, electricity, internet, whatever. Things we rarely see an interruption of, as we have stability. In business we have a culture of 'uncertainty avoidance', but in Africa they can't look that far ahead, as you can't do that in chaos. It's hard enough to keep a business operating, let alone risk-assess it and proactively plan for the future.

If one person does not show up to work, or if a delivery does not arrive, it stops ten people down the line from working. This happens the world over. Here, however, the people downline do not busy themselves with something else, they just sit. Then get annoyed when a customer asks for service. As if the customer should just know the state of affairs and not have come in expecting service today. There is no form of apology, just a negative expression of body language. They seem incapable of seeing it from your perspective, and they don't care to do so. The supply chain scenario happens everywhere, but the response here is different from anywhere else.

There are two conflicting realities at work. On the one hand it's the customer's fault for not immediately getting the state of play and being able to deduce service is not available. *Based on observation.* On the other hand, no one picks up on everyday realities or the school of life, like the fact roads are dangerous. *There is no observation.* These two perspectives don't make sense in our Western system of logic. No one is looking at the bigger picture, just their own viewpoint.

I roll into a petrol station which looks open. People are on the forecourt. As I park by the pump, no one moves. I take off my gear, and reach for the pump when an attendant comes out of the garage and uses his hands to slit his throat, gesturing there is no more petrol. His eyes roll back and he is really pissed off to have to tell yet another customer there is no petrol today, another hassle for him. He does not once think to put up a sign, or stand at the entrance to stop people from coming in. It's the customer's fault, not his.

Walking into the tourist information office in Dar I want to know about ferry times to Zanzibar – one of the top five questions they are asked. There are two ladies at a counter and a man off behind a desk. They are not working, but busy talking with each other and looking at their phones. They greet me nicely, and I ask about times. They don't know the times. The ferry is two hundred metres away and a top activity for tourists to head for. They don't have a timetable either. They don't really care or apologise that they cannot help, they are still having a funny chat amongst themselves, laughing as I flounder. They advise me to go there and ask myself. *Why the fuck are they there? Who pays them to not do a job?* Another Western concept which does not work here.

I walk to the ferry terminal for some answers. As I'm there, I want to ask about taking the bike with me to Zanzibar. The clerk thinks there are two ferries a week, but does not know for sure. It's her company that operates the vehicle ferries. She gives me a card of who I can e-mail to ask, but no one will answer if I do. Everything is word of mouth and you have to spend a lot of time trying to find the right person to talk with. No one trades information, or has the general idea about things on their doorstep or in their town. People come to life when asking you about your trip, or when chatting with friends. When asked about something three doors down the road, however, they clam up and scratch their heads. They rarely know about anything further than their role, often rarely even that. They live in their small world and have no interest in anything else, which is very hard to appreciate. Over time I came to realise, if I asked anyone about anything here, I was fucked. Work it out for yourself, or abandon the idea.

Often we joke about 'island time' in the West when things move slowly. Being green to Africa, I had never heard of the idea of 'polychronic' time, or even our own 'monochronic' sense of time. I had sensed them, but never heard the words. In the West we operate under monochromic time: doing one thing at a time, with a sense of order. We do not value interruptions and believe there is an appropriate time and place for everything. We achieve one thing and move on to the next thing. We make a plan, and try to stick to it. We also have a sense of personal property and dislike borrowing things. We like to get our work done and go home, as we have boundaries.

Conversely, the idea of polychronic time means that things are seen as cyclical, not linear. Multiple things can are done at the same time. Punctuality is not important, and interruptions are acceptable. It's not about where the business is right now, it's more about where it is heading. It's acceptable to change plans frequently. They do certain tasks when the mood suits them and often flit between different tasks for no logical reason. Relationships are valued over the idea of time. 'Polychrons' do not separate business and personal life; they are happy to blend them. Generally speaking, anywhere in the West is monochronic, and everywhere else (most of the southern hemisphere) is polychronic. You might not easily decipher it, but in the service business it quickly becomes apparent.

There is a lack of education, and there is a lack of caring. The first is on the state, and the second on the people. They can trigger each other, but form the nucleus of the overall loop for me – a toxic cycle. I understand the first and feel something should be done about it. I cannot understand the second and have no desire to help people who do not want to help themselves. Can education make them care? *Maybe.* Can their sense of time ever align with ours? Does it need to? *I'm not sure on either.* Can we ever meet in the middle? *Hopefully.* Can they still care, despite being let down by the state? *Definitely.* Understanding polychronic time helps, but I see an overriding lack of caring. Apathy is the dominate force I encountered in Africa. Beyond that, is there anything that needs fixing in Africa? That's a question only Africans can answer.

The Hybrid Culture

It's hard to see what is inherently African and what a developed nation's influence is in Africa. The two overlap, making it hard to decide what causes what. From what I could see, Africa is absorbing certain aspects of modern developed countries, namely television, mobile phones, mass-produced alcohol, automobiles, beauty products and clothing. They are not absorbing democracy, mass consumerism, capitalist notions of business, trade standards, or an economic framework to support the delivery of Western products, forming yet another conflict.

We often talk of syncretism in religion, but not in culture, where different parts of opposing concepts are blended. The amalgamation of different cultures here led me to the expression 'Hybrid Culture'. The positive side of this of often referred to as 'the leapfrog effect' where developing cultures can benefit from developments in technology from developed countries. For example, solar panels were invented in an advanced country, slowly engineered to be better, and then finally mass produced to be made cheaply available. The developing country can just 'leap frog' into the new technology, and skip the costly developmental stages. I have often heard this used in developmental aid discussions, one of their many buzzwords.

Nobody seems to mention the downside of the leapfrog effect, where cultural elements blend to a negative or confusing result. Imagine a pornographic magazine landing in a strict Muslim country as an extreme example. It's the smaller blends which lead to a psychological conflict of identity. Western-style clothing into traditional dress, or make-up to countries that have never had it. These cultural offshoots multiply into a juxtaposition of very old next to very new, not so much in a technological basis, but a more cultural one. Facebook and mobile phones causing the Arab spring was a positive thing (we assume). It also led to the war in Syria and an influx of refugees across Europe, likely causing Brexit and the potential disintegration of the European Union. It's harder to see element by element, but very clear overall when walking down the street and seeing elements of culture clash.

The result looks like a lose-lose situation for them. With television they see the Western lifestyle, as programming only comes from developed countries. This creates an enormous psychological conflict to see how other cultures live and then look out their own front door, if indeed they have one. It's on television, but it's another school of life. You can argue the effect could be both positive and negative. To me it looks like a hybrid culture, half African, half influenced by the rest of the world. This is common in developed countries as well, but more clear here. If the natural African culture is not suitable to certain products of Western development, like TV or Budweiser, then sticking these into the mix only complicates things.

If Africa must build an Africa for Africans, the dubious cultural impacts of the developed world should be restricted, if not ruled out entirely. For argument's sake at least, the cat is out of the bag now. The hybrid culture of Africa I see today will not further develop in any structured direction, without a bedrock of stability, which cannot develop in the loop. Confusing the Western mindset as a result. Africans must drive an African society suitable to the values and customs of Africa, not the developed world. In a way they are cherry-picking the good stuff, without putting in the work or money required to get it, leading to the psychology of apathy and entitlement, and only hurting Africa in the long term. These modern developments within a way of life which remains mostly unchanged for centuries appear as a new form of economic-colonialism. It feeds an immediate need, but it does not build for a strong African tomorrow.

Litter is a prime example of the hybrid culture. It's our invention, which was never in Africa before we created the mass production of goods. We developed it, and over time put a system in place, for better or worse, that collects it and puts it in a huge hole in the ground. Africa absorbed the culture of packaging, but with no system in place to deal with it. A negative leap. As a result, the African continent is awash with litter and hugely depressing to see. They absorb one aspect of the way we do things, but not the evolution of it. It's made worse when we ship our litter to Africa, paying them for the 'service'. They get a small short-term bump in income and a lifelong pile of toxic crap to deal with, as we get yet another new DVD player. African society is out of step with the evolution of the technology and goods now at its fingertips.

Car production is another example of the hybrid culture. Until 2010 not a single everyday-use car was made in Africa, despite it having around two million cars. Until the last ten years, they were not something of the African continent itself, and wholly imported. Why is this? It's a Western invention, which they have absorbed, and helped fuel their economies, but it's also created a significant killer in Africa – road deaths. African culture has absorbed a Western invention, but fails to respect the risks involved, or protect themselves adequately to reduce the harm this commodity can cause. They have taken our invention and are using it in their own way, not as intended, with cultural consequences. You can argue the car has done more good than bad in Africa, but that is not really my point. I'm thinking of the impacts, positive and negative, that an invention from one culture can have on another. In most cultures you probably wouldn't even notice this idea, but in Africa it's very apparent.

The African diaspora across the world further confuses things. Many Africans in the developed world have become extremely successful. Why is this? They have the platform to do so? They have the drive, that's for certain. They clearly have the intelligence. Did that come from developed school or real world school? Did they have supportive services and opportunities within the system to achieve this success? The abolition of slavery and the civil rights movement in the US inspired global change, and eventually better social conditions for black people around the world. However, there is clearly still a lot more work to be done.

Why did it happen in the US and not in Africa first? Why did Africans not throw off the European imperialists who simply divided up their country? Yes, they could not withhold an army invading them, but over time they had the numbers to overthrow the settlers and take their country back. Eventually most did, but it was decades or centuries later, when the Europeans were ready to rescind and had made their trillions. They did rise up then, but when they did, they did so as the countries the Europeans had divided them into, not as a whole continent together. An Africa united could be the most powerful continent, but Africa will never unite, as the loop continues to loop. In the Scramble for Africa, we created a very real Tower of Babel; carving up Africa we blocked Africans from achieving their own self-determination as a collective.

An example: The Bridge

On a motorway somewhere downline, I pass under a footbridge. Simple enough; however, it set me thinking. It's a new concrete footbridge, around twenty feet high. The ramp on either side has three levels looping around to get to the top, with no steps so a bicycle can be ridden over it. The kind we see several times a day in the West. It takes around five minutes to get over the bridge. There is a shanty town either side of the bridge; clearly people were crossing back and forth over the road which had a high accident rate with pedestrians, due to the high speed of the road (70 mph). Some foreign NGO donated the funds to build this bridge, costing well over a million US dollars. The locals don't use it at all. It takes less effort to walk under the bridge and equal (waiting for a break in traffic) or less time. Not hugely surprising; this also happens in the West sometimes.

It develops further here, the bridge now providing shade from the sun. If anyone has to wait to cross the motorway, they want to be in the shade. People used to cross the motorway from several different places, now they converge on the same path when crossing. A vendor saw passing trade, set up a stand selling fruit, and soon competition moved in. Now there are five fruit sellers under the bridge, all selling the same thing. Customers pick up things as they cross the motorway on foot and more foot traffic is flowing to the same spot.

More accidents are happening than before, not less, funded by substantial charity work in the West. People feel positive they have made a difference in African quality of life by giving, and reduced needless deaths, but it's a million dollars wasted. The bridge is causing more traffic accidents on the motorway. We provide a solution based on our culture, which does not fit theirs. Ideas that work well for us will not work well for Africans. They will radically reinterpret things, and never use them in the fashion intended, in a passive form of anarchy. It's also very alarming for Westerners to encounter; it might look normal, but it does not operate 'normally'. Where are the police in this as agents of the state? They are not protecting citizens. This new market should not be allowed to exist, but they do nothing to stop it.

So how should development work for Africans? I have no idea, but I know they must be the ones to drive it. I also know they don't have the determination to drive it. Hence the loop repeats. I don't know any developmental agencies that seek to incorporate this idea of passive anarchy. New technologies (the sharing economy) can unlock more local and radical ways of doing things on a mass scale. The best possible scenario is Africans driving their own solutions to their own problems.

M-Pesa is a wonderful example of Africans harnessing new technology and bypassing the need for historical branch banking. It's a private enterprise, however, seeking to make a profit and adapting to African life. It was driven by the Commonwealth Telecommunications Organisation and funded by the

Department for International Development UK (DFID). Now you might be able to pay for your food or petrol with your mobile, which is great. However, you cannot use it to pay for a train ticket to the capital, as there is no trainline. Nor can you use it to post a letter in the post, as there is no mail service. Short-term positivity, but another leap without years of evolution, creating a hybrid reality.

Conclusion

I'm trying to understand the culture from my experience and why it was so jarring for me to see. I'm trying to judge if I should feel responsible or guilty about the current state of Africa. Finally, I'm trying to deduce if I should help, and if so, what can or should I do?

In a sad way I recuse myself regarding Africa. It's a problem I cannot fix. I meet their apathy with my own. I'm sorry for what my forefathers did. If I could fix it, I would. Western-led social development seems to stifle African entrepreneurship and provide solutions not fit for use on the ground. Giving money to charities is trying to treat, but not curing anything. That giving is perpetuating the loop, driving entitlement and apathy. A radical step change is required to drive Africa forward, and it has to be the Africans that drive it.

I did not sit on my couch in the West and decide all of this by watching mainstream media, or reading Western propaganda about Africa. I went to the place itself and talked with the people there, observing life as I went and forming these opinions first-hand. However, I encourage everyone to make up their own minds. Go to the place yourself and draw your own conclusions. The income from tourism alone will directly boost the economy far better than giving to charity.

If our only tool is our idea of civilisation (the hammer), Africa does not share the same values and aspirations (it's not a nail), our solutions will not work. We do not understand what we are trying to fix. Our influence is arguably making things worse. We do not have a universal truth, only one that (just about) works for us, which we have developed over centuries. Often while exploiting the developing world to our gross advantage. The whole world is failing Africans, including Africans themselves. I can't say I blame them for giving up and being wholly apathetic. When facing such a tidal wave of odds, I would also likely give up. I gave up on the road just passing through it.

How can you make a difference in Africa, assuming you want to? Put pressure on governments and companies that do business there to be leaders in ethical fair trading. Don't buy any products which involve components from Africa (like palm oil, gold, diamonds, oil, cocoa, timber), which are owned by anyone other than African companies. Find 100% African companies, and buy goods from them. That's a hard ask as Africa's top five exports are all raw materials which go on to make other goods, by other countries. Africa does little manufacturing, the loop at work yet again. Overall trade is better than aid, but don't buy diamonds and stop coveting the diamond as the only wedding ring.

Far more qualified people than myself can advise what can be done to help. What I saw is that our established current methods are not working. We need to either back off, or change our approach entirely. Don't give to lame charities which encourage a sense of apathy and entitlement in Africa (and use over half the money just to fund their operation). Go to Africa and dig a well for a six months, learn about the culture, teaching people how to do it in the process, so they can do it for themselves in the future. Create a cure for malaria. Consider small-scale ecological mobile manufacturing capabilities for everyday goods, which require small set-up costs, or can be donated. Encourage African-led entrepreneurship to drive inventions and industries for Africans. Continue to drive eco-energy technologies which can provide energy off-grid and be harnessed by all, for free. Encourage use of the menstrual moon cup as a more natural birth control and donate millions of them.

Overall, stop thinking we know everything and that our way is what's best for Africans – it's not. Either Africa wants to move forward, or it wants to stay put in time as it has mostly done for centuries, and it does not mean they are wrong to do so. Get out of the African agenda, both from an industrial exploration perspective and from the existing aid platform, and leave them to drive their own future. If that is straight into the ground, or to the most dynamic place on earth, then so be it. I never – ever – thought I would agree with Robert Mugabe, but his words resonate: *Zimbabwe for Zimbabweans – Africa for Africans.* Perhaps if ties were severed totally and Africa drove itself, it could finally rise to the superpower it should be. If it did, I would guarantee its cities and culture would not resemble any other in the world and it would be (even more of) an entirely unique place.

This would likely have catastrophic effects on so many levels, that it would never be allowed to occur by the world's superpowers. Nevertheless it's an interesting question. Would Africa descend into pure anarchy if we completely removed ourselves? If it did, from what I saw it would be due to apathy. An apathy which is understandable, but which has strong and deep roots, destroying prosperity and hope. You can lead a horse to water, but you can't make it drink. You can lead an African to self-determination, but you can't make him believe in it.

Stop thinking Africa can only learn from us and consider what we can learn from them. They can teach us a lot about being happy without material goods. A timely lesson as we outstrip the earth for every resource possible, creating nothing but momentary happiness and waste. What African cultural practices concerning family and community can we learn from? What can we learn about everyday happiness from them? We should be more like them and learn how we can exist with less of an impact on the planet. From my perspective it looks 50/50 of information going back and forth, but the current model is 100% from us to them.

We think of Africa as backward, uncultured and antiquated, pushing the holier-than-thou agenda and further driving the sense of apathy. Drive hope by encouraging Africans to be African on a mass scale. Think long and hard about what you might want to do to help Africa, if anything at all. You can't deliver real aid without understanding the people or the problem you are trying to help. I had travelled widely before I went there, but I never really understood it until I stood there seeing it in real life. If you can ever truly understand it.

———————————

Glory and I go onto travel another twelve thousand miles across Asia, but I reason this is a story for another time. In the next chapter I jump ahead to my eventual return to the UK, over ten months since I left, having ridden thirty thousand miles through 33 countries.

Sadly, for various reasons, Jo and I do not go the distance. She is now engaged, and I am very happy for her, wishing her the best.

ELEVEN

REFLECTIONS IN A SNOW-COVERED HILL
Africa and Beyond

'Sometimes following your heart means losing your mind.'
Ernest Hemingway

Africa was a dream to me my whole life, as a promise of adventure. It called to me and I answered, joyously. A chance to drive my own direction, under my own steam, on my own. A quiet rebellion against a loud modern life. In a way, it was not about the journey, or the destination. Not about long uncomfortable days on a bike, or being scared and culturally lost, but about just for once in my life striking out on my own. Putting myself somewhere I would never be, had I not intervened and taken control over my life.

It was about not following a common prescribed formula to life. Not doing what I was 'supposed' to be doing. It was about seeing how far I could drive my own personal will and challenge destiny's plan for me. How much of your life can you control? How far can you pull yourself away from your fate? Your everyday fate, at least, maybe not your ultimate fate. Whatever your dream, can you do it? The rush came from trying, doing and accomplishing. It was not the physical destination, but the mental one. That's what it was about. Afterwards, I realised it was about a lot more than that. It had given me years of meaning and purpose in a meaningless world. It had slowed my depression and tempered my disappointment with the world.

In many ways Africa did not suit me, solo at least. I guess I'm not built for that kind of adventure. If I thought I could leave my depression at home, it came with me every step of the way. Africa scared me more than it inspired me. The fear was my own failing, I am very aware of that. I survived, however, physically at least. No doubt money aided the enterprise. Mentally, I was in pieces on my return. But that is why we travel, to challenge our understanding of the world – and there is no greater challenge in my experience than Africa.

Before departing, I regarded myself as a well travelled and a 'man of the world'. Africa immediately humbled me on that score. I was very sheltered and didn't really know much of the developing world – which is most of the world. I just knew my own little world. Anyone who says, 'It's a small world' has not seen much of it. It's impossibly vast and varied.

It's wonderful to find out that the world is still an infinitely large place, full of surprises. In modern times it appears it is developing into one bland, watered-down vanilla 'global culture' where everyone speaks English and the only culture is the church of Capitalism, but this is not happening any time soon from what I can see. Social democracy and our way of life is not 'a thing' for the majority of the world. Just the opposite, actually, our way of life is the minority. The majority of the world's peoples do not have electricity or running water; they far outweigh us. That took me some time to digest, and it still does. While advanced countries continue to pull together into the vanilla, the underdeveloped countries continue to be left even further behind. The future will look more like Orwell's three superstates, locked in 'perpetual war' over the 'disputed zone'. I have no doubt the forsaken 'disputed zone' will be Africa.

As a traveller, I want to know why I found Africa so difficult. I want to understand how I can learn from this journey. How can I travel better next time, wherever the destination is, and make sure I experience more? I wanted to take what I learned into my daily life, to understand the world better. I needed to process the trip as a whole, and I needed to be home to do it. I returned without a scratch, and oddly thought the whole thing was no big deal, all out of sight now. When I sat down, and re-read all of my notes I had goosebumps, and a day of tears. It most certainly was a big deal.

It was a profound experience, which attacked the way I think about everything. Africa was like a mental freight train I stepped in front of. In business we often talk about learning the most from failures, but the same is true of our personal lives. I failed in Africa, and it was the biggest learning experience of my life. Retrospectively, in many ways I regard it as a degree, fascinating, but more work than fun.

What was I thinking?

In everyday life we compute hundreds of things subconsciously, be it someone walking down the road, walking into a shop and asking a question, waiting for a bus, or talking with someone we know. Within the chain of these events, we have a scale we subconsciously operate. Imagine a volume dial that has 0-10 levels. At our base level – home – most daily events happen from 0-3, which is a very tolerable range. This allows for human personality. Not everyone is the same; people can act and react differently. Occasionally something happens which goes above the 3 and pulls our conscious mind to attention. *This is something I need to think about and act.* This event would be the one we recall for the day. Maybe we saw a car accident, which pushed us up to a 7. Perhaps we saw a shouting match on the street, registering a 5. We only tend to remember things which go over the 5 mark. We will always remember anything above a 9 for the rest of our lives.

Say we process 500 scenarios everyday in the subconscious, using common algorithms we have learned though repetition (in reality its more like millions). When we travel to foreign countries, we may start to stretch a hundred of these daily thoughtstreams. Going to France, for instance, they speak a different language, and this impacts a hundred such events through the day, be it reading a sign, speaking with someone, or trying to buy something in a foreign language. Our common assumptions are slightly rearranged in a way that interrupts our subconscious processing of what we deem 'normality'. At the low level we find this mental stimulation interesting and regard it as 'the excitement of travel'. Thirty things in this example reached 5 on our unconscious scale, which the brain regards as a hard day's work. You're tired, but you had fun.

In Africa, half of these 500 daily thoughtstreams were turned up to somewhere between 5 and 8 on a typical day for me. On a bad day nearly all 500 were turned up over 5, some all the way to 10. At the 10 mark you will never forget that moment. It's ingrained in your mind for life (and part of the learning process should that scenario ever evolve again). When several of these mental calculations happen in a row, it leads to fatigue. The longer the day, the more to process, and the harder things get to work out.

What was once a simple thought process gets harder to complete the more fatigued the brain is, leading to a sense of alienation and distress in the subconscious. In the conscious mind you might think, *'What was that all about?'*, but you register the fact you are physically tired. Africa was exhausting as it's all happening at once, across the full spectrum of thought. There was not a lot of mental downtime for me, despite being physically stationary. When I had a moment to myself in a hotel room, I was still processing the information my mind had absorbed that day. Thus, I found it tiring the whole time. I'm still processing a lot of what I absorbed when there, even in the subconscious.

Separate to the subconscious algorithms we process, our conscious brain also processes what is in our immediate attention. In the same French example (or easy travel), our conscious brain will process around 500 of these 'social' characteristics (poverty, cleanliness, discomfort in others). In an easy country that might be only fifty, but in Africa it was well over 250 a day for me. To the Western mind, Africa represents the greatest rearranging of common assumptions on social characteristics possible. When you alternate so many small social factors like this, it's hard to assimilate with the culture. I struggled to comprehend the society's structure.

Yes, as humans we know Africans need food, shelter and water to survive. Beyond that I couldn't decipher much; it was simply too foreign for me. If it doesn't look like our world, we have to learn it to navigate it. When physically exerting myself already, this was more hard work. Your physical self is tired, your conscious brain is confused, and your subconscious gets muddled. You are not in the best zone to experience new cultures – it's simply more about staying safe. Africa brings this out more so than anywhere else in the world and thus has the greatest ability to instil confusion and fear in visitors. In some ways it's refreshing, but in many others it's terrifying. It confused me: it was too much, on too many levels, too often. Working the bike and working the culture was nudging maximum capacity of my mind every day, for extended periods. People ask me how was it? Did you have the time of your life? I have to say it wasn't about beers on the beach, but more about simply staying healthy, alive and sane.

I had been to China, Russia, Brazil, but I have never seen such a radically different way of life as in Africa. It was not just a foreign language or a foreign custom, it was truly *a foreign world*, in every sense. All of the dimensions were different, every assumption changed out. I did not know humans could flourish in such a way of life. It bent my mind further than any place I've been, undermining my supposed understanding of the world. I expect for most of my life now I will compare what I am looking at to what I saw in West Africa. As uncomfortable as that is, I hope it continues, so I can incorporate that into my outlook on life and understanding of humanity. That was the point after all: I made this trip to learn more about the world.

Most of the world considers Africa as backward or uneducated. If you think like this, you play into the popular narrative and will end up dismissing the place. If you can remove that fundamental bigoted assumption, that in the West we are all-seeing and knowing, you will appreciate our value system is just one interpretation of how life can be lived. There is a variety of human values, and ways of life – plural. *You have to remove the 'right' or 'wrong' viewpoint.* There are different ways to live. Your judgement on them is not relevant. The more of these interpretations you can appreciate, the wider you're understanding of humanity can be. We don't need perfect streets, rigorous social institutions or fifty types of tuna in the supermarket. When you move beyond these ideas, Africa is just another way of living, which is quite efficient.

This is all in hindsight. In the moment I couldn't appreciate it so easily. What was at fault was my inability to be comfortable in different values and realities, my inability to accept that culture. In almost every sense the social structure was too far outside my tolerable limits. That was the disappointment I found in myself when I was in Africa. I did not have the capacity to accept so many shifts on both the conscious and subconscious level. It was too far from my daily normality in every direction I looked. I couldn't get in step with what was happening on the street. It was too alien for me and my mind shut down. It moved to 'safe mode' and in doing so blocked me from fully engaging with the local culture. I was really disappointed in myself, as it had never happened to me before in this way.

It's more complex than the idea of a 'comfort zone', but it's on the same lines. In that framework it's two steps beyond the comfort zone, past the good risk-taking and fearlessness. Past the good stress and into the bad stress. Past moderate risk and into extreme risk. Past good heightened anxiety into bad anxiety and fear. I put myself into bad anxiety and stress for extended periods, where it was new and highly taxing. I had no awareness such a realm existed, or that I would be travelling into it.

At the time I could not put my finger on what I was feeling; retrospectively it was being in this zone. Even at the low end, it's an exhausting sense-confusion. An extended feeling of mental malaise, lasting for days. Knowing what it is now, should I ever get there again it will not be new territory. One day there might be a 'psychology of adventure' for adventure travellers, but that was certainly not on my pre-departure reading list. I didn't even know such a thing existed.

People always jest, 'Did you find yourself on your travels?', a particularly annoying question and total bullshit. I've known myself since birth very well. (If anything, I was trying to get away from him!) I did learn a lot more about how my brain works.

People talk about luck on a trip life this and no doubt it plays a part. Wiser people talk about preparation, which I agree can make a trip, or break it. There is one further step beyond this, however, which is *instinct, and* for me it's the most important factor. In the modern world we are repeatedly driven to switch our instinct off, to try and tame our natural emotions. Modern advice says stay put in a skyscraper when it's on fire and wait for help; instinct says run. Modern practice says trust the sat nav; instinct says look up and absorb the road, see what is happening, and sense the right direction. The map on your phone tells you to walk down the alley in the dark, when your instinct says don't. It's the step beyond the conscious mind when action immediately occurs.

Instinct will operate subconsciously, if you let it flow freely. Instinct is beautiful to tune into and harness its power; however, it's exhausting. Language stops operating in the core of our brains. It's purely emotional in there. There is no science to it, it's the world around us that we tune into.

For me instinct trumps both preparation and luck. Instinct transcends all cultures, and even our species. It is primal, animal. It knows no languages or customs. It operates when you are fresh and when you are tired – if you dial into it and listen. It's naturally inbuilt, but still takes cultivation to master. Across thousands of interactions and scenarios, you always need to be listening to it. Instinct will give you a heads-up to the situation, but you have to be able to find the right responses as there is a huge range of responses between fight or flight.

Heightened awareness takes you through many stages of instinctual gatekeeping. Snap judgements can save your life. If it does not feel right, move on. Call it your gut, call it your heart, call it the creeps – it's instinct. In this respect, I view the trip as a total success. I religiously followed my instinct and had no real problems as a result. This skill needs to be nourished to stay productive and yield constant results. Don't get trapped in your little bubble. It might be painful, but let your animal instinct roam. Moving forward, I must continue to use it on a daily basis, despite the comfortable routine of normal Western life naturally dulling it.

Sitting here after the trip and thinking back, these were my thought processes in Africa deconstructed. For these reasons I found it very difficult there. I find it disappointing to think back on my general state of mind there. It could, of course, just be that I am weak and not very adventurous.

Returning home was bewildering. Many long-term travellers talk about depression and blues, but heading home I was happy and excited. I needed some routine and normality to contextualise what I had seen. Not a 'nice hotel comfort', but genuine 'I'm home' comfort, that you can only get at home. A complete base level reset. The immediate response was of comfort and security. The short to medium-term response was deeper, harder than expected, and harder still to decode. It was hard to reset, given the sheer quantity of new information in my world view. Everything seemed superfluous and over the top. The reset eventually worked; it just hit like a ton of bricks when it came.

Heading into London in the first few days of returning, I see a young beautiful girl get on the train. Her hair is freshly washed, dried and combed. Her fingernails and toenails perfectly polished and painted. Not a hair out of place, in a spotless designer outfit. Perfect in every sense. Post-Africa the facade was lost on me (not the girl though, thankfully). She lives in a bubble, likely of her own making, her own little world where everything is perfect. How would she fare on the dusty streets of Burkina Faso? Where there is no running water to keep that hair clean, no power for that hairdryer, nowhere to get clean, and nowhere to stay clean. We all form our own bubble, based on the reality of where we are. I knew this before, but I see it clearer now.

Sitting on a train like this, my mind is in riot trying to reconcile these worlds I've passed through. How can you compare them? *How can you not?* Nothing seems real anymore, just a pretence. When you boil life down to the essentials, of which running water and power are not, it's very hard to build it back up again. It's all so glaringly superfluous here in the developed world, and all so hopelessly desperate back in Africa. They both sum up the paradox trap perfectly.

This constant toil for outward identity with piercings, tattoos, extreme beauty, make-up, blue hair, shock clothing etc. is so weak. It's just a crisis of identity, 'style' only possible in a culture of excess. We can easily wear goth clothing when there are fifty styles of clothing to choose from. Most people in Africa are happy with clothes. They don't give a fuck what the T-shirt says, as long as it covers them. If it fits, it's a bonus. Here we pay money to have it say something cool – something we like, something that gives us outward identity, expresses who we 'are'. Merely 'being' is not enough for us. We must perpetuate this vast machine, this system. We must *buy buy buy* and keep this machine of comfort ticking over. We must propel it every year to grow the economy and get wealthy, get secure. People express themselves through what they buy, retail shopping some kind of retarded expression. It's insane to think about, utterly futile. Our culture celebrates the style we portray, instead of the thoughts and ideas we convey. To keep this surface identity going, we must keep up with the others, and make a collective bubble.

I find myself wanting to be no one now. An anonymous unremarkable fellow on the train, who doesn't get a look, let alone a second look. I don't wish to advertise any businesses on my being. Remove all the labels and the outward signs of identity. I don't feel part of this culture, or the African one, I am a tourist in all senses and all places – always. None of them are 'my culture'.

The same goes on the streets. I longed for order in Africa. Once the chaos is gone, it seems every imperfection has been covered over. Mother Nature suffocated, ironed flat. I look out and see only the occasional small strip of heavily pruned greenery. All rubbish is firmly in a receptacle (thankfully), the dust swept away by a machine. Everything is so neat and tidy, it induces a state of lethargy. Like being high on opium, it's all just perfect; everything is new and shiny. Elaborate screening protects us from seeing the inner workings of the machinery that makes our lives easier, protecting us from every possible danger. New adverts, new fonts, stuff I've never seen before, begging for my attention. It's the business of business. Yes, I've never seen this billboard, but I've seen millions just like it. Advertising can never be art – it's not expression, it's a business. It's lost on me, all of it.

Paddington Station suffers a signal failure and all trains stop. Paddington is described as 'chaos'. It's not the chaos of Nairobi or Bamako, however. We have systems in place for crowds here, and a culture of order. There it's a different chaos, where people die to qualify for the word 'chaos' being used.

We drive to see the family, and on the way the motorway is a calming and quiet experience. The queues to leave the city seem never-ending, but once we are underway we cover a hundred miles in ninety minutes easily. We stop and have a pleasant lunch at a well-stocked services. We also stop at the supermarket before arriving. It's all innocuous enough; however, I am totally bewildered. As I walk the aisles and take in the sheer quantity of choices I'm bowled over. The supermarket is also selling plastic goods, chairs and other useless one-time-use items made in China.

A tidal wave of confusion washes over me as I look around. It's all overwhelming, and I'm relieved to have the trolley to support me as I feel I could fall over. The mental storm is so absolute it overpowers my physical being. Here in my own country, my own environment – *I am lost.* We are destroying this earth, quickly, for choice and comfort. We can't settle for a potato, we need ten varieties, and ten shapes of potato. The brands and colours seem so aggressive. It's all in my face, a cathedral of the unnecessary. A part of me comes off in every aisle, another strip of my mind, melting me away. My pulse races and my head pounds. I fear a heart attack by the frozen foods aisle. This was once my home? This was once my life? My mind has broken into several pieces across the miles. I was not comfortable there and I'm not comfortable here. Where is my space? Is there one? Do I have to set out again to find it?

Why do I get the choice, and the people in Mali do not? Who decides? Why am I so fortunate? If indeed this is fortunate. Why do these other people not see their good fortune? Why does the world just not make any sense? Why can't I find peace in it all? Working to a trip made sense, but there was no end to the rainbow and here I sit once again, pondering the meaning of it all. I'm no further along than before – drifting on the road, drifting at home. Drifting along the corridors of understanding and thought. They go on forever and never reach a conclusion. Some doors shine and some doors don't, but they all lead to more doors. Not the doors of perception, but the eternal doors of question. They go on forever. They keep you busy, but they reach nowhere. You pass and pass through them, and that is life. Maybe the final one reaches somewhere, maybe not. We won't know until we open it.

This whole thing of life is a grand cycle. This much is clear. Can I outthink the cycle and break the chain? Sometimes I am convinced the human condition is the greatest logic problem of all time. We can eventually outthink it. At other times I think logic is the problem itself, and not the tool to use. I am fixed, I am broken. Still wedged in the fucking paradox of logic. The fog clears for a bit, but never fully lifts. I hear noises, but nothing calls clearly to me. I have urges, but they are on the surface. Deep down my soul sits quiet and watches all. Right back to square one – *is this table real?*

I came back from Africa physically fit, but unwell mentally, troubling thoughts still rumbling through my mind. I struggle to make sense of even home with this new reality. It's too much weight for me to carry and makes me depressed.

Having an 'identity' is totally superfluous when you are not sure you will be alive tomorrow. Consequentially the whole way I viewed the world, the way I was 'me', was violently torn down in this new world. Things I held dear, now slipped into a trivial stupidity. It took some time to realise Africa destroyed a part of me, although I felt demolished at the time, I could not see it. The further I get from it the clearer it becomes. In doing so it also set me free. In my new reality however normal is no longer normal. 0 has been destroyed, so resetting is impossible. Instead I must build up a new world to live in, a new way to make sense of it all, a new 0.

I have to sit down and write this to clear my mind. It's the only way I can compartmentalise my experience. It's not a story of high adventure, but of exposing myself to a difficult part of the world, and trying not to lose my mind in both the process of the trip and more importantly when I return to my own culture.

Fast Forward

In the medium term, things sink in, as time naturally files experience. Reacquainted with family, friends, foods, routines return me completely into the comfort zone. Here, a cold, confused depression takes hold. I feel like I am running around with the whole world in my brain and it hurts. My mind seems sick with all I have seen, but it refuses to go down a dead end and die. It was totally backwards that on the open road I had direction, yet once home I am lost.

In travelling the world, my brain cannot process what we are doing to the Earth. The destruction is so vast and invasive, so permanent. No one speaks on behalf of the Earth. The world over you see faith, be it the Muslim, the Catholic, or the Buddhist. On the road I saw churches, mosques, monasteries and holy places everywhere, regardless of the culture I was in. What do they all have in common? Wisdom? Fear? Stupidity? Weakness, I think. They all share a common weakness, born in the minds of humankind. They cannot face the enormity of meaninglessness, so create a construct of understanding to help them cope. Another bubble. They disparage drug addicts, when they are hooked on the biggest drug of them all. Human, all too human indeed.

The faces may change, the places of worship may change, the cultures may change and the gods, too, but the base weakness of human kind remains the same around the world. Fear is fear, regardless of where you come from, or what colour your skin is. When will people stand on their own two feet, free of self-inflicted guilt and weakness? When will people drive their own reality and change the course of their fate instead of leaving it entirely to fate? When can we take charge of our lives, our world?

The modern age is being driven by people who do not think. Just fleeting scattered thoughts, with no clear vision or goal. We are evolving our own culture of narcotising dysfunction by singular unconnected events. There is no masterplan. The only sense of reality comes though people's 'feeds', delivering endless inane stupidity, an epic distraction. It seems as if everyone is down the rabbit hole, and no one is looking up. We've created a world too complicated for us to understand anymore. It's too scary for people to stare into the vast landscape of the human mind. And I'm the coward.

We celebrate the highest form of fake and long after those most removed from nature. The biggest celebrities are the fakest people; everything is about the appearance, and the appearance is totally fake and heavily pruned. The natural is hidden, covered over, something to be ashamed of. Deep within our society is a sickness, a fear of the natural world. The nicer a place is, the more built up it is (and fake). We've literally lost our roots. When the road is too rocky, we just build an overpass over it.

We are creating products to get rich and live comfortable lives, but slowly killing each other as we do so. We destroy the Earth with needless over-consumption, killing our home. We slowly poison each other, by using synthetic ingredients for profit. Ultra-processed food is cheap to make and buy, but it gives you cancer. Sugar is addictive, so it's pumped into everything, and it's killing us. Fast 'convenience' food is pumped full of toxic chemicals, creating obesity and diabetes. Everyday household products contain volatile organic compounds (VOCs) which are worse than truck exhaust fumes to breathe. It's a great irony that the sanitiser you use to clean your home will poison you. The infection might not kill us, but the cancers will. Our own way of life is making us wealthy and comfortable, but killing our bodies and home in the process. People don't seem to draw the link.

I had many thoughts like this before the trip, but now they seem so much louder, so much clearer. No one asks about your mental state after a trip like this. People are only fascinated by what went wrong. They want to know about the worst parts, the jeopardy. They want bullet points, or 'highlights'. Buzzwords that make me vomit. The same vanilla question over and over: 'What was your favourite part?' How can I take such a vast experience and cut it down into bitesize chunks? What was my favourite part?

'Fully deconstructing my mind and deeply analysing the meaning of life across several varying cultures, then trying to reapply it to my own culture.'

'Oh.'

I didn't get sick, crash, get robbed or end up in jail, but my mind went through all those things. My mind did get sick, it broke down, it crashed several times. It also felt like it was in a prison, of its own making – making it all the more difficult. I can't show anyone a picture of that – it's in these words. I continue to learn the lessons of this trip every day.

Playing Lego with my nephew in Kenya, I held a brick in my hand and studied it. This totally unnecessary piece of plastic perpetuates the destruction of the Earth. It also gives us economic opportunity, drives employment, pays taxes and provides healthcare. It gives us stability. It enables us to live comfortably. It can also teach a young mind how to build and be good fun - but that is not my point. This industry of false needs provides that economic bed of comfort, which I longed for downline. I was disgusted by that – disgusted by myself. As a traveller I regret not pushing myself further and harder. *I should have gotten into the huts.* I should have stayed longer, until the dusty chaos became comfortable and normal.

It strikes me that people are the problem. I am the problem. We run around with preconceptions in our mind as heavy baggage – in my case 'the demons'. As individuals we are beautiful loving humans; as groups we are violent reckless destroyers of the Earth. As Nietzsche rightly said, 'In individuals, insanity is rare; but in groups, parties, nations and epochs, it is the rule.' Somewhere in between the individual and the group, we seem to sour this life. By the time we reach a nation, we strangle it to death. Humans are incapable of balance – there is no balance with the earth. There is no balance between our animal instincts and our supposed 'superior' mental capacity. If anything, this is the heart of the human condition. There is no balance with our human brothers and sisters. Some are more human than others in our twisted grasp for identity, our quest for comfort. Immigrants are a threat and not humans. The sense of 'home' is a sign of weakness. The sense of 'us', a source of conflict. The quest for comfort, a retreat from real natural life itself.

Perhaps human suffering is a fundamental part of life. That's what I thought in Africa. Humans have lived on Earth for at least five thousand years, and the more primitive the society, the less impact they have had on the planet. The more complex the society, the harder the impact is on the planet. The current hyper life is complex, and clearly destroying our home rapidly. African life is simple, but it is full of suffering and hard to process. We feel a sense of guilt around the suffering as we perpetrated so much of it. The guilt feeds into how we think about Africa, and how we react.

Where these cultures mix, conflict arises. Not just physical and political conflict, but a conflict of ideas which debases both cultures, leading to misunderstanding. We don't have to be able to understand Africa. But to do so, we have to be able to step outside the construct of Western logic. We must be able to understand it as a thing in itself. Yes, we have caused several key developments and tried to shape Africa in way that is profitable for us, exploiting it in the process. We should doubtless feel guilt in that, but beyond that is where I'm pointing.

We must be able to understand a potent alternate culture which will not blend with ours. We need to further accept that this is OK, and we cannot bend it into a shape we want. It's not our place to meddle, despite the shit we did in the past. Especially given the shit we did in the past. Not only is it not our place to do so, more importantly it's impossible. If Africa teaches us anything, it's that it will not follow any form we attempt to guide it to, no matter how altruistically or sinisterly motivated it is. It must strike its own form, its own future. To develop its own narrative, to its own set of values. Trying to push development is not wrong; trying to push it into our model is. It won't work for Africa and will only perpetuate the loop.

I did a philosophy degree to answer several key questions on life. Big questions about equality against freedom, or the freedom of the individual in the collective. I sat and listened to a wide range of people from different cultures debate these issues at great length. I threw some rocks of my own at age-old ideas. I determined several of these questions could not be answered, but felt satisfied I had at least asked the questions. I had tried, and gathered some peace from that. I didn't know then that (in the words of Kant) logic is a crooked set of principles from which nothing straight can be built.

I feel the same way about Africa now. I am unsure if I gathered any answers, but my impressions are first-hand, and not from the television or a book. We caused this, so naturally feel guilt, but we can't solve it. Only Africans can fix Africa – if indeed it needs any fixing at all. I take some peace in the fact that at least I asked the question, even if I don't know the answer. Maybe it's us that need fixing. What causes the reaction in us to Africa is the shock of seeing a life so different. If we can get over that, do we still feel Africa needs support?

———————

Comfortable once again, the more familiar 'normal' demons came back to me. They are not really demons anymore, just standard worries and confusion about life. Staring into a vast sea of frantic disillusionment, the desperation wells up inside me. So much wasted effort. So much care in the world, and no heart. My head stops working, my mind only finding dead ends. The paradoxes are only growing, just like the universe, in a way we can never really see, but only feel. Here I sit once again, looking out on this fuckfest of importance and scratching my head. I must be 'home' − it's all so foreign, so blank, so nothing.

How can any of this ever matter, or ever make sense? Why should it? It's easier to believe this is all an error. However, you would be a fool to consider it is not actually happening. The world is too big and nothing crushes it like walking down a street in the US. Everyone strives for an identity, until they all bleed into one singular identity of nothing, so painfully trite. Yet they all force themselves to matter in the world and the saga continues. There may well be an Einstein in their midst, but I can't see him. Every life matters, yet as a collective we are so ugly, so vapid. When people come together in the modern era, it seems to showcase the worst in us, not the best. Can disillusionment ever be clear, or must it be opaque by nature?

I cannot not attach myself to any of it. I am a tourist on the road, and I am a tourist at home. No place, culture, nation or religion do I call 'mine'. My identity is in the wind, as it always has been. At times it blows beautifully on a soft warm scented breeze, inspiring love and warmth. Sometimes it howls through the forests on a cold winter night, driving confusion and hatred. I love it, and I hate it. It sets me free, and imprisons me. It pushes me harder into finding my own truth, but also further from humanity in the process. Without roots, I am unable to grow. But without an anchor, I am able to roam free and flourish. Having no home stops me from feeling home anywhere. However, home is merely a place of comfort, not a place of understanding.

———————

Infinity drives nail after nail into my mind, until it is barely able to function. Each new day the nails are removed and each day they are driven in again, in new places. Each time it's excruciating. I travelled thirty-thousand miles on a motorbike across the world, but my mind went thirty-billion units of infinity through the endless hallways of forever to nowhere. On and on, and on, and on some more. Like a shooting star, ferociously burning across the sky of reason, indifferent to the odds. Charring everything in its beautiful path, onwards to its glorious demise.

The very structure with which we built our world only brings it down. But we can't go on blaming the past, we must face our future ourselves. The world owes us nothing. One is inclined to say, then we owe the world nothing. But this is not the case, as we owe our home everything and must stop destroying it. I see a glass house now, about to shatter. So much falsity surrounds us and the fake must fall. As we shuffle along our busy corridors of man-made importance to activities which simply pass our man-made sense of time away. We think it's all so important – *but it's not.*

We drift further from reality and into a proto-reality of self-importance. The more I open my eyes to it, the further I get from 'this' reality. It's all so important, and it's all so meaningless. We are here, but not here. We are so smart, and yet so stupid. Deep in the mystic I search for clues, but find none.

I'm in pieces on my return and cannot get a grip. England is my home, but nothing seems familiar; it's all completely over the top and ridiculous. I wonder how this was my life before. I see all the people in their shiny new cars. There I am in my shiny new car, wanting for nothing practical, but starving for something mystical. In a feverish search for identity, the trip had become my identity. Ultimately it was a distraction from a lack of identity and bond with my own culture. On returning I feel stripped of all identity I had before and am simply blank. Despite the miles, the memories, the upsets and glories, I'm a blank sheet of paper with no leads on tomorrow. It's not my world, it's this world, merely a place I am in. Just like in Africa, I struggle to accept the reality I find myself in.

The thought of the trip completely, is too much to process. There is no sweet snappy slogan to summarise everything out there. It's no big deal, and yet infinitely complex at the same time. I may not know the exact road to take, but if I travel by logic, I will always arrive at the dead end of a paradox. Logic is not a map of the human mind. It's a half-truth at best. Yet we cling to it, and only get so far down the road. Then we get lost, get drunk and let it all out, citing the 'human condition'. Refreshed, we start again down the same road for another cycle, to the same result. Sometimes we get a bit further, sometimes we don't.

We never reach the end of the road, maybe not even in death. The vast meaninglessness of it all haunts us. I lurk somewhere in the shadows, watching it all. The journey of a million miles starts with one step. One word or one thrust of life. As we kill – with one step, one sentence or one thrust of death. But no one ever talks about how it ends. A journey of a million miles also ends with just one step. A step from one journey into another. Some you cover distance on, and some you sit still for.

We continue to hurtle through space. An explosion of life, and all the important things we hold dear. Where is the world spinning? Where are we headed? Why is it all so bloody important? What the fuck does it all matter for? I am no wiser in returning than when I left. The world fills me with wonder, and fear. I revel in being alive, and at times I loathe it. However I never, ever take it for granted. There is more good than bad, but overall it's a global mess. Surely there has to be another way? The confusion clears now and then, but it's still rooted in confusion, so will return. My view of the confusion is bigger now, I see more of it. Some things are clearer, but overall it's still cloudy. Nudging the void, and often slipping into it. The fissures of logic, the cracks of humanity, the pointlessness of it all. The anger and frustration. Circling the emptiness, driving straight north in circles.

Blasting off on the bike through the streets in a reckless rage affirms some kind of life in me. A celebration of the futility. I don't care what cool shoes you wear, or what your T-shirt says. I want to know why you exist. I want to know what you think. Your choice in car, or music, does not inform me of that. I want to know why. Why you deserve to breathe this sweet air? Maybe you can help me understand if I deserve to do the same.

I want to leave my blood on these pages. Let me fuel this vast meaningless, this unchecked energy that propels 'humanity' forward, deep into infinity. I hope these words upset you. Defend your mind, question your life, for I demand answers – *I demand blood!* Distort the neat rows of perfection and tidy the chaotic mess on the other side. Change the world, and show we are alive, celebrate the life, you bunch of glorious bastards!

The whole narrative of Western thought is building towards a universal tomorrow, a universal truth. We are all equal, we all deserve to live, every voice counts. Yet we grossly overpopulate the world, to a point it cannot handle. There is no universal point to head for. It's a myth; it merely makes us comfortable. It provides a basic framework to train an understanding of things we will never fully understand. We are merely treating the human condition, never curing it. We will never be happy in a system, and we will never survive comfortably outside of one.

If we travel to gain a new way of seeing things, then the trip was a fantastic success. However, I never thought it would undermine my view of Western society even more. Now I feel even more unbelonging at home, and wholly unbelonging of life on the road. Our 'world' has become an even more bemusing place than before. Once again I am surrounded by people, and totally alone. Once again, like in Africa, I'm uncomfortable. Unlike there, however, here I have everything I need, but still cannot find respite. In Africa getting a bottle of water was a small victory in the effort to live. Here it's all so easy that it has no sweetness, no sense of triumph.

A trip like this becomes your identity. Every channel of thought leads to it – it's all you see. After the trip it's stripped from you and you are not sure on which road to take. I flew Glory home, as being on the earth without her seemed alien and strange. I needed her back by my side quickly. I couldn't be apart from her at this crucial stage. Ironically, at my own front door, and not the other side of the world. Through so much change our relationship remains a constant. To have no trip and no bike is too daunting. Even if she sits on the driveway, that tangible reality is key to my identity. I need her in my life right now. Over time that might change, but for now she is essential. With the spacecraft nearby, the spaceman can blast off quickly. I likely never will, but the peace she brings is priceless. She is my own weakness as she is an identity for me now. I feel a sense of solace from the meaning she gives me, but I also create a barrier to drive conflict. I can see it clearer now.

There was muted celebration for 'the intrepid traveller' returning, but I could not bask in it without my girl. She did all the hard work, after all. I still can't say my heart was completely in love with her. I can't say my heart can completely love. But I could not deny the bond we had forged: we are a team. I had tended to her physically and she had done so to me mentally. We never really fell hard, we never really stopped, she never left me in the lurch. When she groaned, I listened and acted. As such she stayed ever faithful, even when I put her through hell. I could learn something from all this. However, physically repairing a bike is a lot easier than repairing a mind. I'm sure a human gives out sounds and vibrations of anguish, but I struggle to pick them up. Struggle further how to fix them. There is no Nick to call, no manual to consult. The human condition is far more complex than any machine will ever be. Glory is easy love – my kind of love.

Perhaps the meaning of your life is to make meaning in your life. The sun will always rise on a new day, until it doesn't. Truth is an error, the quest is to not seek it. The great push for human understanding will involve the destruction of logic. These words we craft need to be destroyed. It's not just Africa that has a loop, all humans do. Push your mind farther than it has ever gone and you might just break the loop. Of course, it will also break you in the process. I might be in pieces, but I will put myself back together again. For some reason my meaning is running headlong at these unseen walls, not to shake them, but to try and destroy them completely.

POSTSCRIPT

'The Universe is transformation. Life is opinion.'
Marcus Aurelius

It took months of being home to really 'return'. There were, and still are many sleepless nights to try and understand it all. I'm not just thinking about Africa, but the whole of my life. I knew I was back when that cold empty feeling of depression returned. Without a great project to focus on, the fire goes out, and I am forced once again to face a life I do not understand.

The world is a mess. My family is a mess. I am a mess. I can function, even steer things to work better, and show signs of success. But it's under some childish assumption that things will eventually work out, when they never will. *Is it all in my head?* Here we are in the most stable, secure and prosperous times the human race has ever seen, yet here I am feeling empty and rootless. Unable to sleep again, and unable to slow a constant rumble of thoughts about our world.

The trip was everything. It was the ultimate goal, steering my life choices for years before embarking, a reason in the madness. Without it, I am more lost than when I set out. Whatever identity I had before is even weaker now. If you travel through enough borders, countries become irrelevant. In a way we need to destroy the idea of nationalism to see the world clearly. It's one Earth full of humans. The wind knows no borders, nor the sun. Our frameworks of understanding are irrelevant. The conflict we inflict on each other is fruitless. The enemy is just someone whose point of view you don't understand yet. The enemy is you. Factually there is, and there is not. Nature gives us a beautiful spark; our reaction is the conditioning of human interpretation. A belief structure which helps us get up in the morning and sleep at night. But it's all human weakness. We are prisoners of ideas.

The demons are still with me, but they have a different form now, one which is more familiar now. I have taken my framework of understanding down so many times, I cannot rebuild it anymore. It falls to pieces when I try to get a hold of it. Love is a folly, which will never last. All the possessions in the world just mean the destruction of it. At some point I will have to take a chance and try to love someone, but the thought just scares me. The greatest question remains the greatest question: why are we here? Occasionally there is a moment of clarity, of calm. It's mostly never-ending suffocating waves of meaninglessness, however, with the occasional glimpse of freedom.

Everyone says they want to do a trip like mine one day. You know they won't. They might have the stones, but they don't have the commitment. I struggled a lot on the road, but time heals. There was a lot of frustration, but now and then I crack a smile when I remember beasting it out on the open piste in Southern Mali. *High on Coca-Cola and dreams, scared shitless, but free.* I get Goosebumps remembering back on charging the road in Tanzania full tilt. Oddly when I look out on the rows of miserable winter commuters on my trudge to work, this is what I see, and it warms me.

At least I can say for once I changed the course of my fate and forged my own path. There is no way my life would have placed me on that road for so long, through so many foreign lands by fate alone. There is no way I would have challenged my framework of understanding so ruthlessly at home. There is a victory in that at least, however deluded it is.

Despite all of this, I am still eternally happy to have a roof over my head, a warm bed to sleep in, food in the fridge and money in the bank. Things could certainly be a hell of a lot worse. Materially, things have never been better, but mentally I'm awash. Just like the road, the real battle is always in your mind. I can't see it, but I can feel it. I know I am up against the unseen wall of the human condition.

On the surface this trip was a success. I returned healthy and whole having seen a lot. Inside, however, it was the greatest failure of my life. I did not have 'the time of my life', but instead spent a great deal of time in fear and discomfort, more a nightmare than a dream. We rarely learn from success, however. It's taken me months to realise how profound this experience was. It's still happening now and will continue to do so. If we are here on Earth to learn, which I believe we are, the scale tips back to success. A lot of this story, and my mental health in general do not sound great – but the process of writing this has been hugely cathartic. I would not do this again, however, I would not change a thing I did, and I am grateful for this lesson.

The journey was a rebellion, neat and tidy. Back home, however, every day I am rebelling against myself and my society, which is not neat or tidy. I remain searching for something, still yet unfound.

London, January 2018

Acknowledgements

Many people help with a journey like this, some by mere words of encouragement, others by huge effort and support.

First and foremost I would like to thank my mother, Grace, and my English brother Neil for always being there as base camp, no matter how far I roamed. Having you both there through all of this in case of the worst was a great comfort, and I cannot thank you enough. A huge thanks to the one and only living legend Nick Lloyd (and Linda!). All I wanted was a bike ready for the task. I got that and a new friend for life on top. I can't thank you enough for your work, support and guidance, mate.

Thanks to my inspirations and teachers and the many travellers who paved the way: Ted Simon, Oisin Hughes, Adam Lewis, Chris Scott, Dr Pat Garrod, Keith Code, Elsbeth Beard, Dan Walsh, Rory Stewart, Yuval Noah Harari, Tim Butcher, Jay Griffiths and many, many more ...

My (very few) fellow riders: Nick Marler - my first! - great times, my friend! The crazy Brazilians – hope to meet you again somewhere down the road – whoever you are.

Thanks to those who helped on the way: Kevin Ames for preparing Glory so nicely, and selling her to me! Alan Arnold at Infinity Motorcycles, Grant & Susan at Horizons Unlimited, Jill Collard at Masta UK, Charlie Hay at Afrikids, La Familia en Corse – Coralie and Amandine et al, Sylvie & Gil in Dakar, everyone at Afrikids, Cedric at Amarante, Mario & Yahn in Duneworks Yamaha Swakopmund, Roan at Helderburg Yamaha Cape Town, Pete and Kerry in Cape Town – thanks for some quality down time in your place! Foxy Roxy for being the one and only SA Superstar (wish we could hang out more, love)! Freddie and Lizzie Grounds, Philippa and Jamie at Tropic Air/Jack's bar Nanyuki (for some great nights and mighty hangovers!), Chris at Jungle Junction Nairobi (your jokes are even worse than mine, well done), Alice, Will and Johnny Harries (including the new additions) in Nairobi, Peter at Nascer do Sol Lodge, Kathy at Moto Freight, James Cargo, Sukkie at Cars UK (you're a star!), Billy and Ryan at the Bourne Valley Inn, Laura Gray for the beautiful home in Yorkshire to write this, and the sage advice!

Spotracker for keeping my mother sane, and the FCO for your tireless work advising travellers down line.

And of course Jo. I hope you had as much fun as me. Sorry it didn't work out, love, xx.

A big thanks my friends and supporters: the following extended families: the O'Tooles, Casas, Simonpietris, Walmsleys, Brix/Rossensteines, Bibbys, Gastmans, Levett Prinseps, Sarins and the extended Bacardi famila. And the following individuals in particular: Lorraine Bevan (more than words I can say. Thanks for teaching me to play the long game!), Emily Blount (forever x), Karolina Jendras, Josh Jordan, Chloe Crowther, Sam and Angela Carter, Ellie Grudgings, Michael Maylon, Vaughn Yates, the Laverstoke team – Amy, Suzi, Helen, Safety Sam, Debs, Jodi, and the wider team that actually made it all happen. Thanks to my employer for giving me this year off to chase my crazy dream, I am eternally grateful.

In the prepartion of this book: Thanks for Hilary Johnson (for teaching me the basics of grammer and some good chats). Lynne Bridges for the wonderful map illustrations. The Escape - of Basingstoke - particularly Ian Mumford & David Oswald, and especially Guy Nicholson for the wonderful cover. Thanks for all my friends & family for putting up with me talking about it a lot and offering words of encouragement along the way…here is if (finally).

And, of course, those who need shaming:

The Government of Nigeria – *Fuck you.* Seriously.
Conship shipping of Ghana
South African Air – thanks for wasting days of my time.
Mr Holt – my old English teacher – who says nothing good comes from bullying and Xenophobia?